MARTIN LUTHER KING, JR.

Also by James A. Colaiaco

JAMES FITZJAMES STEPHEN AND THE
CRISIS OF VICTORIAN THOUGHT

Martin Luther King, Jr.

Apostle of Militant Nonviolence

James A. Colaiaco

St. Martin's Press   New York

All rights reserved. For information, write:
Scholarly and Reference Division,
St. Martin's Press, Inc., 175 Fifth Avenue, New York, N.Y. 10010

First published in the United States of America in 1988
Reprinted 1990, 1993

Printed in the United States of America

Library of Congress Cataloging-in-Publication Data
Colaiaco, James A.
Martin Luther King, Jr./James A. Colaiaco.
p.   cm.
Bibliography: p.
Includes index.
ISBN 0-312-02365-0 (hc)
ISBN 0-312-08843-4 (pbk.)
1. King, Martin Luther, Jr., 1929-1968.   2. Afro-Americans-
-Biography.   3. Baptists—United States—Clergy—Biography.   4. Afro
-Americans—Civil rights.   5. United States—Race relations.
I. Title.
E185.97.K5C65 1988
323.4′092′4—dc19
[B]   88-14900
                                                                        CIP

10 9 8 7 6 5 4 3 2

To Nancy, my kindred spirit

Contents

Acknowledgements

Anyone who studies the American civil rights movement must acknowledge the efforts of the many scholars who have contributed to our understanding of the role of Martin Luther King, Jr. and the nonviolent method. Their research and writings have assisted me in forming my own views of King, his nonviolent method and the black freedom struggle. In addition, I wish to thank my colleague Marc Crawford, who shared with me his first-hand knowledge of the civil rights movement, and gave the entire book a perceptive reading. I was privileged to have brief conversations with James Baldwin, Floyd McKissick and James Forman. I am grateful to my parents, Helen and Alfred Colaiaco, for their abiding support. My father also gave each chapter a careful reading. I wish to thank Sam Ruggeri, my computer consultant, whose expert advice saved me hours of labour. My mother-in-law, Josephine Ruggeri, provided some important articles and video tapes. The resources of the Bobst Library of New York University were of immense help to me. I also wish to express my gratitude to the General Studies Program of New York University for providing me with the time necessary to pursue my scholarly interests. My greatest debt is to my wife, Nancy Ruggeri Colaiaco, who read each draft of the book, offering many suggestions for its improvement. Over the past few years, we have engaged in continual discussion of King and the civil rights movement. I am deeply grateful for her insight, encouragement and love. Needless to say, although this book has profited from the readings and assistance of others, I alone bear responsibility for its contents.

Baldwin, New York   JAMES A. COLAIACO

The author and the publisher wish to thank the following who have kindly given permission for the use of copyright material:

'The Letter from Birmingham Jail', in *Why We Can't Wait* by Martin Luther King, Jr.
Copyright © 1963 by Martin Luther King, Jr.
Excerpts reprinted by permission of Harper & Row, Publishers, Inc., and by permission of Joan Daves.

Chapters 5 and 8 in this book are expanded versions of two articles by the author published in *Phylon*:
'The American Dream Unfulfilled: Martin Luther King, Jr. and the Letter from Birmingham Jail'.
Phylon 45 (Spring 1984), pp. 1–18.
'Martin Luther King, Jr. and the Paradox of Nonviolent Direct Action'.
Phylon 47 (Spring 1986), pp. 16–28.
Permission to reprint excerpts granted by *Phylon – The Atlanta University Review of Race and Culture*.

Preface to the
Paperback Edition

As the nation marks the twenty-fifth anniversary of the assassination of Martin Luther King, Jr., we must conclude that his dream of a society providing equality and justice for all Americans remains a dream deferred. The nation is still unwilling to make a total commitment to wipe out the effects of racism and reconstruct a society that fulfills the ideals of democracy. In the years since King's death, the federal government has failed to provide the leadership necessary to resolve our pervasive economic and social problems. Poverty, unemployment, and inadequate education, health care and housing continue to afflict the nation's underclass, especially black Americans. During the 1970s, the controversies over busing and affirmative action showed that the nation had still not developed an equitable solution to discrimination against blacks in employment and education. The black family, whose stability is essential to the successful integration of black Americans into the mainstream of American life, continues to languish. At the same time, the nation's inner cities, where blacks are imprisoned by poverty and institutional racism, remain in deterioration.

During the late 1960s and early 1970s, black activists saw the necessity of altering their methods and broadening their goals. While litigation, court decisions, and nonviolent direct-action protest had been effective in overturning legal segregation, they proved to be limited in combatting deeply rooted economic and social problems. Moreover, as King himself realized during the last years of his life, the struggle had to be broadened beyond civil rights to include economic or human rights. Since King's death, blacks have attempted to influence government policy by placing a greater emphasis on electoral politics. Reaping the benefits of the Voting Rights Act of 1965, a landmark victory of the civil rights movement, many blacks have been elected to important political offices on the state and local levels. Atlanta, Birmingham, Chicago, Los Angeles, Memphis, New York, and Washington, D.C., are among the major cities that have elected black mayors.

Blacks have also recognized the potential of the ballot to influence

politics on the national level. The 1984 presidential campaign of
Jesse Jackson not only mobilized black voters, but also drew
considerable support from non-blacks as part of a "Rainbow
Coalition." The campaign, which reached a climax with Jackson's
televised address to the Democratic National Convention that
summer, succeeded in highlighting the need to guarantee human
rights to all Americans, regardless of race. Four years later, Jackson
again received substantial voter support in his second effort to gain
the Democratic nomination for the presidency. He remains today an
eloquent spokesman for the human rights issues that continue to
plague the nation. The urgency of resolving these issues was
dramatized in the spring of 1992, when blacks in Los Angeles,
California, rioted in response to the acquittal of four white police
officers in the videotaped beating of a black motorist. The ensuing
violence left many dead, thousands injured and arrested, and
massive destruction throughout the city—an ominous flashback to
the Watts riot of 1965, the Detroit and Newark riots of 1967, and the
violence that erupted in cities throughout the country following
King's assassination on 4 April 1968. With most black Americans
economically and socially worse off today than at the time of King's
death, many would concede that it is not King's dream of a society
of black and white together that is closer to becoming a reality, but
rather the nightmare forecast in 1968 by the Kerner Commission—
that the United States is moving towards two societies, one black,
one white, separate and unequal.

The author wishes to reiterate that this book is not a biography, but
a narrative of the black freedom struggle from 1955 to 1968, with the
principal focus upon the achievement of Martin Luther King, Jr. The
book discusses the nonviolent protest campaigns led by King and
the Southern Christian Leadership Conference, the strategies
employed, and the philosophy of King as expressed in the classic
"Letter from Birmingham Jail" and other writings. The book is
intended for general readers who wish to deepen their comprehen-
sion of one of the most significant protest movements in the annals
of human history. Only by understanding the past can we discern
where we must go from here.

Baldwin, New York   JAMES A. COLAIACO

                                           September, 1992

Introduction

Martin Luther King, Jr. ranks among the greatest political strategists of all time. From the mid-1950s until the late 1960s, he was the most important leader of a nonviolent civil rights movement that transformed the politics of America and inspired oppressed people throughout the world. During this period, black Americans attained more progress than in the previous century. The system of *de jure* segregation was overturned in the South and essential legislation was enacted, enabling blacks to make significant strides toward resolving what Swedish sociologist Gunnar Myrdal called in 1944 the American Dilemma – the conflict between the nation's democratic ideals of freedom and equality, and its practice of denying basic rights to black citizens.

It has become well-known that King's fame was created by the movement. He never failed to give due credit to those dedicated leaders and organizations, in addition to the thousands of local activists, who were instrumental in generating the support necessary to make the black freedom struggle a mass movement. Nevertheless, under King's leadership, more blacks than ever before were inspired to protest for constitutional rights they had been deprived of for generations. Even in a democracy, recognizing the right of citizens to petition for a redress of grievances, some injustices cannot be rectified through institutionalized political channels. Denied the right to vote, oppressed by segregationist legislatures, frustrated by the gradualism of the courts and virtually ignored by the federal government, blacks had to find an alternative means to bring about reforms in accord with racial justice. By the early 1960s, King and the Southern Christian Leadership Conference (SCLC) – the protest organization he headed since 1957 – had perfected a method of militant nonviolent direct action to confront Jim Crow in the South and awaken the conscience of America to the evils of racism. Although numerous individuals contributed to the success of the movement, the black freedom struggle would not have taken the same direction or achieved as much without King.

The American civil rights movement was not the first twentieth-century example of the success of the nonviolent method on a mass scale. In India, Mohandas K. Gandhi recognized that the nonviolent method was not passive and submissive, but a powerful and coercive instrument for social change. Using the tactics of nonviolent resistance, Gandhi led a movement that liberated his people from the British Empire. He succeeded largely because he was able to dramatize before the court of world opinion the contrast between Britain's imperialism and its cherished democratic tradition. Applying Gandhian strategy and tactics, King emerged as the apostle of militant nonviolence in America. Working in the context of a democracy, he took full advantage of the constitutionally guaranteed freedom of organized protest, in addition to the opportunity for publicity afforded by the media. King himself played an essential role in the nonviolent strategy, leading marches and rallies, going to jail for civil disobedience, giving press conferences, delivering public speeches and publishing articles and books explaining the civil rights movement to the American people and the world.

King and Gandhi were successful because they realized that nonviolent protest is basically an art – and they were quintessential artists. By inspiring and leading a mass following, by carefully selecting their protest tactics, by creative use of the media and by making themselves integral to the overall strategy, King and Gandhi orchestrated dramatic moral confrontations with their adversaries, compelling them to make reforms in the interest of justice. In 1961, two years prior to King's triumph in Birmingham, Alabama, Indian writer Ved Mehta predicted in the *New York Times* magazine that when the twentieth century came to a close, King and Gandhi would be judged the influential men of our time, neither because they were religious leaders, nor because they achieved political success, but because 'they were imaginative artists who knew how to use world politics as their stage'.[1]

This book is not a biography of King; the details of his life have been sufficiently recounted. Instead, the reader will find here a study of King's contribution to the black freedom struggle through an analysis and assessment of his nonviolent protest campaigns. This book also traces the development of the nonviolent method as applied during the civil rights movement in America from the mid-1950s to the late 1960s. During the initial stage of the movement, from 1955 to 1962, the nonviolent method was perfected. These years included the Montgomery bus boycott, in which King emerged as a national black leader; the founding of the Southern Christian Leadership Conference (SCLC); the student sit-ins; the Freedom Rides, led by the Congress of Racial Equality (CORE) and the Student Nonviolent Coordinating Committee (SNCC); and the Albany, Georgia campaign, from which King and SCLC learned valuable lessons in nonviolent warfare.

Nonviolent protest recorded its greatest triumphs from 1963 to 1965, when King and SCLC were its pre-eminent practitioners. This period included the Birmingham campaign, the March on Washington, the St Augustine campaign and the Selma campaign, a watershed in the civil rights movement. These years also witnessed the 1964 Mississippi Freedom Summer, forecasting the fragmentation of the black freedom struggle; and the enactment of the Civil Rights Act of 1964 and the Voting Rights Act of 1965, testimony to the power of nonviolent direct action to effect legislative reform.

This book contains two interlude chapters. One is an analysis of King's 'Letter from Birmingham Jail' – a manifesto of the civil rights movement and a defence of nonviolent protest, including civil disobedience. King's Letter, a model of expository prose and argumentation, has not received the scholarly attention that it deserves. The other interlude chapter is an analysis of the paradox, inherent in the nonviolent strategy, that the campaigns of King and SCLC were most successful when peaceful protesters provoked white racist violence. By thus exposing the brutality of Southern racism, King and SCLC were able to prod the federal government to intervene on behalf of black citizens, and attract national sympathy for civil rights legislation. Many critics either overlooked or did not accept the provocative and militant nature of the nonviolent method, blaming King and SCLC for the violence and civil disruption that often accompanied their campaigns.

Beginning in 1966, the black freedom movement took a new direction, as reflected in SCLC's Chicago campaign. After the defeat of *de jure* segregation in the South, the movement became national and broadened its goals beyond civil rights to human rights such as employment, quality education, housing and health care. King was among the first black American leaders to shift his focus from civil rights to human rights. As the nation became engulfed by domestic turmoil, manifested by ghetto riots, the emergence of Black Power and protests against the war in Vietnam,

King moved to the left politically, embarking upon a radical critique of American institutions and foreign policy. During the final days of his life, with the nonviolent method on trial, King was preparing to launch the 1968 Poor People's Campaign as a first step toward the elimination of poverty and a substantial alteration of American society.

1

Montgomery: The Walking City, 1955–6

I

The nonviolent civil rights movement that overthrew legal segregation in the South of the United States originated in Montgomery, Alabama, the cradle of the Confederacy. On Thursday, 1 December 1955, Mrs Rosa Parks, a 42-year-old black seamstress at a downtown Montgomery department store, and a respected member of the National Association for the Advancement of Colored People (NAACP), was arrested for violating the city's segregated transportation ordinance by refusing to relinquish her bus seat to a white man. Her arrest galvanized the black community. That evening, Jo Ann Robinson, president of the local black Women's Political Council, telephoned Mr E. D. Nixon – a Pullman porter who was a veteran civil rights activist and former president of the local NAACP – to discuss what action should be taken to protest the arrest of Mrs Parks. The Women's Political Council had been pressuring the city to reform its segregated transportation system since 1953. Robinson and Nixon decided to call for a boycott of the Montgomery City Lines. On Friday morning, after posting bond for the release of Mrs Parks, pending a trial, Nixon telephoned the city's black clergymen to enlist their support. Reverend Ralph Abernathy, pastor of the First Baptist Church, received the initial call. On the advice of Abernathy, Nixon also telephoned Reverend Martin Luther King, Jr.

Over the years, blacks in Montgomery had suffered repeated indignities and abuses while riding segregated buses. They constituted 70 per cent of the passengers on the Montgomery City Lines, and 50 000 of the total city population of approximately 130 000. White racism permeated Montgomery, as it did the entire South. The United States Supreme Court's historic 1954 decision in *Brown v. Board of Education*, outlawing racial segregation in public schools, was disregarded, and the vast majority of the city's black citizens

5

were denied the constitutional right to vote. On 25 November 1955, the Interstate Commerce Commission issued a ruling that prohibited racial segregation on interstate buses and trains and in interstate terminal facilities, effective by 10 January 1956. Because of the ruling, blacks throughout the South expected that segregation on intrastate transportation would soon also be banned. According to Montgomery law, blacks were seated in the 'colored section' at the rear of the bus, while the front ten seats were reserved exclusively for whites. If white passengers had already filled the front reserved seats and more whites boarded, blacks in the unreserved section immediately behind were legally obligated to give up their seats to whites who were left standing. Even if a bus were crowded with blacks alone, they were prohibited from occupying the first ten seats. Black passengers were also required to pay their fare at the front of the bus, and then get off and enter at the rear. It was not uncommon for a bus to drive off before a black person had re-boarded. Even while obeying the law, black passengers were frequently subjected to racial slurs and physical assaults from white drivers.

On Friday evening, 2 December, a meeting of black leaders was held at the red brick Dexter Avenue Baptist Church of Reverend Martin Luther King, Jr., across from the Alabama State Capitol where Jefferson Davis had taken the oath of office as President of the Confederacy. Over 40 prominent black ministers and civic leaders attended the meeting, at which they planned a one-day bus boycott, to be held on Monday, 5 December, the day of Mrs Parks' trial. Several thousand leaflets, mimeographed by Jo Ann Robinson, were distributed, presenting the reasons for the protest, and urging blacks not to ride the buses that Monday. Since the vast majority of bus riders were black, the Montgomery City Lines would be particularly vulnerable to a boycott. The local newspaper, the *Montgomery Advertiser*, published a copy of the leaflet on its front page, thus spreading the news about the protest throughout the city. On Sunday morning, the word went out from Montgomery's black churches exhorting everyone to support the boycott. To plan further action, a mass meeting was scheduled for Monday evening at the Holt Street Baptist Church.

II

The black church played an essential role in the Montgomery bus boycott and in the struggle for civil rights in the South. As the centre of the black community, it provided both a refuge from a hostile white society and a place for political and social activities. Leaders also came from the church, for educated black men were often drawn to the ministry. Financially supported by a loyal congregation, the black preacher could afford to remain independent of white society. The black church spawned many leaders of the civil rights movement in the 1950s and 1960s, from Martin Luther King, Jr. and Ralph Abernathy to Andrew Young and Jesse Jackson.

The black church also provided the spiritual basis for the nonviolent method of protest that transformed race relations in America. As King noted: 'Through the influence of the Negro church, the way of nonviolence became an integral part of our struggle'.[1] The philosophy of nonviolence was preached from pulpit to pulpit in the South. The Southern Christian Leadership Conference (SCLC), headed by King, trained blacks in the nonviolent method and directed protests throughout the South. Deprived of access to community centres or public school auditoriums, the nonviolent army was recruited and trained in the church. Within its walls, blacks held protest meetings, planned strategies, listened to sermons on nonviolence, printed leaflets explaining their grievances, sang inspirational hymns and united in prayer. During the height of the civil rights movement, it was from the church that the nonviolent army marched, and to the church that, when necessary, it retreated. Black churches in the state of Alabama are monuments to the struggle for black equality in America: the Dexter Avenue Baptist Church and the Holt Street Baptist Church in Montgomery, the Sixteenth Street Baptist Church in Birmingham, and Brown's Chapel African Methodist Episcopal Church in Selma. In the words of Reverend Wyatt T. Walker, executive director of SCLC during the early 1960s: 'If there had been no Negro church, there would have been no civil rights movement today'.[2]

III

On Monday, 5 December 1955, the white population of Montgomery was astonished as thousands of blacks walked, took cabs or private cars rather than ride the segregated buses. Some were seen riding mules to work; others went by horse-drawn buggy. Having expected only about 60 per cent cooperation, King and other black leaders rejoiced when the boycott was 99 per cent effective. That morning, Rosa Parks was tried, convicted, and fined $14, including court costs. Her attorney, Fred D. Gray, immediately filed an appeal. The Parks case was one of the first resulting in the conviction of a black person for violating a segregation law. In the past, those who defied Jim Crow, the name applied to the legally sanctioned system of segregation, were either charged with lesser offences, such as disorderly conduct or disturbing the peace, or their cases were dismissed. By charging Parks with violating the segregated public transportation law, the city made a tactical error that cleared the path for an appeal to the higher jurisdiction of the federal court, and ultimately to the United States Supreme Court, where the constitutionality of segregated intrastate public transportation could be decided.

The protest gathered momentum. On the afternoon of the 5 December bus boycott, 16 black leaders met to organize the mass meeting scheduled for that evening at the Holt Street Baptist Church. To direct the protest, they formed the Montgomery Improvement Association (MIA), a name proposed by Reverend Ralph Abernathy. Martin Luther King, Jr., the 26-year-old pastor of Montgomery's Dexter Avenue Baptist Church, was elected president.

Born into a black middle class family in Atlanta, Georgia, on 15 January 1929, King graduated from Morehouse College at the age of 19, and received a Bachelor of Divinity degree from the racially integrated Crozer Theological Seminary in Chester, Pennsylvania, in June 1951, graduating at the head of his class. Four years later, in June 1955, King received a Ph.D. in systematic theology from Boston University. Pursuing his interest in philosophy, he took supplementary courses in the subject at the University of Pennsylvania while at Crozer, and at Harvard University while in Boston. In 1953, King married Coretta Scott, a native of Marion, Alabama, who was studying to be a concert singer at the New England Conservatory in Boston. The following year, he returned with his wife to the South to assume the pastorate of the 400-member Dexter Avenue Baptist Church. His congregation was among the best educated and wealthiest in Montgomery. During the first year of his pastorate, King completed his doctoral dissertation, organized a political and social action committee within his congregation, and was elected to the executive board of the local NAACP. Although he had lived in Montgomery only 15 months when the bus boycott began, King was considered the wisest choice to head the MIA because he was not embroiled in the factionalism that divided the city's black leadership. Moreover, he had already established a reputation as a well-educated minister with extraordinary oratorical skills. In the following months, King would succeed in uniting the city's black people into a powerful nonviolent force for social change.

On the evening of 5 December, King set the tone and the ideal for the rest of the protest when he addressed the mass meeting at the Holt Street Baptist Church. The church was packed to capacity, and some three or four thousand blacks had to stand outside and listen to the proceedings on loudspeakers. Following an opening inspirational hymn, 'Onward Christian Soldiers', and a reading from Scripture, King was introduced to the crowd. He spoke without notes. After recounting the arrest of Mrs Parks, and the unjust conditions that prevailed on the Montgomery buses, he declared: 'There comes a time when people get tired. We are here this evening to say to those who have mistreated us so long that we are tired – tired of being segregated and humiliated, tired of being kicked about by the brutal feet of oppression'. As the audience shouted in agreement, King went on to proclaim: 'One of the great glories of democracy is the right to protest for right'. Insisting that the protest must be nonviolent, he said: 'Love must be our regulating ideal'. He then invoked the words of Booker T. Washington: 'Let no man pull you so low as to make you hate him'. King concluded with an eloquent peroration:

> If you will protest courageously, and yet with dignity and Christian love, when the history books are written in future generations, the historians will have to pause and say, "There lived a great people – a black people – who injected new meaning and dignity into the veins of civilization." This is our challenge and our responsibility.[3]

The civil rights movement had found its greatest leader and most inspirational orator. Under the direction of Martin Luther King, Jr., the black freedom struggle would no longer be confined to courts of law, but would move to the streets of the South with the rest of the nation looking on.

Following King's speech, Rosa Parks was introduced and received an ovation. Ralph Abernathy then read the demands which an MIA committee had prepared to present to the Montgomery City Lines:

1. courteous treatment of blacks by bus drivers;
2. passengers on city buses to be seated on a first-come, first-served basis – blacks sitting from the back forward, whites from the front to the rear, with no section reserved for either race;
3. black bus drivers to be employed on predominately black routes.

Blacks unanimously agreed to continue the boycott until the Montgomery City Lines accepted these demands. Surprisingly, they were limited and moderate, and fully consistent with the city's segregated transportation ordinance. The seating arrangement called for was not new to the segregated South – it prevailed in Atlanta, Georgia and Mobile, Alabama. Nevertheless, it would at least eliminate the humiliation of Montgomery blacks who, under the existing interpretation of the segregation law, were compelled to stand while seats reserved for whites were unoccupied. At this time, King and the MIA did not intend to challenge the legality of segregated transportation. They were content to accept separate, but somewhat more equal and humane, treatment under the existing law.

The presence of reporters and television cameras at King's dramatic 5 December speech focused widespread attention upon the Montgomery protest. In the ensuing years, King would become a master at utilizing the media to further the civil rights cause. He was the ideal media hero, commanding respect not only as a charismatic leader and captivating speaker, but also as the recipient of a doctorate in theology who was conversant with the great books of the Western tradition. His sermons were filled with as many references to Plato and Aristotle as to St Paul. As the drama unfolded in Montgomery, the media impressed upon the minds of millions of Americans, and people throughout the world, the oppression inherent in 'separate but equal'. Not only did the media help to propel King to international prominence, but it would provide the publicity essential to the success of the militant, nonviolent method he espoused.

IV

The Montgomery boycott required superior planning and organization. Four committees – strategy, finance, transportation and programme – were created. King headed the strategy or negotiating committee, which also included Ralph Abernathy, E. D. Nixon, and Jo Ann Robinson. To keep the black population united and informed, mass meetings took place twice a week, on Monday and Thursday nights, in various city churches. The MIA raised money for legal fees and transportation costs by collections from the black congregations, and – after media coverage transmitted news of the protest throughout the world – by donations from across the United States and from as far away as Tokyo.

During the first days of the boycott, the city's 18 black-owned cab companies helped by transporting protesters in 210 cabs for the same ten cent fare they had to pay on the buses. But boycott leaders feared that the city might soon invoke an existing law imposing a minimum fare for cab rides. To provide blacks with an alternate means of transportation, a car pool was formed and an elaborate system of dispatch and pick-up stations set up. In organizing the car pool, King sought the advice of Reverend Theodore Jemison. In June 1953, Jemison had led the blacks of Baton Rouge, Louisiana in a boycott against the city's segregated buses. Although the Baton Rouge boycott won a compromise settlement from the white power structure, the protest lasted only one week and failed to attract national attention.

On Thursday, 8 December, at the request of the interracial Alabama Council on Human Relations, a meeting was held at City Hall between the MIA, Mayor W. A. 'Tackie' Gayle, Commissioners Clyde Sellers and Frank A. Parks and two representatives of the Montgomery City Lines. The proceedings, which lasted four hours, were attended by newspaper reporters and television cameramen. While the bus company was willing to improve courtesy toward black passengers, its lawyer, Jack Crenshaw, argued that, contrary to the MIA's claim, the seating arrangement requested would violate the city's segregation law. Crenshaw was immediately supported by the Mayor and Commissioner Sellers, and soon by Commissioner Parks. Moreover, the bus company refused to consider hiring black drivers. On 17 December, another meeting was held, this time including C. K. Totten, vice president of the National City Lines in Chicago, which owned Montgomery's bus company. In the spirit of conciliation, the MIA moderated one of its demands; the bus company would not have to hire black drivers until vacancies occurred. Nevertheless, Totten merely echoed the objections voiced by the City Commission and Crenshaw at the previous meeting. When this session also failed to yield a settlement, Mayor Gayle scheduled a third meeting for Monday morning, 19 December. But when the Mayor invited the secretary of the· local racist White Citizens' Council to participate, the negotiations dissolved.

The city's rejection of the MIA's modest demands enhanced the determination of blacks to continue the boycott, which had already begun to hurt the Montgomery City Lines. By Christmas, the city's black population was united as never before. Company revenues having declined by over $2000 a day, 32 drivers were dismissed on 27 December, and additional lay-offs would occur the following year.

The city next attempted to divide the black leadership. Prominent white citizens ridiculed older black ministers for surrendering direction of the protest to King, the young newcomer to Montgomery. False rumours were spread that the MIA leaders were concerned less about the welfare of the black community than their personal financial advantage. The Montgomery City Commission also tried to crush the boycott by a clever ruse designed to lure blacks back on the buses. On Sunday, 22 January 1956, the *Montgomery Advertiser* announced that a settlement had been achieved. According to the story, three 'prominent Negro ministers', allegedly representing the MIA, met with the City Commission and reached an agreement which would reserve the first ten seats at the front of the bus for whites, the ten seats in the rear for blacks; the remaining sixteen seats in the unreserved middle section would be filled on a first-come, first-served basis, whites sitting from the front, blacks from the back. This seating arrangement would be consistent with the city's segregation law. But by this time, the MIA was resolved to continue the protest until Montgomery's buses were completely integrated, and would not have consented to such a modest accord.

Fortunately, King was informed of the 'settlement' on Saturday evening by a telephone call from Carl T. Rowan, an editorial writer for the *Minneapolis Tribune*. King and other protest leaders immediately embarked on a tour of the city's night clubs and taverns to inform the black community that the boycott was still in effect. Black ministers were also telephoned and instructed to announce to their congregations on Sunday morning that there had been no settlement. When King finally located the three black ministers connected to the 'settlement', they told him that they had not agreed to any accord, but had been duped into meeting with the City Commission.

The city next launched a 'get tough' policy. On 24 January, Mayor Gayle condemned the boycott on television, declaring it a threat to law and order, and announced that he and Commissioner Parks had become members of the White Citizens' Council, joining Police Commissioner Clyde Sellers. 'We have pussy-footed around on this boycott long enough', the Mayor said. 'The white people are firm in their convictions that they do not care whether the Negroes ever ride a city bus again if it means that the social fabric of our community is destroyed'.[4] Police harassment of blacks followed. Drivers in the car pool were arrested for minor or illusory traffic violations. On 26 January, King was arrested for allegedly driving 30 miles per hour in a 25 miles per hour zone, and jailed for the first time in his life. He was released on his own recognizance.

Unable to break the boycott, the city resorted to more extreme measures. King received threats daily by telephone and mail, causing him to fear for the safety of his family and himself. On 30 January, the anniversary of the assassination of Gandhi, King's home was bombed while he attended a mass meeting, and his wife Coretta and their first child Yolanda narrowly escaped serious injury. Rushing home, King implored a crowd of angry blacks to refrain from retaliatory violence: 'We must meet violence with nonviolence. Remember the words of Jesus: "He who lives by the sword will perish by the sword".'[5] According to King's biographer, Lerone Bennett, Jr.: 'This moment changed the course of the protest and made King a living symbol'. Before this, he and other boycott leaders had spoken of love and forgiveness. 'But now, *seeing the idea in action*, . . . millions were touched, if not converted'.[6] Two nights later, a stick of dynamite was tossed on the lawn of the home of E. D. Nixon.

Undaunted by violent opposition, the MIA decided to institute a court action. Fearing that the Parks case might be stalled indefinitely in the Alabama state courts, on 2 February, the MIA's NAACP attorneys, representing five Montgomery black women, filed a suit, *Browder* v. *Gayle*, in the United States District Court in Montgomery, requesting that segregation on buses not only in Montgomery, but also in the entire state of Alabama be declared unconstitutional as a violation of the Equal Protection Clause of the Fourteenth Amendment. On 11 February, while the MIA suit was pending, the White Citizens' Councils, which then boasted 250 000 members throughout the South, held a rally in the Montgomery coliseum, drawing a crowd of 12 000. The keynote speaker was Senator James Eastland of Mississippi, a champion of segregation. As the Senator spoke under the waving flag of the Confederacy, leaflets were distributed to the crowd which contained the words: 'We hold these truths to be self-evident, that all whites are created equal with certain rights, among these are life, liberty and the pursuit of dead niggers'.[7] Meanwhile, the Men of Montgomery, an organization of leading businessmen concerned about the economic effect of the boycott, which by March had cost city merchants an estimated $1 million, attempted to pressure city authorities and the bus company to work out a compromise.

Responding to the MIA's federal suit, the City Commission undertook legal action of its own. On 21 February, King and 89 leaders of the boycott, including 24 ministers, were indicted by the Montgomery County grand jury for violating a remote 1921 Alabama anti-boycott statute, recently exhumed by a city attorney, which made it a crime to hinder lawful business without 'just cause or legal excuse'.[8] The grand jury made no attempt to conceal its prejudice. 'In this state', the indictment declared, 'we are committed to segregation by custom and law; we intend to maintain it'.[9] But this tactic also failed to crush the boycott. To the surprise of city authorities, blacks considered it an honour to be arrested.

When the indictments were announced, King was away lecturing at Fisk University in Nashville, Tennessee. He returned to Montgomery to be the first to stand trial, despite the reservations of his father, Martin Luther King, Sr., who feared for his son's safety. After four days of court proceedings, King was convicted by Judge Eugene Carter and released on 23 March, pending an appeal, after which the other cases would be considered. King's trial attracted international attention, giving the protest greater unity and momentum. Scores of reporters from the United States, Europe and some from as far as India were present to hear the testimony of 28 witnesses for the defence who described in detail their mistreatment on Montgomery's buses. As King and his wife Coretta left the courtroom, they were greeted by hundreds of people, including reporters, photographers and television cameramen. After a crowd of supporters shouted 'Long live the King' and 'We ain't gonna ride the buses no more', King emphasized: 'We will continue to protest in the same spirit of nonviolence and passive resistance, using the weapon of love'.[10]

As the spring of 1956 came to a close, Montgomery's blacks continued to walk. The sentiments of the black community were perhaps best expressed by an impoverished and uneducated elderly woman, known affectionately as Mother Pollard, who, when asked whether she was weary after several weeks of walking, replied: 'My feets is tired, but my soul is at rest'.[11] Blacks appeared to have gained a victory when the Montgomery City Lines, acting on orders from their Chicago parent company, the National City Lines, decided to desegregate buses on 23 April. But the order was rescinded on 9 May, when the City Commission secured a state court injunction prohibiting desegregation of the buses. Meanwhile, arguments in the *Browder* v. *Gayle* case concluded in the United States District Court. On 4 June 1956, the protest received a substantial boost when a special three-judge panel declared that bus segregation in Montgomery was unconstitutional. Nevertheless, this decision would be ineffectual unless the MIA also prevailed in the appeal that the City Commission immediately made to the Supreme Court. The protest continued through the summer, and King embarked on a nationwide speaking tour, bringing the Montgomery story to thousands.

In desperation, the city sought to cripple the boycott by attempting to destroy the MIA's transportation system. After insurance companies were pressured to cancel coverage of the MIA car pool in September, Lloyd's of London provided a substitute policy. On 30 October, the city requested the state court to issue an injunction against the car pool on the grounds that it was a private enterprise illegally operating without a franchise. A hearing before Judge Eugene Carter was scheduled for 13 November, almost a year after the boycott had begun. The city was in a strong legal position, and King and the MIA expected the court to rule against them. Deprived of its car pool, the boycott would be crushed. On Tuesday, 13 November, a worried King went to court. During a brief mid-day recess, there was a commotion in the courtroom. Suddenly, a reporter for the Associated Press rushed to King and handed him a paper which read: 'The United States Supreme Court today affirmed a decision of a special three-judge U.S. District Court in declaring Alabama's state and local laws requiring segregation on buses unconstitutional'. The boycott had been saved. 'God Almighty has spoken from Washington, D.C.', a jubilant black exclaimed.[12] Later that day, the Alabama state appellate court ruled in favour of the city and enjoined the car pool. But the decision was now moot, for the Supreme Court had outlawed all forms of segregated public transportation throughout the nation.

On the evening of 14 November, some 8000 Montgomery blacks crowded into two churches and celebrated their victory simultaneously. Reverend Robert Graetz, a white member of the MIA executive board, read from St Paul's Letter to the Corinthians: 'Though I have all faith, so that I could remove mountains, and have not love, I am nothing'.[13] The MIA executive board officially called off the boycott, but decided that blacks would not ride integrated buses until the Supreme Court mandate became effective in Alabama. Later that night, when about 40 carloads of hooded Ku-Klux-Klan members drove through the black neighbourhood, they were viewed like a circus parade. The black citizens of Montgomery could no longer be intimidated.

At this time, King and the MIA leadership began to prepare Montgomery's black population for the anticipated hostile reaction of whites to integrated buses. Aware that violence would detract from the moral significance of their victory, King's philosophy of nonviolence was preached at mass meeting after mass meeting. A mimeographed set of 'Integrated Bus Suggestions' was distributed, calling upon blacks to ride the buses without violence 'either in word or deed'.[14] In early December, King and the MIA sponsored a week-long Institute on Nonviolence, which brought black and white religious and political leaders to Montgomery to reflect on the lessons of the boycott. In his keynote speech, 'Facing the Challenge of A New Age', King praised the motto adopted by the Institute, 'Freedom and Justice through Love', and emphasized the power of nonviolence to challenge and awaken the conscience of white racists. He concluded by urging blacks to unite in a mass nonviolent movement to overcome segregation and bring about 'the beloved community'.[15]

On 18 December, the city government of Montgomery responded to the Supreme Court's decision by issuing the following statement:

> The City Commission, and we know our people are with us in this determination, will not yield one inch, but will do all in its power to oppose the integration of the Negro race with the white race in Montgomery, and will forever stand like a rock against social equality, intermarriage, and mixing of the races under God's creation and plan.[16]

This declaration, manifesting a blatant defiance of the law of the land, represented segregationist sentiments throughout the South.

On 20 December, the Supreme Court's bus integration order became legally effective in Montgomery. Later that day, King concluded a sermon at the St John A.M.E. Church by reminding his audience to behave in a manner that would promote harmony and understanding between blacks and whites: 'We seek integration based upon mutual respect'.[17] The following morning, before television cameramen and reporters, Martin Luther King, Jr., Ralph Abernathy, E. D. Nixon, Rosa Parks and Glenn Smiley, a white minister, boarded the first integrated bus in Montgomery.

Nevertheless, while laws and court decisions declare rights, they cannot change hearts. After a few days of apparent compliance with the court decision, Klan members fired gunshots at integrated buses throughout Montgomery, especially during the evening hours. A pregnant woman was wounded in the leg; and a black, teenage girl was beaten by a group of white youths as she left a bus. The Montgomery City Commission responded by temporarily suspending evening bus service for 'the protection of life, limb, and property of the people of Montgomery'.[18] The violence persisted. In early January, several black churches and the homes of Ralph Abernathy and Robert Graetz were bombed. By this time, even moderate supporters of segregation began to fear the consequences of the breakdown of law and order. After the *Montgomery Advertiser*, white ministers and members of the business community denounced the spreading violence, the bombings ceased, allowing bus services to resume on an integrated basis.

V

The victorious Montgomery bus boycott inaugurated the era of mass nonviolent protest for civil rights in the South. For the first time in American history, an entire black community had resisted Jim Crow successfully. For 381 days, thousands of blacks walked to work, some as many as 12 miles a day, rather than continue to submit to segregated public transportation. The protest had been 95 per cent effective, proving that blacks possessed sufficient economic leverage to influence reform. While the MIA expenses totalled some $225 000, the bus company lost more than $250 000 in revenues, the city several thousand dollars in taxes, and the merchants several million dollars in sales. The success in Montgomery had repercussions throughout the South. In 1956, bus boycotts were organized in Birmingham, Mobile, and Tallahassee, and many Southern cities desegregated their buses voluntarily, without court intervention.

Some underestimated the achievement of the Montgomery boycott by claiming that the federal judiciary rather than the boycott was responsible for the victory. Thurgood Marshall of the NAACP remarked: 'All that walking for nothing! They could just as well have waited while the bus case went up through the courts, without all the work and worry of the boycott'.[19] But when the boycott began in 1955, there was no indication that the federal courts were prepared to enforce integration in public transportation within the Southern states. Without the protest, it is unlikely that there would have been a legal challenge to Montgomery's segregated transportation ordinance. The boycott not only created the situation that allowed NAACP attorneys to institute the federal suit, but it also mobilized national sympathy for the black cause which the courts could not ignore.

The civil rights movement could not have overturned *de jure* segregation in the South without the complementary action of nonviolent protest and litigation. Nonviolent direct action disrupted segregated communities, focused attention on racial injustice, stirred the national conscience, raised issues to be adjudicated, and was instrumental in implementing court decisions. At the same time, the federal courts gave legitimacy to the black freedom struggle, and helped sustain nonviolent direct action by rendering scores of decisions in support of civil rights. As King advised the NAACP in a letter to Thurgood Marshall in 1958: 'You continue winning the legal victories for us and we will work passionately and unrelentingly to implement these victories on the local level through nonviolent means'.[20] Litigation alone, without the pressure of nonviolent direct action, is intolerably slow, while nonviolent direct action, without the support and intercession of the courts, has nothing to sustain it or to consolidate its gains.

The Montgomery bus boycott launched King virtually overnight into a position of national and international prominence, marking his emergence as a symbol of racial justice. Not since Booker T. Washington had a national black leader emerged from the South. On 18 February 1957, *Time* magazine featured a cover story on the Montgomery boycott, and hailed King as 'one of the nation's remarkable leaders of men'.[21] Under his charismatic leadership, the blacks of Montgomery had conquered fear and apathy, casting off the crippling psychological chains that had made them unconscious participants in their own oppression. Blacks throughout the entire nation followed the startling events that turned Montgomery into a 'walking city', and witnessed the power of nonviolent protest. 'I am an invisible man', proclaimed the protagonist of Ralph Ellison's great novel in 1953, 'I am invisible, understand, simply because people refuse to see me'.[22] After the Montgomery bus boycott, black Americans were no longer invisible; they had impressed themselves indelibly upon the national consciousness.

2

Nonviolence Spreads in the South, 1957–61

I

Until the Montgomery bus boycott, the battle for civil rights in the South was led by the National Association for the Advancement of Colored People. Founded in 1909, the NAACP resorted to a combination of public education, legislative lobbying and court action in an effort to attain equality for black Americans. Its strategy sought to undermine the legal basis of segregation by plodding away, case by case, through the courts. During the 1940s and 1950s, the Association won a series of important victories, placing it in the forefront of the civil rights movement. In 1944, the United States Supreme Court upheld the right of blacks to vote in Southern primaries by banning all-white primary elections. In 1946, in *Morgan* v. *Virginia*, the Court prohibited segregated seating on buses engaged in interstate travel. In 1948, it outlawed racially restrictive covenants in housing. Two years later, it upheld the right of blacks to enrol in publicly supported institutions of higher learning. The greatest NAACP triumph was the 1954 United States Supreme Court decision in *Brown* v. *Board of Education*, declaring racial segregation in public schools unconstitutional. This landmark decision overturned the 'separate but equal' doctrine formulated in *Plessy* v. *Ferguson* in 1896, which had given legal sanction to segregation. Speaking for a unanimous Supreme Court on 17 May 1954, Chief Justice Earl Warren proclaimed: 'We conclude that in the field of public education the doctrine of "separate but equal" has no place. . . . Separate education facilities are inherently unequal'.[1]

Brown was a monumental victory, and appeared to signal the demise of the entire Jim Crow system. But, in the months following the decision, the expectations of black Americans were unfulfilled, for public schools and accommodations remained segregated as the Southern states mounted a campaign of 'massive resistance'.

White Citizens' Councils were instituted throughout the South to resist integration, and new life was breathed into the Ku-Klux-Klan. The legal strategy of the NAACP was virtually impotent against such defiance. Moreover, between 1956 and 1959, the Southern states attacked the NAACP, either outlawing it, as in Alabama, or passing laws and issuing injunctions to impair its operation.

Encountering staunch opposition to desegregation, the Supreme Court itself proceeded to weaken the effectiveness of the *Brown* decision. Instead of ordering immediate and total compliance, the Court succumbed to what it considered political necessity, ruling on 31 May 1955 that desegregation should merely be carried out 'with all deliberate speed'.[2] This ruling, known as *Brown II*, provided a loophole for Southern segregationists, who responded with a policy of deliberate delay and evasion. Blacks could not depend upon the federal executive for a vigorous enforcement of *Brown*. President Dwight D. Eisenhower, with a cautious eye focused on the Southern white electorate, refused either to approve or disapprove of the decision. Perhaps the most flagrant expression of Southern resistance to federal law occurred on 12 March 1956, when 101 Southern members of Congress signed the 'Southern Manifesto', condemning *Brown* as 'a clear abuse of judicial power . . . contrary to the Constitution'.[3] Such contempt for the Supreme Court by the Southern leadership encouraged many segregationists to resist the law. 'The true meaning of the Manifesto', wrote Anthony Lewis of the *New York Times*, 'was to make defiance of the Supreme Court and the Constitution socially acceptable in the South – to give resistance to the law the approval of the Southern Establishment'.[4]

II

In the face of such a concerted effort to defy the law of the land, blacks lost confidence in legislation and court action as the means to achieve full citizenship. The law merely declares and defines rights, it does not fulfil them; laws and court decisions must be enforced to be meaningful. A more militant method was needed, supplementing the moderate legalist strategy of the NAACP, that would compel the Southern states to comply with the law, and induce the President and Congress to take a more active part in support of civil rights. This method, forged in the crucible of the Montgomery bus boycott, was mass nonviolent direct action. Montgomery had expanded the arena of black protest from the courts and legislatures to the streets. In the hands of King, the nonviolent method would revolutionize race relations in the South and affect the politics of the entire nation.

By the mid-1950s, a number of factors coalesced to contribute to the emergence of a mass civil rights movement in the United States. At the outset of the twentieth century, more than 90 per cent of American blacks lived in the South; by 1960, almost half lived in the North. The decline of cotton agriculture and the industrialization of the South forced millions of blacks to migrate from the rural plantations to the cities – mostly to the North – in search of employment opportunities. Urbanization helped to politicize poor blacks, concentrating them in ghettos, and led to the development of a black middle class. Freed from the controls of the plantation system, urban blacks were able to develop leaders and unite to protest their oppression in the North and the South. Beginning with the New Deal of President Franklin D. Roosevelt, black Americans also began to exert a growing influence upon national politics. As blacks began to shift their allegiance from the Republicans to the Democrats, both political parties saw the need to solicit their vote. When the Second World War established the United States as the dominant power, its international responsibilities were enhanced. Having defeated fascism and its racist doctrines, thus emerging as a worldwide symbol of freedom, the United States was vulnerable to international criticism for its unjust treatment of black citizens. Moreover, as the peoples of Africa and Asia attained independence from colonial rule during the postwar period, black Americans became increasingly conscious and resentful of their inferior status.

Although nonviolent direct action became the dominant method in the black freedom struggle during the decade of 1955–65, neither the advocacy nor the use of nonviolence was new to blacks in America. As early as 1932, theologian Reinhold Niebuhr suggested in *Moral Man and Immoral Society* that nonviolent action, such as boycotts and refusal to pay taxes, could be effective in accomplishing black emancipation. During the 1930s, Reverend Adam Clayton Powell, Jr. organized boycotts and mass marches to help members of his Harlem church in New York City secure better jobs and higher pay. Black leaders also perceived a valuable lesson in the achievement of Mohandas K. Gandhi, who employed nonviolent direct action to liberate India from British imperialism. In 1936, Gandhi told Dr Howard Thurman that he foresaw a special mission for the black American: 'It may be through the Negroes', the Indian leader declared, 'that the unadulterated message of nonviolence will be delivered to the world'.[5] The following year, Gandhi told Dr Channing Tobias and Dr Benjamin Mays, later president of Morehouse College and mentor of King, that nonviolent action would be a valuable weapon for black Americans in their struggle for civil rights.

Prior to the Montgomery bus boycott, the most famous example of the power of mass nonviolence in the United States was the proposed March on Washington in 1941. A. Philip Randolph, president of the Brotherhood of Sleeping Car Porters, summoned a massive march in the nation's capital to protest nonviolently against racial discrimination in the defence industries. The protest was cancelled after President Franklin D. Roosevelt responded to the threat of thousands of marching blacks by issuing an executive order that abolished discrimination in all government defence jobs, and created the Fair Employment Practices Commission. One year later, in an address to the policy conference on the March on Washington Movement, Randolph pointed out the inadequacy of the prevailing gradualist methods and applauded Gandhi's use of civil disobedience to protest injustice. Testifying before the Senate Armed Services Committee in 1948, Randolph warned that unless the army was desegregated, blacks would engage in massive civil disobedience and resist the draft. 'I reported last week to President Truman', he informed the Committee, 'that Negroes are in no mood to shoulder a gun for democracy abroad so long as they are denied democracy here at home'.[6] President Truman answered the threat of civil disorder by issuing a directive desegregating the armed services.

The application of Gandhian nonviolent tactics was pioneered in the United States by the Congress of Racial Equality (CORE). Founded in Chicago in 1942 by James Farmer as an outgrowth of the Fellowship of Reconciliation, a Christian pacifist organization, CORE successfully employed nonviolent direct action against racial discrimination in the North. Until the 1960s, the organization comprised a small, predominantly white, membership, and confined its activities largely to the North. In 1943, CORE integrated several Chicago restaurants by means of sit-ins. In 1947–48, a

CORE campaign desegregated the pool at the Palisades Amusement Park in New Jersey. In 1947, CORE sponsored a 'Journey of Reconciliation' – forerunner of the Freedom Rides of 1961 – through the Upper South to test compliance with the 1946 United States Supreme Court decision in *Morgan* v. *Virginia*, banning segregated interstate bus transportation. An interracial team of 16 riders, including Bayard Rustin, a future advisor to King, embarked on Greyhound and Trailways buses, challenging Jim Crow transportation by blacks sitting in the front and whites in the back. Arriving in North Carolina, some riders, including Rustin, were arrested for refusing to leave their seats when ordered to do so.

Although CORE initiated the use of nonviolent direct action in the struggle for racial justice in America, the method became effective on a mass scale only with the emergence of King. As James Farmer, national director of CORE from 1961 to 1966, later observed, during the early years of the organization, 'nonviolence was still an unknown technique and the word caused adverse reaction. It only began to grow at the time of the Montgomery bus boycott of King in 1956'.[7] In his autobiography, Farmer assessed the contribution of King to the nonviolent movement: 'If we [CORE] had plowed the ground for a decade and a half, the Montgomery movement had fertilized it and put the seed in, . . . No longer did we have to explain nonviolence to people. Thanks to Martin Luther King, it was a household word. CORE was a beneficiary of the emergence of King'.[8]

III

King's philosophy of nonviolence was a synthesis of the teachings of Jesus Christ and Mohandas K. Gandhi. While the Sermon on the Mount provided the motivating ideal of love, Gandhi provided the method of mass nonviolent direct action. As King observed, the love advocated by Jesus was expressed by the Greek word *agape*, defined as unconditional, disinterested goodwill toward all men. Agape aims 'to preserve and create community'.[9] King first became interested in Gandhi when, as a young student at Crozer Theological Seminary, he travelled to Philadelphia to attend a lecture on the Indian leader by Mordecai W. Johnson, president of Howard University, who had recently returned from a trip to India. At that time, King had been searching for a method to combat social evil. He was so moved by Johnson's lecture that he decided to pursue the subject further and bought a number of books on Gandhi's life and works. King was deeply impressed by the Indian leader's famous Salt March to the Sea, and by his nonviolent tactics – boycotts, strikes, marches and mass civil disobedience. He was also influenced by Gandhi's concept of *Satyagraha*, or Soul Force, which embodied love as an instrument for overcoming evil. According to King, Gandhi had developed a powerful method to implement the ideals of Christianity.

While committed to the love ethic of Jesus, King initially questioned how such love could be used to combat injustice. His reading, while a student in college, of Henry David Thoreau's classic essay 'Civil Disobedience' convinced him that one has a moral obligation to refuse to cooperate with an unjust social system. To remain passive in the face of evil is to condone it. Moreover, King's study of Gandhi taught him that Christianity did not mean nonresistance to evil, but nonviolent resistance to evil. Nonviolence is an active and coercive form of resistance. The Christian may confront evil forcefully, but with nonviolence and love rather than violence and hate. King pointed to his reading of Gandhi as the source of his belief that nonviolence was 'the only morally and practically sound method open to oppressed people in their struggle for freedom'.[10]

The Montgomery bus boycott convinced King that the nonviolent method could be applied to the civil rights cause. A week after the boycott began, an elderly white woman wrote a letter to the editor of the *Montgomery Advertiser*, pointing out the parallel between the protest and the method of Gandhi. King had previously given merely an intellectual assent to nonviolence, but his experience in Montgomery did more to clarify his thinking on the question of nonviolence than all the books he had read. His views were further clarified by discussions with two pacifists: Bayard Rustin and Glenn E. Smiley. Rustin had been an office holder in the Fellowship of Reconciliation (FOR), and was then executive secretary of the War Resisters League. Smiley was a white Methodist minister and a FOR field secretary. Both men, disciples of Gandhi and the American pacifist A. J. Muste, arrived in Montgomery in February 1956 to assist in organizing the protest.

After the boycott, King's devotion to Gandhi's nonviolent method increased. While most civil rights advocates employed nonviolence for pragmatic, tactical reasons, King, like Gandhi, embraced nonviolence as a philosophy of life. Visiting India with Coretta in 1959 as the special guests of Prime Minister Nehru, King had the opportunity to discuss nonviolent techniques with some of Gandhi's disciples, and to pay tribute to the memory of the late Indian leader. Arriving in New Delhi, King told a crowd of reporters that he came not as a tourist, but as a pilgrim.

IV

Inspired by the success in Montgomery, King and other black leaders founded an organization to coordinate nonviolent direct-action campaigns throughout the South. In January 1957, King met in Atlanta with more than 60 black ministers and formed the Southern Leadership Conference on Transportation and Nonviolent Integration. In addition to King and Ralph Abernathy from Montgomery, the ministers included Fred Shuttlesworth from Birmingham, Joseph Lowery from Mobile, and C. K. Steele from Tallahassee. The new organization voted to petition President Eisenhower to deliver a major policy speech in the South, demanding compliance with the anti-segregation decisions of the United States Supreme Court; to invite Vice President Richard Nixon to visit the South and confer with its black and white leaders; and to ask Attorney General Herbert Brownell, the chief law enforcement officer of the nation, to urge Southern authorities to abide by the law. Though the federal government rebuffed these petitions, the black freedom struggle received valuable publicity.

On 14 February 1957, the Southern Leadership Conference, now consisting of 97 members from ten Southern states, reconvened in New Orleans and changed its name to the Southern Christian Leadership Conference, or SCLC. King was unanimously elected president, and Ralph Abernathy became treasurer. SCLC, with its headquarters established in Atlanta, was the first civil rights organization to be born in the South. Within a short time, it became what Bayard Rustin called 'the dynamic center of the civil rights movement'.[11] Unlike the other civil rights groups, it was not a membership organization, but consisted of local affiliates, grouped by state, and drew its strength from the black church – ministers and their congregations. By 1962, SCLC had 65 affiliates throughout the South. By 1967, the number had risen to 270.

One of the first official acts of the newly-formed Southern

Christian Leadership Conference was to dispatch a telegram to President Eisenhower, requesting that he convene a White House Conference on Civil Rights. Reflecting the new black militancy, the telegram stated that if 'effective remedial steps were not taken', SCLC would be 'compelled to initiate a mighty Prayer Pilgrimage to Washington'.[12] When their request was denied, King and SCLC announced plans to carry out their threat. On 17 May 1957 – the third anniversary of the *Brown* decision – King, along with Roy Wilkins, executive secretary of the NAACP, and A. Philip Randolph, sponsored a Prayer Pilgrimage to the nation's capital. The Prayer Pilgrimage – the largest civil rights demonstration in the United States until that time – drew an estimated 15 000 to 37 000 participants (including about 3000 whites) from 33 states. After a number of speeches were delivered at the Lincoln Memorial – including those by Randolph, Wilkins and Adam Clayton Powell – Randolph, father of the 1941 March on Washington Movement, introduced the keynote speaker – Martin Luther King, Jr.

As King approached the podium, the crowd rose to its feet. He began by deploring the fact that Southern states had defied the *Brown* decision with a policy of massive resistance. They had gathered in Washington that day, King proclaimed, to demand the democratic right to vote for blacks throughout the South. Recognizing that the ballot would give blacks political power to secure other fundamental freedoms, King appealed to President Eisenhower and Congress to enact legislation protecting the right to vote. King then inspired the crowd to join him in the refrain 'Give us the ballot':

> Give us the ballot and we will no longer have to worry the federal government about our basic rights . . . Give us the ballot and we will fill our legislative halls with men of good will, and send to the sacred halls of Congress men who will not sign a Southern Manifesto, because of their devotion to the manifesto of justice . . . Give us the ballot and we will quietly and nonviolently, without rancor or bitterness, implement the Supreme Court's decision of 17 May 1954.[13]

King concluded by calling for strong leadership in the struggle for civil rights from the federal government, from both the Democratic and the Republican parties, from white, Northern liberals, from white, Southern moderates, and from the black community.

Reaction to the speech, King's first before a national audience, gave clear indication that he had become the foremost spokesman of the black protest movement. New York's *Amsterdam News* said that king 'emerged from the Prayer Pilgrimage to Washington as the number one leader of sixteen million Negroes in the United States'.[14] Shortly after, the NAACP officially recognized King's contribution to the cause of racial justice by awarding him the organization's Spingarn Medal.

The Prayer Pilgrimage helped to garner support for the Eisenhower Administration's proposal for civil rights legislation. In 1957, Congress passed the first major civil rights law since the Reconstruction era, following the American Civil War. Signed by the President in September, the Civil Rights Act of 1957 created the United States Commission on Civil Rights, established a Civil Rights Division in the Justice Department to be headed by an Assistant Attorney General, and empowered the federal government to obtain injunctions preventing deprivation of the right to vote. To enable blacks to take full advantage of the legislation, SCLC inaugurated a Crusade for Citizenship, a voter-registration drive with the idealistic goal of doubling the number of black voters in the South by the next national election. Failure of the 1957 Civil Rights Act to protect black voting rights induced the Eisenhower Administration to propose a new statute, which was passed three years later. The Civil Rights Act of 1960 authorized the federal district courts to appoint 'voting referees' to safeguard the right to vote in areas where it was denied or obstructed by local officials. The act also authorised the Department of Justice to file suits in defence of voting rights. While the Civil Rights Acts of 1957 and 1960 marked some progress, this legislation was still insufficient to guarantee the right to vote for black Americans, and did nothing to remedy the problems of segregated schools and public accommodations.

In the wake of the Prayer Pilgrimage, King and SCLC sought to rally blacks to launch a nonviolent offensive against segregation in the South. In preparation, SCLC undertook to improve itself as an organization. In the fall of 1959, King announced that he was resigning as pastor of the Dexter Avenue Baptist Church in order to be more effective as president of SCLC. He would be moving to Atlanta, the site of SCLC headquarters, to assume the co-pastorship, with his father, of the Ebenezer Baptist Church. The following year, Reverend Wyatt T. Walker became SCLC's executive director. Prior to joining the SCLC staff, Walker had been active in organizing civil rights protests in Petersburg, Virginia during the late 1950s. He was an ex-president of the Petersburg Improvement Association, and was instrumental in establishing SCLC affilitates throughout the state of Virginia. According to Louis Lomax: 'Walker was master of all he surveyed in Petersburg, his home-grown protest movement was one of the best in the nation'.[15] Bold and aggressive, Walker brought important administrative and leadership skills to SCLC. He would also contribute to shaping SCLC into an effective nonviolent fighting force.

By 1960, King believed that the time was ripe for a massive nonviolent assault upon Jim Crow, employing the tactics of sit-ins, mass marches, and civil disobedience. Black youth would play an instrumental role. In 1958 and 1959, several thousand black students had participated in two youth marches to Washington in support of the *Brown* decision. Addressing the second march, on 18 April 1959, King told the crowd that their presence in the nation's capital proved that 'the only answer you will settle for is – total desegregation and total equality – now'.[16] In a speech to the 1959 annual convention of the pacifist Fellowship of Reconciliation, King predicted that blacks throughout the South would employ 'direct action against injustice without waiting for other agencies to act. . . . We will not obey unjust laws or submit to unjust practices'.[17]

V

King's faith in black youth was confirmed. On Thursday, 1 February 1960, four black students from North Carolina Agricultural and Technical College entered a Woolworth store in Greensboro, sat down at a lunch counter legally reserved for whites, and ordered coffee. Denied service, Ezell Blair, Jr., Franklin McCain, Joe McNeil and David Richmond – each a member of the NAACP Youth Council – politely refused to leave. They were soon joined by hundreds of other students from the same college and other local black colleges. The sit-in movement, a milestone in the struggle for black equality, was born.

Though CORE had pioneered the tactic in the field of civil rights in 1942, and sporadic sit-ins had occurred throughout the South during the late 1950s, not until 1960 were they employed on a massive scale, attracting national publicity. The sit-ins reflected the development of locally-based black movements throughout the South. Most of the protests were organized and supported by SCLC affiliates, local CORE chapters and NAACP Youth Councils. By 10 February 1960, sit-ins had taken place in 15 cities throughout five Southern states. Protests were conducted not only at lunch counters, but also at department stores, libraries, supermarkets, theatres and hotels.

One of the most successful sit-in movements developed in Nashville, Tennessee, and was led by members of the Nashville Christian Leadership Council (NCLC), an SCLC affiliate. In 1959, black students from local colleges underwent training in workshops on nonviolence under the direction of Reverend James Lawson, and staged 'test sit-ins' at some Nashville department stores. On 13 February 1960, inspired by the Greensboro protest, members of the NCLC – including John Lewis, James Bevel, Diane Nash, Bernard Lafayette, and C. T. Vivian – led a series of sit-ins and a boycott against Nashville's downtown retail stores, disrupting business and publicizing black grievances. After hundreds of protesters were arrested, and many became victims of white violence, a number of stores consented to desegregate their lunch counters. Sit-ins continued to spread through the South; by the end of 1961, nearly 200 cities in the upper South and in the border states had begun to desegregate.

Though King did not lead the Southern sit-in movement, he was a major influence. According to James Farmer of CORE: 'This new surge of nonviolent activity was without question inspired by the example of Martin Luther King, Jr. in Montgomery. Nonviolence was now a "respectable" tactic, the mightiest weapon for the weaponless'.[18] King had a profound effect upon young activists. Throughout the South, student protesters read his book, *Stride Toward Freedom*, an account of the Montgomery bus boycott, and carried a statement with them which read: 'Remember the teachings of Jesus Christ, Mahatma Gandhi and Martin Luther King. Remember love and nonviolence'.[19] Addressing a church rally in Durham, North Carolina, in February 1960, King called for a united assault upon all forms of segregation, and termed the student sit-ins 'one of the most significant developments in the civil rights struggle'.[20] The outstanding success of the sit-ins substantiated King's conviction that nonviolent direct action could overturn segregation in the South.

The sit-ins projected the students to the forefront of the civil rights movement. In an effort to coordinate and centrally organize future protests, SCLC's executive secretary, Ella Baker, arranged for a meeting of student leaders. On Easter weekend, 15–17 April 1960, more than 200 student delegates from 58 Southern communities convened at Shaw University, in Raleigh, North Carolina. In her opening address, 'More Than a Hamburger', Baker told the audience to consider that the struggle for equality would entail not merely integration of lunch counters, but broad social change. King also addressed the students, preaching his philosophy of nonviolence. The greatest impression was made by Reverend James Lawson, the pacifist leader of the Nashville sit-ins, who criticized the inadequate legalistic methods of the NAACP, and called upon the students to engage in nonviolent protest. 'The pace of social change is too slow', he lamented. 'At this rate, it will be at least another generation before the major forms of segregation disappear. All of Africa will be free before the American Negro attains first-class citizenship'.[21]

Before the Raleigh conference concluded, the students rejected a proposal that they become part of SCLC, choosing instead to form an independent Temporary Coordinating Committee. On the final day of the conference, the students overwhelmingly endorsed King's philosophy of nonviolence. 'We affirm', they announced in a published statement, 'the philosophical or religious ideal of nonviolence as the foundation of our purpose, the presupposition of our faith, and the manner of our actions'.[22] Within a few months, the Temporary Coordinating Committee was transformed into a permanent protest organization: the Student Nonviolent Coordinating Committee (SNCC), which became popularly known as 'Snick'.

VI

The presidential campaign of John F. Kennedy in 1960 kindled hopes among black Americans for a new birth of freedom. Kennedy had endorsed the Democratic Party's strong civil rights platform – hailed as 'the most far-reaching stand of any major political party in American history' – which promised to end racial discrimination in voting, public schools, employment and housing.[23] The accomplishment of their civil rights goals, the platform concluded, 'will require executive orders, legal action brought by the Attorney

General, legislation and improved Congressional procedures to safeguard majority rule'.[24] In accepting the nomination of his party, Kennedy praised the platform, declaring it one 'on which I can run with enthusiasm and conviction'.[25] He also instructed Senator Joseph Clark and Representative Emanuel Celler 'to prepare a comprehensive civil rights bill, embodying our platform commitments, for the introduction at the beginning of the next session'.[26]

Nevertheless, early in his campaign, Kennedy began to de-emphasize the need for new civil rights legislation, stressing instead the importance of executive initiative. In the second of his televised debates with Richard Nixon, the Republican candidate, Kennedy said that the President has a responsibility to provide 'a moral tone and moral leadership' in the area of civil rights.[27] Accordingly, Kennedy pledged more vigorous enforcement of the Civil Rights Acts of 1957 and 1960 to protect voting rights, and proclaimed that federally-assisted housing could be 'desegregated by the stroke of a presidential pen'.[28]

In October 1960, the month prior to the presidential election, King made national headlines when he was arrested, along with 36 students, for sitting-in at Rich's Department Store in Atlanta, Georgia. Five months before, soon after moving to Atlanta, he had been arrested and placed on one year's probation for driving without a valid Georgia licence in DeKalb County. Although the Atlanta authorities were prepared to release him, the DeKalb County judge sentenced King to four months of hard labour in Reidsville State Prison for violating probation. Knowing the possible consequences of such a sentence for a black person in Georgia, many feared for his safety. King's imprisonment prompted John F. Kennedy to make a highly-publicized telephone call to a worried Mrs King in Atlanta, expressing his concern. The following day, Robert Kennedy convinced the DeKalb County judge to grant King his constitutional right and release him on bond, after spending one day in jail. John F. Kennedy's intervention led King's father, a Republican, to announce that he was endorsing the Democratic nominee for the presidency. That November, Kennedy received almost 75 per cent of the black vote, which played a decisive role in his slim victory over Nixon in the election.

Soon after Kennedy took office in 1961, King published an article in *The Nation*, 'Equality Now', urging the new President to undertake 'a radically new approach to the question of civil rights' by sponsoring far-reaching legislation and issuing executive orders to wipe out racial discrimination.[29] But the President was constrained to bow to political realities. He did not want to alienate the Southern Democrats, who were strong enough in Congress to defeat any proposed civil rights legislation, in addition to the rest of his ambitious legislative programme, which included tax bills and Medicare. With Nixon having received the majority of Southern votes in 1960, Kennedy wanted to insure another Democratic victory in the election of 1964. He hoped that vigorous enforcement of current civil rights laws would be sufficient to maintain the confidence of black voters, without risking the loss of his political support in Congress. Kennedy appointed several highly qualified blacks to important federal posts – including Thurgood Marshall as a United States Circuit Court Justice, Carl Rowan as assistant secretary of state for public affairs, Robert Weaver as head of the Housing and Home Financing Agency, and Andrew Hatcher as associate press secretary. But Kennedy was careful to placate Southern Democrats by appointing a number of ardent segregationists to the federal bench in the South.

In place of new civil rights legislation, Kennedy decided to pursue a policy that would guarantee blacks the right to register and vote. The Administration concluded that a massive voter-registration drive would direct the attention of blacks away from protests and increase the number of Democratic voters for the next election. To educate blacks in understanding the electoral process, the Administration sponsored a Voter Education Project, financially underwritten by philanthropic organizations such as the Taconic and Field Foundations.

But many black Americans became disappointed with Kennedy's 'New Frontier'. During its first two years, the Administration failed to protect adequately civil rights in the South. Not until 21 November 1962 did the President fulfil his campaign pledge to issue an executive order banning discrimination in federally-funded housing. The order was so poorly implemented that it had minimal effect. Even the Voter Education Project was a disappointment. Although the Justice Department initiated a number of voting rights suits, it was hampered by weaknesses inherent in the Civil Rights Acts of 1957 and 1960. By 1964, only 40 per cent of the black population of voting age in the South would be qualified to vote, as compared with 70 per cent of adult whites.[30]

VII

The weaknesses in the Kennedy Administration's civil rights policy were first dramatized to the entire nation by the Freedom Rides of 1961. Soon after becoming CORE's national director in February, James Farmer announced a plan to test Southern compliance with a December 1960 United States Supreme Court decision in *Boynton* v. *Virginia*, prohibiting segregation in interstate transportation facilities. On 4 May 1961, after informing President Kennedy of their route, an interracial group of 13 Freedom Riders boarded two buses, a Greyhound and a Trailways, in Washington, D.C., and set out on a trip to challenge segregation throughout the South. New Orleans was their destination. The CORE-sponsored Freedom Ride was modelled on the organization's 1947 Journey of Reconciliation, and would, in effect, put the sit-ins on the road. The Freedom Riders would challenge Jim Crow in terminal restaurants, restrooms and waiting rooms, exposing the blatant defiance of federal law throughout the South. The Riders pledged to remain nonviolent, and to accept the legal penalty of imprisonment for their civil disobedience. Whereas the 1947 Ride had been confined to the Upper South, the 1961 Ride would penetrate the more resistant areas of the Deep South, taking the Riders through the states of Virginia, the Carolinas, Georgia, Alabama and Mississippi. The Freedom Ride went beyond the nonviolent strategy implemented by the sit-ins, and was calculated not only to disrupt public order in the South, but also to compel the federal government to fulfil its responsibility to protect citizens attempting to exercise their civil rights. As James Farmer recalled: 'Our intention was to provoke the Southern authorities into arresting us and thereby prod the Justice Department into enforcing the law of the land'.[31]

During the first few days, the Freedom Riders travelled unmolested through Virginia and North Carolina. But upon reaching Rock Hill, South Carolina, violence erupted. Whites attacked the Riders at the Greyhound station, beating John Lewis, future leader of SNCC, and Albert Bigelow, a white pacifist, when they attempted to integrate the 'whites only' waiting room. Trained in nonviolence, the Freedom Riders offered no resistance. Only after a white woman member of CORE was knocked to the ground did police intervene. Relentlessly, the Freedom Riders proceeded without incident through Athens and Augusta, Georgia, arriving in Atlanta on 13 May, where they spent the night, before heading into Alabama.

On Sunday, 14 May, the Greyhound bus pulled into Anniston, Alabama, where an angry white mob, armed with iron bars and chains, punctured the tires and smashed the windows. After police arrived, the crowd allowed the bus to depart, only to pursue it in cars. When the bus tires finally went flat six miles outside of Anniston, the mob again encircled the bus, tossing in an incendiary bomb. As the Freedom Riders escaped from the burning bus, they were beaten. One hour later, when the Trailways bus arrived in Anniston, whites jumped aboard and beat the Freedom Riders. When the Trailways bus finally reached the Birmingham terminal, the Riders were set upon by a mob who beat them mercilessly while police were conspicuously absent. One Rider, James Peck, a white veteran of CORE's 1947 Journey of Reconciliation, was knocked unconscious.

By this time, the Freedom Ride was making national headlines, and pictures of the beaten Riders were widely circulated by the media. Attorney General Robert Kennedy responded by telephoning Alabama Governor John Patterson to request that the state authorities provide for the protection of the Riders. Although at first the governor refused to cooperate, avoiding calls from both the Attorney General and the President, he was soon persuaded to meet with a representative of the federal government. Justice Department attorney John Siegenthaler, Robert Kennedy's administrative assistant, was immediately dispatched to Alabama. Meanwhile, after bus drivers refused to transport them to their next destination of Montgomery, the battered Freedom Riders elected to complete their journey to New Orleans by aeroplane, where they attended a mass rally on 17 May, marking the seventh anniversary of the Supreme Court's *Brown* decision. Thus concluded the CORE phase of the Freedom Ride.

At this point, SNCC students from Nashville and Atlanta intervened. Convinced that the protest must continue, 21 SNCC Freedom Riders, including John Lewis, left Birmingham for New Orleans. Arriving *en route* at Montgomery on the morning of 20 May, they were assaulted by a savage mob as they came off a bus. Across the street from the terminal, a horrified John Doar of the Justice Department described the scene to Attorney General Robert Kennedy by telephone. 'The passengers are coming off', Doar reported. 'A bunch of men led by a guy with a bleeding face are beating them. There are no cops. It's terrible. It's terrible. There's not a cop in sight. People are yelling, "Get'em, get'em." It's awful'.[32] Among those injured was John Siegenthaler, who was knocked unconscious while attempting to rescue two white women Freedom Riders in his car.

Police were absent in Montgomery as the white racist mob swelled to over a thousand. Governor Patterson called the Riders 'rabble rousers', and claimed that he could not guarantee their protection.[33] In Washington, President Kennedy issued a public statement requesting that local authorities prevent further outbreaks of violence. He also instructed the Attorney General to take whatever action was appropriate. The Justice Department had assumed that the rules of federalism dictated that the federal government could not intervene in any state to enforce the law unless it was clear that the local authorities could no longer maintain order. As noted earlier, the Freedom Ride was based upon a strategy designed to provoke such dramatic conflict and disorder that the federal government would have no alternative but to intervene. Convinced by the mob violence in Montgomery that the local authorities alone were insufficient to protect the rights and lives of American citizens, Attorney General Robert Kennedy dispatched some 400 federal marshalls under the command of Byron White to the city on 20 May.

King served as chairman of the Freedom Ride Coordinating Committee, organized by CORE, SCLC, and SNCC. The committee's objective was to 'fill the jails of Montgomery and Jackson in order to keep a sharp image of the issue before the public', and force the Justice Department to protect the lives of interstate travellers.[34] On Sunday, 21 May, King arrived by aeroplane in Montgomery from Chicago to address a mass rally in support of the Riders at Ralph Abernathy's First Baptist Church. As King assailed the Alabama authorities for failing to protect the Riders, an angry mob of several thousand whites surrounded the church and shattered the windows with rocks, bricks and bottles, prompting him to telephone the Attorney General with a request for federal protection. While King led those inside the church in freedom songs, federal marshalls arrived and restrained the mob with truncheons and tear gas. Throughout the night, blacks remained inside the First Baptist Church, until Governor Patterson, bowing to federal pressure, finally declared martial law and sent the Alabama National Guard and state troopers to Montgomery to disperse the mob.

Determined to continue the protest, King and the Freedom Ride Coordinating Committee rejected Attorney General Robert Kennedy's call for a 'cooling off period', and prepared to continue the Ride. As James Farmer explained: 'We had been cooling off for a hundred years. If we got any cooler, we'd be in a deep freeze'.[35] Additional Riders were recruited and participated in workshops on the techniques of nonviolence. Addressing the final training session on the evening of 23 May, King reiterated the objectives of the Freedom Ride: 'To test use of transportation facilities, according to federal law; to encourage others to demand use of the facilities; and to direct the spotlight of public attention to areas which still segregate'.[36] Joined by additional students from Washington, Nashville and Atlanta, the Riders planned to pass through Mississippi before reaching their destination of New Orleans.

On 24 May, 27 Freedom Riders left Montgomery for Jackson, Mississippi in two buses. The Attorney General had prevailed upon Mississippi's Senator James Eastland and Governor Ross Barnett to promise protection for the Riders, with the understanding that they would be arrested as soon as they arrived in Jackson. They were escorted along the road to Jackson by the Mississippi National Guard and patrol cars, while aeroplanes and helicopters scouted overhead. Invited by the Riders to accompany them, King declined because he could not risk another violation of his parole.

When the two bus loads of Freedom Riders arrived unharmed in Jackson on 24 May, they were arrested for attempting to integrate the terminal. That evening, King called Attorney General Kennedy, who wanted the Riders released from jail, informing him that they would refuse release on bail. King went on to explain the basis for their nonviolent civil disobedience: 'It's a matter of conscience and morality. They must use their lives and their bodies to right a wrong. Our conscience tells us that the law is wrong and we must resist, but we have a moral obligation to accept the penalty'. When King said that the Riders might be joined by thousands more, Kennedy warned him against such a threat. After reflecting, King responded: 'It's difficult to understand the position of oppressed people. Ours is a way out – creative, moral and nonviolent. . . . You must understand that we've made no gains without pressure and I hope that pressure will always be moral, legal and peaceful'.[37]

Meanwhile, King continued to prod the federal government to act more decisively in support of civil rights. On 5 June, he called upon President Kennedy to issue a 'second Emancipation Proclamation'.[38]

Throughout the summer of 1961, the Freedom Ride continued to capture national headlines as students and ministers, mostly black but some white, streamed into Jackson. The Freedom Ride had become a mass movement, dramatizing the defiance of federal law in the South. Among those arrested were Stokely Carmichael, Ralph Abernathy, Wyatt T. Walker, James Farmer, James Lawson, John Lewis and Yale chaplain William Sloane Coffin. By the end of the summer, more than 300 persons had been arrested in Jackson, and over 1000, from every part of the nation, had participated in Freedom Rides in the South.

The Rides bore substantial results, inspiring the Southern nonviolent protest movement. On 29 May 1961, at the suggestion of King, Attorney General Kennedy formally petitioned the Interstate Commerce Commission (ICC) to act against segregation in interstate bus terminals. On 22 September, the ICC responded by issuing an order banning segregation in both interstate carriers and terminal facilities, effective on 1 November 1961. The ruling was designed to implement the United States Supreme Court decisions of 1946 and 1960. Although some areas of the South continued to resist, CORE reported in 1962 that scores of communities had voluntarily complied with the ICC ruling.

The Freedom Rides supplied an important strategic lesson for King and SCLC: in order to arouse public sympathy sufficient to pressure the federal government to enforce civil rights in the states and localities, white racists had to be provoked to use violence against nonviolent protesters. As James Farmer later reflected: 'Our philosophy was simple. We put pressure and create a crisis and then they react. I am absolutely certain that the ICC order wouldn't have been issued were it not for the Freedom Rides'.[39] This lesson received dramatic reinforcement in 1962, when James Meredith attempted to become the first black man to enrol in the University of Mississippi, precipitating what has been called 'the gravest federal–state crisis since the Civil War'.[40] After Mississippi Governor Ross Barnett defied a federal injunction by preventing Meredith's enrolment, President Kennedy sent federal marshalls to the university campus at Oxford, Mississippi to enforce the court order. When they were rebuffed by a rioting white mob, the President was compelled to dispatch several thousand federal troops and National Guardsmen. Before the violence ended, two persons died and 375 were injured. On 1 October 1962, James Meredith, escorted by federal marshalls, registered as a student at the University of Mississippi.

In the years ahead, provoking crises to stir publicity and prod the federal government to take decisive action in support of civil rights would become an integral part of the strategy of nonviolent direct action implemented by King and SCLC.

3

The Lessons of Albany, Georgia, 1961–2

The first test of SCLC's capacity for nonviolent warfare occurred in Albany, Georgia, in 1962. The fifth largest city in the state, with a population of 56 000, 40 per cent black, Albany was a stronghold of racism in the Deep South. The Albany *Herald*, published by staunch segregationist James Gray, regularly featured editorials and stories supporting white supremacy and urging the City Commission to resist requests by blacks for desegregation. In 1961, most Albany blacks were not registered to vote, and the city's public facilities, including the bus and railway stations, lunch counters, schools, parks, hospitals and libraries, were completely segregated. As historian Howard Zinn, then a reporter for the Southern Regional Council, observed: 'In the year 1961, a Negro arrived in Albany on the colored part of the bus, entered a colored waiting room, drank from a colored water fountain, used a colored restroom, walked eight blocks to find a restaurant which would feed him, and travelled six miles to find a good Negro motel'.[1] Albany's entire justice system was white: the courts were segregated, the jails were segregated; the judges, juries, sheriffs, deputies and the city police were white. Nevertheless, by late 1961, the student sit-ins and the Freedom Rides had exerted an effect upon the city's black population. The Jim Crow South was stunned when, after generations of apathy, Albany blacks engaged in massive nonviolent protests that rocked the community, disrupting civil order for almost a year.

Civil rights agitation began in Albany, Georgia in the fall of 1961, when SNCC field workers Charles Sherrod and Cordell Reagon arrived and established a voter registration drive. SNCC also organized black students at local high schools and at Albany State College to protest segregation, and held workshops to instruct blacks in the tactics of nonviolence. On 17 November 1961, encouraged by the efforts of SNCC, Dr William G. Anderson, a black osteopath, consolidated a number of local organizations to form the Albany Movement. Anderson was president; Slater King, a real estate broker, vice president; and Marion Page, a retired railway worker, secretary. The goal of the Movement was to overturn segregation not only in bus stations and lunch counters, but in all forms of public facilities within the city.

On 22 November, five blacks were arrested by Police Chief Laurie Pritchett when they attempted to integrate a Trailways bus station lunch counter. The protesters sought to compel the city to comply with the Interstate Commerce Commission ruling of 1 November, banning segregation on bus and train facilities. The protest gathered momentum when, on 10 December, a group of ten Freedom Riders, including SCLC's Youth Director, Bernard Lee, and SNCC's James Forman, was arrested by Chief Pritchett for trying to integrate the waiting room of the Albany railway station. Pritchett told the press: 'We will not stand for these trouble-makers coming into our city for the sole purpose of disturbing the peace and quiet of the city of Albany'.[2]

To protest the arrest of the Freedom Riders and the failure of the federal government to enforce the ICC ruling, meetings were held in black churches throughout Albany. Massive demonstrations followed, in which over 500 high school and college students were arrested for parading without a permit. After negotiations between the city and the Movement quickly broke down, Mayor Asa Kelley requested that the state National Guard be mobilized. On 14 December, when the protest began to falter, Dr Anderson tele-phoned King and Abernathy, who had been following the develop-ments in Albany from SCLC headquarters in Atlanta. Anderson issued a formal invitation to King to assist the protest by speaking at a Movement meeting.

The following evening, Friday, 15 December, King, Abernathy and Walker arrived at Albany's crowded Shiloh Baptist Church. King's presence brought the protest valuable publicity. 'When Martin Luther King came to town', Dr Anderson recalled, 'there was worldwide press immediately present in Albany'.[3] King had no intention of leading a protest campaign; he merely hoped that his presence would revive the Movement. Addressing the audience of over a thousand, he exhorted them to continue the fight against racial injustice: 'We shall overcome. Don't stop now. Keep moving. Walk together children. Don't you get weary'.[4] Blacks responded by singing choruses of 'We Shall Overcome' – the anthem of the civil rights movement. Before closing the meeting, Dr Anderson suddenly asked King to lead a protest march to City Hall the next day. Taken by surprise, he consented before the cheering crowd. King and SCLC had become part of the Albany Movement.

But not all blacks welcomed King to Albany. Movement secretary Marion Page objected to what he considered an SCLC intrusion. SNCC, having prepared the groundwork for the Albany protest by organizing the black community, resented that King – whom they contemptuously dubbed 'De Lawd' – would come to town, draw most of the publicity, and win most of the credit. According to SNCC members: 'We plant the seed. Dr. King reaps the harvest'. Others complained: 'We were working here long before De Lawd showed up to pull his miracles'.[5] Cordell Reagon, who had been in Albany more than two months before SCLC arrived, explained that King 'didn't come there by our request. . . . He came there by Dr Anderson's request . . . we were not even consulted. . . . There was no necessity for King to come to town'.[6] SNCC's James Forman recalled: 'I opposed the move [to invite King to Albany], pointing out that it was most important to keep the Albany movement a people's movement – the presence of Dr King would detract from, rather than intensify this focus'.[7] Forman believed that for blacks to attain freedom, they must rely upon local organization rather than charismatic leaders such as King. Commenting upon what he regarded as SCLC's imperialistic tendency, Julian Bond observed that when SNCC finished working in an area, it left behind 'a community movement with local leadership, not a new branch of SNCC'.[8] As blacks throughout the South began to view King as a Messiah, SNCC members resented being regarded as mere John the Baptists.

II

The afternoon of 16 December, King, along with Abernathy and Dr Anderson led a procession of 264 marchers to Albany City Hall. They were arrested for parading without a permit. By this time, more than 700 protesters had been arrested, over 400 remained imprisoned, and the disruption had begun to hurt business for the city merchants. Wyatt Walker announced that SCLC would commit its 'total resources' to the Albany campaign.[9] King vowed to stay in jail until the Movement's demands were met, hoping that the resulting publicity would pressure the federal government to intervene to enforce the ICC ruling, and bring the city to the negotiating table. He appealed to blacks throughout the nation to join him in Albany: 'If convicted', he promised, 'I will refuse to pay the fine. I expect to spend Christmas in jail, and I hope thousands will join me'.[10] The city responded by re-opening negotiations.

On Monday morning, 18 December, two days after his arrest, the nation was surprised to learn that, contrary to his original intention, King had posted bond and was released from jail. Movement leaders Dr Anderson and Marion Page had reached a verbal 'truce' with the city commissioners, who were anxious to prevent masses of sympathizers from flocking to join King in the Albany jail. According to the 'truce', bus and train facilities would be desegregated, all demonstrators released on bond, and a biracial committee established to work out a schedule for desegregating the city, in return for a moratorium on protests until a hearing before a newly-elected City Commission on 23 January. After Dr Anderson explained that the verbal agreement was the 'practical course to take', a sceptical King had no choice but to accept release on bail and return to Atlanta. Before departing from Albany, he praised the agreement at a press conference. When asked by reporters why he had reneged on his pledge to remain in jail through Christmas, King pointed out that his release was essential to the agreement. 'I would not want to stand in the way of peaceful negotiations', he responded.[11]

The 'truce' assured Albany of a peaceful Christmas, but it did not bring any substantial gains to the black community. Released from jail, the demonstrators found no change in the unjust conditions that had given rise to their protest. Albany was still thoroughly segregated, and the protest had merely extracted a promise from the city that it would hear black grievances. On 23 January, after having halted demonstrations for more than a month, King's scepticism was vindicated when the new City Commission refused to act upon black grievances. 'The demand for privileges will scarcely be heard', the Commission insisted in a public statement, 'unless . . . arrogance, lawlessness, and irresponsibility subside'. Movement leaders, the statement concluded, would 'earn acceptance of their people by encouraging the improvement of their moral and ethical standards'.[12]

Thus, by the end of January, 1962, the Albany Movement had been outmanoeuvered by the white power structure, and seemed on the verge of defeat. King accepted the blame. Had he remained in jail, perhaps hundreds of supporters would have joined him in Albany, and the meaninglessness of the verbal agreement might have been exposed. As King later stated: 'I'm sorry I was bailed out. I didn't understand at the time what was happening. We thought that the victory had been won. When we got out, we discovered it was all a hoax. We had lost an initiative that we never regained'.[13] According to the New York *Herald Tribune*, the Albany 'truce' was 'one of the most stunning defeats of King's career'.[14]

Having been outsmarted by the City Commission, the Movement decided to renew the protest with a boycott of Albany buses which led to a meeting with the city's private bus company. On 29 January, black leaders offered to end the boycott in return for a written pledge from the company that it would desegregate the buses and hire blacks. Company officials replied that before they would issue such a pledge, the city must sign an agreement that it would no longer enforce the segregated transportation ordinance. When the City Commission rejected this proposal on 31 January, the boycott continued, causing the bus company to go out of business by early February. Meanwhile, a selective boycott of downtown Albany stores, begun shortly after the December 1961 truce, failed to apply sufficient pressure to extract concessions from the business community.

III

On 27 February 1962, King and Abernathy returned to Albany to stand trial for the 16 December march. Lawyers for the defence argued that their arrest had violated the First Amendment rights of free speech and peaceful assembly. Found guilty of disorderly conduct and of parading without a permit, sentencing was postponed until 10 July. King then embarked on a speaking tour to raise funds for the Albany Movement. When the day of sentencing arrived, the judge presented King and Abernathy with a choice of either a fine of $175, or 45 days in jail. Before television cameras, King announced that he and Abernathy would go to jail as a moral protest. They hoped that the national publicity would revitalize the Albany Movement and induce federal intervention.

A concerned President Kennedy requested that Attorney General Robert Kennedy report to him on the Albany situation. Assistant Attorney General Burke Marshall telephoned Coretta King to inform her that the Justice Department would use its influence to secure her husband's release. Meanwhile, Albany's black community prepared to mount another series of nonviolent demonstrations.

But once again, King did not remain imprisoned long enough to help the Albany Movement. On 13 July, after only three days in jail, he and Abernathy were told by Chief Pritchett that they were being released because an 'unidentified, well-dressed Negro man' had paid their fines. Some members of the Albany Movement speculated that the Justice Department had arranged the release. In fact, Mayor Asa Kelley, after a meeting between white segregationists and conservative blacks, had ordered King's removal from jail to deprive the protest of a galvanizing issue. As Pritchett later admitted, 'it was a matter of strategy. . . . An arrangement was made'.[15] The Albany Movement had been outsmarted. As a perplexed Ralph Abernathy expressed at a mass meeting: 'I've been thrown out of lots of places in my day, but never before have I been thrown out of jail'.[16]

Refusing to relent, King announced on 16 July that he would soon intensify the nonviolent crusade to even greater proportions. '[Our] protest', he proclaimed to crowds in Shiloh Baptist and Mount Zion churches, 'will turn Albany upside down'.[17] Faced with the threat of massive disruption, the city responded with a move calculated to destroy the protest by gaining the sympathy of the federal government. Attorneys for the city went to the United States District Court to request an injunction against the protests on the grounds that they disturbed the peace and prevented other city residents from exercising their constitutional rights. Throughout the civil rights movement, injunctions – court orders requiring that individuals do, or refrain from doing, acts specifically described in the order – were effective weapons of segregationist authorities in attempting to impede nonviolent protests. At the same time, an injunction banning demonstrations would not only attract public attention to a campaign, highlighting the confrontation between the protest movement and the racist order, but also raise the issue of the constitutional right of blacks to protest peacefully.

On 20 July, District Court Judge J. Robert Elliott, a segregationist recently appointed to the bench by President Kennedy, enjoined King and other Albany Movement leaders from engaging in unlawful picketing, congregating or marching in the streets, and from 'any act designed to provoke breaches of the peace'.[18] The injunction banned demonstrations for ten days, until 30 July, when a hearing would determine whether the ban would be permanent. King's attorneys immediately sought to overturn the order in the United States Court of Appeals.

The federal District Court injunction posed a dilemma for King and SCLC. Defying it might alienate the Justice Department and the federal courts, upon which blacks depended for protection of their civil rights. As King explained: 'The federal courts have given us our great victories, and I cannot, in good conscience, declare war on them'.[19] On the other hand, if the protests paused, the resulting loss of momentum might doom the Albany campaign. Believing that blacks had more to lose by defying the federal courts, King decided to obey the injunction, halting the protests that had disrupted Albany for the past eight months. He announced to the press: 'Out of respect for the leadership the federal judiciary has given, we have agreed to obey the order issued by Judge Elliott and to work vigorously in higher courts to have it dissolved'.[20] King's decision angered Cordell Reagon, Charles Sherrod and other members of SNCC, who argued that the court order was unjust. But King was encouraged by the prediction of his legal staff that the injunction would be overruled as a sweeping restriction of the demonstrators' constitutional rights.

On 24 July, the Albany Movement's petition was successful when the federal Fifth Circuit Court of Appeals, presided over by Judge Elbert P. Tuttle, rescinded the injunction of the lower District Court, thus permitting demonstrations to resume after a costly delay of five days. That evening, a crowd of some 2000 black youths rioted, throwing stones and bottles at police. 'Did you see them nonviolent rocks?', Chief Pritchett sarcastically asked the press.[21] The violence by blacks was in response to an incident of the day before, when Mrs Slater King, the pregnant wife of the Movement's vice president, was beaten unconscious while attempting to deliver packages to prisoners in the Mitchell County Jail. To prevent further violence, King suspended demonstrations – over the objections of SNCC – and declared 26 July a 'Day of Penitence'. He followed the example of Gandhi, who, after his people resorted to violence in the Punjab in 1919, stopped protests until nonviolent discipline was restored. For the remainder of the week in Albany, direct action was confined to prayer vigils. When King, Abernathy and Anderson led a vigil in front of City Hall on 27 July, they were again arrested and imprisoned. Within his jail cell, King wrote an article for the New York *Amsterdam News*, describing Albany as 'a symbol of segregation's last stand'.[22] Meanwhile, Chief Pritchett complained in a hearing before Judge Elliot that King's presence in Albany had 'raised community tension to the kindling point'.[23]

By this time, the Movement had begun to attract greater attention from the federal government. On 1 August, President Kennedy gave a moral boost to the Movement by saying publicly at a nationally televised press conference that he did not understand why the United States could negotiate with the Soviet Union, while Albany officials were unwilling to do the same for black American citizens. Mayor Kelley responded by announcing that the city would 'never negotiate with outside agitators whose avowed purpose is to create turmoil'. If King left Albany, he added, the City Commission would be 'happy to discuss problems with local Negroes'.[24] While King was in jail, an interracial group of clergymen travelled to Washington to urge federal intervention in Albany. A bipartisan group of United States Senators requested that the Justice Department take 'all possible steps' to assist those imprisoned in the city.[25] When Albany authorities sought another federal injunction, this time a permanent banning of the protests, the Justice Department entered an *amicus curiae* brief in the federal court on behalf of the Movement. Though King was grateful to the Kennedy Administration, he nevertheless pointed out that its moral and legal support offered 'no solution to the problems' in Albany.[26] Rather than directly intervening to enforce civil rights, the Administration seemed to prefer public order over racial justice, alleging that the federal system prevented it from exercising police power in a state unless the local authorities were incapable of upholding law and order. As long as Chief Pritchett continued to meet nonviolent protests with nonviolent law enforcement, federal intervention would not be forthcoming in Albany, Georgia.

On Friday, 10 August, King and his associates were tried for their arrests of 27 July, on the usual charges of parading without a permit and disturbing the peace. Though convicted, King again lost the opportunity to stir publicity for the Movement when he and the others were given suspended sentences instead of being jailed. On Friday evening, King announced that he was halting demonstrations and leaving Albany to spend the weekend in Atlanta, hoping that his absence would encourage negotiations. After the City Commission refused to bargain in good faith, King returned to Albany on 13 August and denounced the Commission for its intransigence. The following day, having failed to win concessions from the city, a frustrated Dr Anderson declared that the demonstrations would cease, and that henceforth the Movement would concentrate on voter registration. Within a short time, a disappointed King announced that SCLC was departing from Albany. 'There comes a time to leave', concluded Ralph Abernathy.[27] King and SCLC had exhausted their efforts to bring racial justice to one of the South's most segregated communities.

The Albany campaign was pronounced a dismal failure by the press and many civil rights leaders. After months of demonstrations, and some 1200 arrests, few tangible results had been achieved. By the end of 1962, the Movement had failed to reach its goal of comprehensive desegregation, and racial conditions in the city were much the same as the year before. Mrs Ruby Hurley, Southeastern regional NAACP director, expressed frustration: 'Albany was successful only if the goal was to go to jail'.[28] Though the city reluctantly complied with the ICC ruling and desegregated its terminals, the remaining public facilities – including the parks, swimming pools and libraries — were either closed, or kept segregated after being 'sold' to a group of Albany businessmen. No efforts were made to hire black bus drivers, policemen or sales clerks, and department store lunch counters remained segregated. As Chief Laurie Pritchett proudly observed: 'Albany is as segregated as ever'.[29] Malcolm X considered the Albany campaign the 'lowest point' in the civil rights struggle in America.[30] According to author Lerone Bennett: 'Albany, by any standard, was a staggering defeat for King and the Freedom Movement', and the 'darkest hour' of Martin Luther King, Jr.'s public career.[31] One year after King left Albany, Reese Cleghorn rendered the following verdict in *The New Republic*: 'Albany remains a monument to white supremacy'.[32] Conditions would remain virtually the same until the enactment of the Civil Rights Act of 1964.

IV

A number of cogent reasons have been suggested to explain the defeat of the Albany campaign. The absence of careful planning impaired the campaign from the beginning. King and SCLC did not choose Albany, the Movement chose them. When King spoke at the Movement rally on the night of 15 December, 1961, he had no idea that he would become committed to a protest campaign for several months. SCLC had no opportunity to study its opponents in Albany beforehand. According to Dr Anderson, when he went to jail with King and Abernathy on 16 December 1961, the day after SCLC first arrived in Albany, 'we left no instructions, we left nobody in charge . . . we had no plans. We had not even planned another mass meeting'.[33] SCLC's Andrew Young explained: 'There wasn't any real strategy in Albany. . . . We didn't know then how to mobilize people in masses. We learned in Albany'.[34]

The campaign was also plagued by disunity. Friction between SCLC and SNCC worked to the advantage of the white power structure. 'They clashed over everything', said SCLC's James Bevel, referring to the Albany Movement. 'They clashed over who would be in a news conference . . . who would be on the front page'.[35] Charles Sherrod said that there was a 'constant war' between SNCC and SCLC.[36] After SCLC took the lead in Albany, SNCC was excluded from strategy sessions and press conferences. SNCC members not only resented the presence of King, but they also attacked his judgement throughout the campaign. They thought that he was too conciliatory. They criticized him for obeying the federal injunction, and for halting the campaign with a 'Day of Penitence'. Whatever happened to 'Christmas in jail?', they asked. The Movement also failed to gain the support of Albany's entire black community; many members of the older generation, fearing the disruptive potential of nonviolent direct action, preferred the more conservative, legalist methods of the NAACP. Older blacks also objected to 'outsiders' such as King coming to the city to settle their affairs. There is, moreover, evidence that the campaign was betrayed by paid black informants who reported to Chief Pritchett the decisions made at Movement meetings.[37]

Post-mortem assessments of the Albany campaign cannot ignore the shrewd tactics of Police Chief Laurie Pritchett. Having read about King's achievement in Montgomery and studied his tactics, Pritchett was determined to undermine the effectiveness of the Albany Movement by meeting nonviolence with nonviolence. As the sit-ins and Freedom Rides revealed, nonviolent direct action was most effective when protesters incited white racist violence, creating local crises, and compelling the federal government to enforce basic constitutional rights. Because Chief Pritchett succeeded in preserving a semblance of order in Albany, the Kennedy Administration felt justified in its policy of nonintervention. The insensitivity of the federal government to the plight of Albany's blacks, indeed of blacks throughout the South, was epitomized when, after the Albany 'truce' in December 1961, Attorney General Robert Kennedy telephoned Mayor Kelly to compliment him on the 'orderly manner' in which the disturbances had been handled by the city.[38] As NAACP's Roy Wilkins later reflected: 'The situation in Albany affirmed more than ever my own belief that we would gain our goals only when the White House and Congress, as well as the Supreme Court, were all acting on our side'.[39]

The Albany Movement could not fulfil its Gandhi-inspired goal of clogging the judicial system. To prevent the Movement from filling the jails, Pritchett arranged to have demonstrators incarcerated outside Albany, in neighbouring counties, once the jails in Albany proper were filled. As SNCC activist Bill Hansen lamented: 'We were naive enough to think we could fill up the jails. . . . We ran out of people before [Chief Pritchett] ran out of jails'.[40] Albany's Police Chief also perceived the importance of the media to the nonviolent movement. Unlike King's later opponents, Bull Connor in Birmingham and Jim Clark in Selma, Pritchett denied the protest movement valuable publicity by not resorting to fire hoses, police dogs, and clubs to breakup demonstrations. The few incidents of police brutality that did occur were committed away from the view of newspaper photographers and television cameras. As Pritchett proclaimed in triumph: 'We, the duly constituted authorities and citizens of this city, met nonviolence with nonviolence and we are, indeed, proud of the outcome'.[41] Pritchett's method was simple: he peacefully arrested every man, woman and child in Albany who attempted to exercise the constitutional right to protest. Even Coretta King felt obliged to recall his achievement:

Police Chief Laurie Pritchett was not at all typical of Southern policemen. He was not brutal, though some of his officers engaged in brutality. He tried to be decent, and as a person, he displayed kindness. . . . Our people were given fair warning. Often they would refuse to disperse, and would drop on their knees and pray. Chief Pritchett would bow his head with them while they prayed. Then, of course, he would arrest them and the people would go to jail singing.[42]

The Albany city authorities also made a number of tactical moves that crippled the protest. Not only did the City Commission encourage Pritchett's nonviolent law enforcement policy, but it also managed to prevent King from taking advantage of his arrests to spur the campaign. Each time King was jailed, his premature release deprived the campaign of necessary publicity. The first time, he was lured from jail by a bogus truce between the Movement and the city; the second time, he was bailed out; and the third time, he received a suspended sentence. The City Commission, steadfast in its refusal to grant blacks any concessions, was also shrewd in offering a mere oral truce on 18 December 1961, halting demonstrations for more than a month. In addition, city attorneys were able to secure the federal injunction that halted demonstrations for ten days, destroying the momentum that was vital to the success of the campaign. Although King obeyed the court order out of deference to the federal judiciary, the injunction exacerbated divisions within the Movement, and, according to Andrew Young, 'broke the back' of the protest.[43]

In retrospect, the Albany Movement attempted to achieve too much. In nonviolent direct action, as in warfare, attention must be focused upon the weakest points in the opponent's defence. Instead of attempting to overturn the entire system of segregated public facilities in Albany, one or two targets should have been chosen. Howard Zinn, in a perceptive analysis of the Albany campaign, observed: 'There are advantages to singling out a particular goal and concentrating on it. . . . The community is presented with a specific concrete demand rather than a quilt of grievances and demands which smothers the always limited ability of society to think rationally about their faults'.[44] King conceded that the Albany campaign lacked a clear focus, and concluded that 'in hard-core communities' nonviolent direct action was more effective if 'concentrated against one aspect' of the segregationist system.[45] More limited objectives would have also made it easier for the media to communicate the grievances of Albany's black community to the nation.

V

Yet the Albany campaign did yield some positive results. It showed that blacks in the Deep South could be united to respond to the call for nonviolent protest. Not since the Montgomery bus boycott had so many blacks been mobilized to protest for their rights. In December 1961 and the spring of 1962, more than a thousand Albany blacks marched peacefully to jail in an effort to overturn the segregationist system. Wyatt Walker maintained that Albany marked 'a big beginning in the Deep South', in which blacks combined to achieve 'a milepost in the early stage of the nonviolent revolution' to resolve the American Dilemma.[46] As King said: 'Negroes have straightened their backs in Albany, and once a man straightens his back you can't ride him any more'.[47] In the aftermath of the campaign, thousands of blacks were added to the voting registration rolls. As a testing ground for the developing method of nonviolent direct action against racism, Albany also provided valuable strategic lessons for SCLC. As Wyatt Walker assessed: 'SCLC came of age in Albany'.[48]

Moreover, SCLC continued to improve its organization during and after the Albany campaign, attracting several talented individuals. Between 1960 and 1963, King, Abernathy and Walker assembled a group of staff members who were not only able leaders, but also knowledgeable in the tactics of nonviolent direct action. According to Walker, SCLC 'had a front-line staff equal to any corporate giant in America'.[49] The staff included ministers James Lawson, C. T. Vivian and James Bevel, each a veteran of the 1960 Nashville sit-ins. Lawson had been expelled from Nashville's Vanderbilt University Divinity School for his leadership role in the sit-ins. Vivian became a director of SCLC affiliates, and future head of the Anti-Klan Network in Washington. Bevel became head of direct action, and later played an important role in the movement to end the war in Vietnam. Fred Shuttlesworth, a founder of SCLC in 1957, became head of the organization's Birmingham affiliate. As a leader of civil rights protests in Birmingham, he had gone to jail eight times by 1963. Walter Fauntroy became Washington bureau director of SCLC in 1960. In 1971, he would become the District of Columbia's first non-voting congressional delegate. Bernard Lee, a veteran of the student sit-ins in Montgomery, was recruited in late 1961. The same year, Andrew Young, future mayor of Atlanta, joined the staff. A skilful speaker, he became SCLC's chief negotiator. From Savannah came Hosea Williams, a superb grass roots organizer who was appointed head of voter registration. In addition to the executive staff, there was a cadre of field organizers. The full-time staff grew from five in 1960 to 60 in 1964, and to about 150 in 1966.[50]

Though SCLC affiliates gathered in various Southern cities for annual conventions, the executive staff in Atlanta controlled policy. Decisions were reached at staff meetings in which each member contributed, offering suggestions and participating in what sometimes became heated discussions. King always had the final word, and the staff usually agreed with his decisions. Though friction among members sometimes occurred, Fred Shuttlesworth recalled: 'We recognized that we had to exist as an organization and once the disagreements were stated we proceeded as a united team'.[51] King was the heart of SCLC; his charismatic leadership held the organization together. But he tried not to stifle the individual initiative and creativity of his staff members. As Andrew Young explained, although King 'really directed it all and he called the shots', SCLC was like 'a jazz combo', in which each staff member had 'a chance to solo'.[52]

4

Birmingham and the March on Washington, 1963

I

By 1963, nonviolence had come of age. Launched on a mass scale in Montgomery in 1955–6, refined by the student sit-ins of 1960, the Freedom Rides of 1961 and the lessons of Albany, Georgia of 1962, militant nonviolent direct action had become a formidable weapon in the movement for black liberation. Having expanded their knowledge of the nonviolent method, King and SCLC would now confront the white racist community of Birmingham, Alabama.

Birmingham was an ideal site for SCLC's next protest campaign. In the year 1963, the city was the embodiment of the American Dilemma. King said that a visitor to Birmingham might have concluded that it had been caught for years in a Rip Van Winkle slumber. A century after the signing of the Emancipation Proclamation, the city was apparently ignorant of the Preamble to the Constitution, the Bill of Rights, Jefferson, Lincoln, the Thirteenth and Fourteenth Amendments and the *Brown* decision. Birmingham was a centre of Southern massive resistance to desegregation. According to King, it was 'the most segregated city in America'.[1] Representatives of the city power structure had stubbornly refused to discuss grievances with leaders of the black community. Rather than submit to integration, Birmingham had closed its parks. The city had abolished its baseball team to prevent it from playing in the integrated International League. The Metropolitan Opera, having adopted a policy of not performing before segregated audiences, no longer visited Birmingham. Most touring theatrical companies followed the example of the Metropolitan.

Although blacks constituted 40 per cent of the Birmingham population of 350 000, only 10 000 of a total of 80 000 registered voters were black. For the most part, blacks were confined to menial jobs, while those who managed to secure better employment were discriminated against in salary and promotions. For years, blacks were also victims of violence as the white establishment attempted to keep them subjugated. They were intimidated, beaten and even murdered with impunity. In May 1961, Freedom Riders were brutally attacked by white racists when they arrived at the bus terminal. Between 1957 and January 1963, there were 17 unsolved bombings of black churches and the homes of civil rights leaders. The only unsegregated places of public accommodation were the bus and railway stations, and the airport. The city was even free from the legal activism of the NAACP, Alabama having outlawed the organization as a 'foreign corporation' in 1956. As people approached Birmingham – the largest industrial centre in the South – they were greeted by chamber of commerce signs that read, ironically: 'It's So Nice To Have You In Birmingham'. The city's racist policies were endorsed by Alabama's governor, George Wallace, who had pledged in his January 1963 inaugural address: 'Segregation now, segregation tomorrow, segregation forever'.[2]

In focusing on Birmingham, SCLC would face its most difficult test in the South thus far. As King concluded: 'The challenge to nonviolent direct action could not have been staged in a more appropriate arena'.[3]

II

Birmingham had experienced nonviolent protest prior to 1963. Inspired by the Montgomery bus boycott, Reverend Fred Shuttlesworth organized the Alabama Christian Movement for Human Rights (ACMHR) in Birmingham in 1956, and led a boycott that succeeded in integrating the city's buses. The ACMHR soon became one of the strongest SCLC affiliates, and instituted a series of lawsuits and petitions against segregation in the city. Early in 1962, Shuttlesworth's organization joined local college students in a boycott of downtown Birmingham stores that displayed Jim-Crow signs, refused to integrate lunch counters, and discriminated against blacks in employment. The boycott was effective, for business declined as much as 40 per cent in some stores.

At its May 1962 board meeting in Chattanooga, Tennessee, SCLC gave serious consideration to Shuttlesworth's proposal that it join ACMHR in a massive assault upon segregation in Birmingham. But King's preoccupation with the Albany campaign precluded a combined protest at the time. Nevertheless, the continuing

ACMHR boycott was aided by the fact that Birmingham was scheduled to be the site of the annual SCLC convention in the autumn. The threat of a prolonged direct-action campaign, occurring simultaneously with the convention, prompted the city's business community to negotiate with ACHMR. The boycott was suspended after some merchants consented to remove their offensive Jim-Crow signs and join in a suit to integrate the lunch counters. Shuttlesworth warned that if the business community reneged on these pledges, SCLC would join ACMHR in a non-violent protest. Shortly after the SCLC convention, blacks realized that they had been misled. The Jim-Crow signs reappeared, and segregation continued. Following a series of telephone conversations between King and Shuttlesworth in September, SCLC decided to proceed with the proposed joint protest. If successful, King declared, it would 'break the back of segregation all over the nation'.[4]

From its inception, the Birmingham campaign revealed that SCLC had learned valuable lessons from its mistakes. After the disappointment in Albany, King and SCLC were under great pressure to achieve a victory that would vindicate the method of nonviolent direct action. Unlike in Albany, the Birmingham campaign was preceded by thorough planning and preparation, including meetings with local black leaders to ensure support. SCLC was determined to mobilize blacks to direct an overwhelming attack upon segregation. The campaign was given a code name: Project C – the 'C' stood for confrontation. A dramatic encounter with a segregationist power structure would nationally expose the evils of racism and attain necessary reforms. Hence, King instructed SCLC executive director Wyatt Walker to 'find some way to create a crisis' in Birmingham.[5] Walker agreed: 'We've got to have a crisis to bargain with. To take a moderate approach, hoping to get help from whites doesn't work. They nail you to the cross'.[6]

Planning for the Birmingham campaign began at a three-day strategy meeting in January 1963 at the SCLC Dorchester training centre near Savannah, Georgia. A timetable was devised, and every possible contingency discussed. Avoiding a major error of the Albany campaign, King and SCLC decided that, instead of assaulting all forms of segregation, they would focus on the downtown Birmingham business community. The success of Shuttlesworth's boycott had shown that blacks had sufficient buying power to pressure city merchants. Using the economic power of blacks to coerce the opposition to negotiate reforms was an important ingredient in SCLC's nonviolent strategy. Two weeks after the Dorchester conference, King, Ralph Abernathy and Wyatt Walker met with Shuttlesworth and the ACMHR board at Birmingham's Gaston Motel for further preparations. The Gaston Motel, owned by black millionaire A. G. Gaston and located near Kelly Ingram Park in the city's black district, would be the campaign headquarters.

SCLC planned a two-pronged assault: a boycott and sit-ins at downtown stores, combined with the constant pressure of disruptive street demonstrations. Initially, mobilizing for Project C was scheduled to begin the first week of March. This would allow six weeks to organize blacks so that protests could be launched during the height of the busy Easter shopping season, Easter falling on 14 April 1963. King and SCLC hoped that the Birmingham business community, faced with the prospect of a great financial loss at this time, would make concessions. But some local black leaders were at first reluctant to support the campaign, fearing that it might encourage the city's white voters to choose a racist in an election for mayor scheduled to be held on 5 March. The previous November, Birmingham had voted to replace its government of three commissioners by one with a mayor and a city council. Although each of the three candidates – Albert Boutwell, Eugene 'Bull' Connor and Tom King – was a confirmed segregationist, Connor was the most extreme and the least acceptable to the black community. Rather than risk encouraging more whites to vote for Connor, SCLC decided to postpone the protest until after the election.

The next phase of the planning was entrusted to Wyatt Walker. By 1 March, Walker had already visited the city several times to prepare for the campaign. He consulted with lawyers regarding the city code on picketing and demonstrations. He recruited volunteers and set up workshops to teach them the methods of nonviolence. He organized a transportation corps. He made a thorough reconnaissance of downtown Birmingham, plotting the main streets and landmarks. He surveyed the eating facilities, sketching their entrances and exits, and recording the number of tables, chairs and stools to determine exactly how many demonstrators would be needed at each store. He also designated a number of secondary targets, in case demonstrators were unable to reach their primary destinations.

Though the Birmingham campaign was ready to begin by the

first week of March, the results of the election forced a second postponement. Neither Connor nor Boutwell having received a clear majority, a run-off election was scheduled for 2 April. Not wishing to aid Connor by antagonizing white voters, SCLC again agreed to delay the start of demonstrations until the day after the run-off election. Meanwhile King had been busy mustering support for the forthcoming campaign. In mid-January, he had embarked on a whirlwind tour, giving 28 speeches in 16 cities outside the South, soliciting financial assistance. SCLC also sent confidential letters to the NAACP, CORE, SNCC and the Southern Regional Council, apprising them of the imminent demonstrations and requesting their help. Early in March, King was in New York City to attend a meeting of 75 prominent citizens at the apartment of black entertainer Harry Belafonte. Present were newspapermen, clergymen, businessmen and professionals, along with representatives of Mayor Wagner and Governor Rockefeller. King and Shuttlesworth explained their plans and financial needs to those assembled, and received their support.

On Tuesday, 2 April, Albert Boutwell was victorious. Regarded as a moderate segregationist, many hoped that his election would initiate a period of racial harmony in the city. Indeed, readers of the *Birmingham News* awakened the next day to the following headline: 'New Day Dawns For Birmingham'. Nevertheless, King and SCLC refused to be deceived. According to Shuttlesworth, Boutwell was 'just a dignified Bull Connor'.[7] As Shuttlesworth explained: 'We have been asked to wait. We're tired of waiting. We've been waiting for 340 years for our rights. We want action. We want it now'.[8] Besides, there was a possibility that Boutwell's election would be voided. Taking advantage of an ambiguity in the city charter, the old administration, including Mayor Arthur Hanes and Bull Connor, defied the election results and refused to vacate City Hall on the grounds that they were legally in office until 1965. Consequently, until the courts decided the issue, Birmingham would literally have two governments, and King and SCLC would have to contend with the irascible Connor, who remained Police Chief.

III

On Wednesday, 3 April, the day after the run-off election, King formally launched the Birmingham campaign, pledging that the protest would not cease until 'Pharaoh lets God's people go'.[9] After postponing the protest two times, blacks would wait no longer. King and SCLC then issued the 'Birmingham Manifesto', an eloquent statement of purpose, and a review of the deplorable conditions that made direct action necessary:

> The patience of an oppressed people cannot endure forever. The Negro citizens of Birmingham for the last several years have hoped in vain for some evidence of good faith resolution of our just grievances . . . . We have been segregated racially, exploited economically, and dominated politically.

The black community of Birmingham had exhausted all possible channels to secure the redress of their grievances. Their petitions had been summarily rebuffed; the courts had brought only limited success; and solemn promises by the city to reform had been unfulfilled. Blacks had no recourse except to protest. The 'Birmingham Manifesto' emphasized that the protest was consistent with America's democratic ideals:

> We believe in the American Dream of democracy, in the Jeffersonian doctrine that "all men are created equal and are endowed by their Creator with certain inalienable rights, among these being life, liberty and the pursuit of happiness" . . . . We act today in full concert with our Hebraic-Christian tradition, the law of morality and the Constitution of our nation. The absence of justice and progress in Birmingham demands that we make a moral witness to give our community a chance to survive. We demonstrate our faith that we believe that The Beloved Community can come to Birmingham.[10]

The first demonstrations, on 3 April, were small, and confined to lunch counter sit-ins at the downtown stores. The plan was to begin slowly, testing the city's response, and to escalate gradually to provoke a crisis. During the first three days, Bull Connor made 35 arrests. On Saturday, 6 April, the second stage of Project C began when Fred Shuttlesworth led a procession of marchers toward City Hall. Refusing to disperse, 42 marchers were arrested for parading without a permit, and escorted by police into paddy wagons while black sympathizers lined the street and sang freedom songs.

On Palm Sunday, 7 April, the campaign stirred the racist violence necessary to draw national publicity. As Birmingham minister A. D. King, younger brother of Martin Luther King, Jr., led a group of 25 demonstrators toward downtown, they were met by Connor and his police, who brought dogs along. Nearby, a large crowd of black spectators had gathered to watch the police make arrests. When a dog lunged at one of the spectators, who tried to defend himself with a knife, the police charged the crowd with clubs and allowed two more dogs to attack. Connor had been provoked into creating an incident that supplied press coverage for the protest. James Forman of SNCC recalled the ensuing reaction at SCLC headquarters: 'Dorothy Cotton and Wyatt Walker were jumping up and down, elated. They said over and over again, "We've got a movement. We've got a movement. We had some police brutality. They brought out the dogs. We've got a movement" '.[11]

Wyatt Walker later said that during the initial days of the campaign, when King and SCLC encountered difficulty gaining recruits, the protest benefited from the inability of the white press corps to distinguish between black demonstrators and black spectators: 'So we devised the technique, we'd set the demonstration up for a certain hour and then delay it two hours and let the crowd collect'.[12] In reporting demonstrations, such as that of Sunday, April 7, Walker pointed out, the white press invariably overestimated the number of actual participants, to the benefit of the civil rights cause.

During the ensuing weeks, the frequency and the size of the demonstrations increased, as King and SCLC attempted to implement the Gandhian principle of filling the jails, straining the judicial process. The boycott also began to hurt the downtown business community. Meanwhile, newsmen from throughout the nation and the world began converging on Birmingham to record the unfolding drama. As Ralph Abernathy told a reporter: 'Tell 'em we're going to rock this town like it has never been rocked before'.[13] King and SCLC aimed to create a crisis that would compel Birmingham to negotiate four demands: desegregation of store facilities and lunch counters; hiring of blacks in local business and government; amnesty for all jailed protesters; and creation of a biracial committee to establish a timetable for the desegregation of the city.

IV

From the outset, the black church played a vital role in the Birmingham campaign. Nightly mass meetings were held in various churches throughout the city, including the Sixteenth Street Baptist Church, Thurgood Church, New Pilgrim Church and Zion Hill Church. As in the Montgomery and Albany campaigns, the church served as the base of operations and recruitment centre for the nonviolent army. During meetings, the black community was informed of progress and subsequent steps in the developing strategy. The correspondence between nonviolence and the teachings of Jesus was stressed repeatedly. United in their struggle, blacks locked arms and sang freedom songs such as 'Woke Up This Morning with My Mind Stayed on Freedom', 'Ain't Gonna Let Nobody Turn Me Round' and the ubiquitous 'We Shall Overcome'. Near the close of each church session, either King, Abernathy or Shuttlesworth would issue an appeal for volunteers for the nonviolent army. These invitations resembled those that occur each Sunday morning in black churches throughout the nation when the pastor calls upon those present to bear witness to their faith. Hundreds of volunteers came forward in Birmingham.

Volunteers had to complete rigorous preparation. During the Albany campaign, King and SCLC had learned the importance of training participants for nonviolent protest. Birmingham demonstrators attended workshops on nonviolent techniques where they listened to sermons and took part in socio-dramas that were designed to simulate the violent reaction they might face. The workshops were conducted by SCLC staff members, including James Lawson, James and Diane Bevel, Bernard Lee, Andrew Young and Dorothy Cotton. Under their supervision, blacks would role-play, some posing as white segregationists, others as black demonstrators. These socio-dramas were an essential part of the training for King's nonviolent campaigns. Their purpose was to instil the discipline necessary to withstand severe provocation and physical violence without retaliating. By maintaining nonviolent discipline, the protester would manifest a moral superiority over his oppressor. Volunteers for the Birmingham campaign had to sign a 'Commitment Card', pledging obedience to the Ten Commandments of the nonviolent movement. Among them, the first required that volunteers 'meditate daily on the teachings and life of Jesus'; the third, that they 'walk and talk in the manner of love, for God is love'; the eighth, that they 'refrain from violence of fist, tongue, or heart'.[14] Only after instilling such discipline could King be confident that his direct-action campaigns would adhere to nonviolence.

King and SCLC knew that the success of the protest would depend to a great extent upon unifying Birmingham's black leaders. Factionalism had disabled the Albany Movement in 1962. At the outset of the Birmingham campaign, some of the city's black leaders either resented King and SCLC for interfering in their local affairs, or were intimidated by the white power structure. To gain support, King and members of his SCLC staff held a week of meetings in early April to explain their method and goals, and to answer criticisms. King also delivered several speeches at the Gaston Motel to different groups, including 125 businessmen and professionals, and 200 ministers. After a strenuous week, King and SCLC attained the support of numerous black leaders.

V

On 10 April, the city administration secured an injunction from Alabama State Circuit Court Judge William A. Jenkins, Jr., banning further demonstrations. The segregationist authorities of the South continued to use injunctions to cripple nonviolent protests. Even manifestly unconstitutional injunctions were extremely difficult to overturn, for litigation often took as long as two or three years. King and SCLC remembered that the Albany Movement had been derailed by a court order that interrupted demonstrations, impairing the momentum of the campaign. The opposition in Birmingham had to be subjected to the relentless pressure of nonviolent marchers.

King was prepared by his legal staff for the inevitable injunction in Birmingham. SCLC was assisted by an outstanding group of attorneys including Clarence Jones, William Kunstler and Harry Wachtel of New York, Orzell Billingsley, Jr. and Arthur Shores of Birmingham, and lawyers of the NAACP Legal Defense Fund, popularly known as the 'Inc. Fund', led by Jack Greenberg.[15] After conferring with his lawyers, King had decided that when the injunction came, he would defy it as an act of civil disobedience and accept the legal penalty for contempt of court. The injunction would focus attention upon the city's violation of the constitutional liberties of black citizens. King's lawyers would argue that the court order was invalid because it denied the First Amendment rights to free speech and peaceful assembly. Until this time in the campaign, King had deliberately avoided arrest in order to organize the back community. His arrest and imprisonment would be an important part of SCLC's strategy, calculated to attract national sympathy for the campaign. Advised that in Birmingham, unlike in Albany, the injunction would come from a state rather than a federal court, King saw that he could violate the court order without antagonizing the federal judiciary.

King decided to carry out his civil disobedience on Good Friday, 12 April, a day chosen for its religious significance. By this time, between 400 and 500 demonstrators had been arrested, and about 300 were still in jail. At noon on Thursday, 11 April, King held a press conference to present his reason for violating the state court order the next day. In the past, he explained, he had obeyed federal court injunctions out of respect for the supportive role the federal judiciary had played in the civil rights struggle. In contrast to the federal courts, the state courts in Alabama and throughout the Deep South had been used 'to perpetuate the unjust and illegal system of racial separation'.[16] Faced with such flagrant defiance of federal law and the United States Constitution, King and the protesters had no alternative but to violate the Alabama state court injunction: 'We cannot in all good conscience obey such an injunction which is an unjust, undemocratic and unconstitutional misuse of the legal process. We do this not out of any disrespect for the law but out of the highest respect for *the* law'.[17]

Following the press conference, King learned that the protest movement had run out of bail money. This posed a dilemma. If King were to go to jail, in his absence the movement might not be able to raise money for the release of hundreds of imprisoned demonstrators that were needed to continue the campaign. King alone had the prominence to attract significant financial contributions. On the other hand, if King avoided jail, he would have to answer all those whom he had urged to submit to arrest. The movement could not afford a decline in morale. After much deliberation, King chose to violate the injunction, hoping that his imprisonment would bring national attention to racial injustice in Birmingham.

On Good Friday, 12 April, nearly a thousand blacks lined the streets as King and Ralph Abernathy led a group of 50 marchers from Zion Church toward downtown Birmingham. After marching eight blocks, they were arrested by Bull Connor and escorted to jail as a crowd of supporters sang 'We Shall Overcome'. As expected, King's arrest made national headlines. For the thirteenth time he had been arrested and jailed for the cause of civil rights. Placed in solitary confinement, he would devote himself to composing his 'Letter from Birmingham Jail', one of the most important documents of the civil rights movement. With the Letter, King succeeded in further dramatizing the Birmingham struggle, etching in the minds of millions of Americans the brutality of Southern racism. On 15 April, King was removed from solitary confinement after his wife Coretta made a telephone call to President Kennedy, pleading with him to exert the influence of his office on her husband's behalf. The same day, King was relieved to learn that Harry Belafonte had raised $50 000 for bail bonds.

VI

On 20 April, King and Ralph Abernathy were released on bond after spending eight days in Birmingham jail. Tried and convicted of criminal contempt of court six days later, they were fined $50 and released, pending an appeal. King and SCLC could now map out the strategy for the next phase, the crisis-provoking climax, of the Birmingham campaign. To multiply the number of demonstrators and enhance the drama of the protest, King followed the advice of one of his most able strategists, James Bevel, who urged that SCLC involve hundreds of black children in the demonstrations. Bevel, Andrew Young, Bernard Lee and Dorothy Cotton began visiting local colleges and high schools. Hundreds of black youths – teenagers, even elementary school children – were invited to attend mass meetings and nonviolent training sessions. By 2 May, some 6000 were set to march in a Children's Crusade for freedom.

On Thursday, 2 May – 'D' Day – the city of Birmingham, was stunned when more than a thousand black children, ranging in age from six to sixteen, emerged from the Sixteenth Street Baptist

Church and marched downtown singing freedom songs. That day, over 900 youths were arrested, offering no resistance. The Children's Crusade focused the eyes of millions on racial injustice in Birmignham. Not only did the children swell the ranks of King's nonviolent army, but, more importantly, the sight of thousands of them marching for freedom touched the heart and conscience of America. The children, many of them just awakening to the evils of racism, served as perfect foils to Bull Connor and his club-wielding policemen.

Lerone Bennett characterized King's use of children as 'one of the most momentous decisions in the history of Negro protests'.[18] According to James Bevel: 'We wanted to get the nation involved in Birmingham, and get a larger segment of Birmingham involved. We knew if the students were involved the parents would come out to find out what was going on'.[19] King and SCLC were now able to fill the jails, and put a spotlight upon racism in Birmingham. As Fred Shuttlesworth recollected: 'Once I saw the waves of children going downtown, and the police couldn't handle it, I knew that the victory was won'.[20] Though some attacked the use of children as a dangerous ploy, King asked his critics why they had neglected to speak out while these children had been victims of segregation. Involving children in Birmingham was, he later said, 'one of the wisest moves we made. It brought a new impact to the crusade, and the impetus we needed to win the struggle'.[21]

The sight of thousands of Birmingham's black youth marching for freedom pushed Bull Connor beyond the limits of his patience, providing King and SCLC with the dramatic crisis they needed. Connor had hoped to destroy the protest by emulating the tactics of Police Chief Laurie Pritchett, who had checkmated demonstrations in Albany, Georgia in 1962 by meeting nonviolence with nonviolence. During the first weeks of the campaign, Connor, expecting an injunction to halt the demonstrations, simply arrested all protesters and politely escorted them to jail. The only violent incident had occurred on Palm Sunday, 7 April, when police dogs had attacked a crowd of innocent bystanders. Confronted now by a steadily escalating protest, and by massive civil disobedience, Connor would be unable to restrain himself.

On 3 May – King proclaimed it 'Double D Day' – the Birmingham campaign reached a climax. After nearly a thousand black children jammed the Sixteenth Street Baptist Church, Connor ordered police to bar the doors. A large crowd of demonstrators and onlookers had gathered across the street in Kelly Ingram Park. Under Connor's command, police with clubs and dogs, and firemen with high pressure hoses, were prepared to attack the demonstrators. Suddenly, about half of the children who had been trapped in the church managed to escape, joining the crowd that had assembled in the park. When they refused to return to the church, Connor gave the order: 'Let 'em have it'. Police charged the crowd, swinging their clubs. Vicious dogs lunged forward, biting several blacks. When firemen turned on their hoses, the torrents of water knocked scores of blacks off their feet, pinning some against buildings, and ripping the bark off trees. While the vast majority of blacks did not retaliate, some spectators untrained in nonviolence resorted to throwing rocks and bottles at police and firemen, injuring several. This violence prompted SCLC's James Bevel to borrow a police megaphone and plead: 'If you're not going to demonstrate in a nonviolent way, then leave'.[22] More than 200 persons were arrested that day.

VII

The evening of 3 May, television brought the horrors of racism in Birmingham into the living rooms of millions of Americans, creating a wave of indignation throughout the country. Bull Connor had been provoked to use violence in defence of white supremacy. As one NBC correspondent observed: 'Before television, the American public had no idea of the abuses blacks suffered in the South. We showed them what was happening; the brutality, the police dogs, the miserable conditions . . . . We made it impossible for Congress not to act'.[23] On the morning of 4 May, newspapers featured pictures of dogs biting black children. A *New York Times* editorial described the Birmingham 'barbarities' as 'revoltingly reminiscent of totalitarian excesses'. In Washington, U.S. Senator Wayne Morse said that Birmingham 'would disgrace South Africa'.[24]

Responding to the public outcry, the federal government finally intervened and began to pressure Birmingham's business leaders to relent. President John F. Kennedy dispatched Assistant Attorney General Burke Marshall to Birmingham to mediate a settlement. Attorney General Robert Kennedy expressed concern: 'Everyone understands that their [the blacks'] just grievances must be resolved. Continued refusal to grant equal rights and opportunities to

Negroes makes increasing turmoil inevitable'.[25] At the Attorney General's request, Defence Secretary Robert McNamara and Treasury Secretary Douglas Dillon made dozens of telephone calls, seeking the cooperation of Birmingham's industrial and business community. Eugene V. Rostow, dean of the Yale Law School, telephoned Yale alumnus Roger Blough, board chairman of United States Steel, who in turn called his associates in Birmingham. Yale law professor Louis H. Pollack, whose work with the NAACP had earned him great respect among civil rights leaders, was asked by Rostow to attempt to persuade Birmingham's black leaders to moderate their demands. At the same time, secret negotiations began between black leaders and the Senior Citizens Committee, a group of prominent Birmingham businessmen.

Sunday afternoon, 5 May, brought hope of ultimate victory to the protesters. Reverend Charles Billups led a group of several hundred marchers from the New Pilgrim Baptist Church. Confronted by police and firemen, they halted and knelt in prayer. When the marchers politely refused to disperse, an infuriated Connor ordered his men to turn on the hoses. After a tense few moments, it became obvious that Connor would not be obeyed. The surprised marchers rose from their knees and proceeded to pass through the police line while Connor's men stepped aside.

During the next two days, the demonstrations intensified. By this time, Connor had added an armoured police car to his arsenal. Almost 3000 protesters were in jail, and several thousand more were ready to march. On 6 May, celebrity Dick Gregory, carrying a sign that read, 'We Want Freedom', led a group of 19 children from the Sixteenth Street Baptist Church. They were promptly arrested. For the next hour, wave after wave of children poured out of the church and were herded by police into paddy wagons and taken to jail. About a thousand persons were arrested that day. The following morning, newspapers featured a shocking photograph, showing three Birmingham policemen pinning a black woman to the pavement, one of them pressing his knee to her throat. On Tuesday, 7 May, almost 3000 blacks amassed in the downtown Birmingham business district. At the same time, fire hoses were turned on demonstrators who had congregated near the Sixteenth Street Baptist Church. After some blacks hurled rocks and bottles at police, Fred Shuttlesworth, who had attempted to calm the crowd, was injured by a blast of water from a fire hose and taken away in an ambulance. Informed of the incident, Connor remarked: 'I wish he'd been carried away in a hearse'.[26] Meanwhile, Governor George Wallace answered Connor's appeal and sent more than 800 state troopers to Birmingham and the outskirts, armed with tear gas, submachine guns, and shotguns. The city took on the appearance of a battlefield, and more serious outbreaks of violence seemed imminent.

As Birmingham's merchants continued to suffer heavily from the economic boycott, the city's 125-member Senior Citizens Committee redoubled its efforts to negotiate a settlement, holding all-night sessions with protest leaders. On Wednesday, 8 May, to express goodwill and encourage a settlement, King and his aides called a 24-hour truce. That day, President Kennedy opened a press conference by urging both sides in the Birmingham confrontation to reach an accord that met 'the justifiable needs of the Negro community'.[27] Finally, on Friday, 10 May, following weeks of demonstrations, an accord was reached that met the most important demands of the protesters. After Fred Shuttlesworth, having recovered sufficiently from his injuries suffered on 7 May, read a statement to the press announcing the terms of the settlement, King told reporters: 'I am very happy to be able to announce that we have come today to the climax of a long struggle for justice, freedom, and human dignity in the city of Birmingham . . . . We must now move from protest to reconciliation'.[28]

According to the settlement, the city's downtown eating facilities, restrooms and drinking fountains would be desegregated; blacks would be hired on a nondiscriminatory basis by business and industry; and a permanent biracial committee would be established within two weeks. In the spirit of compromise, the protesters had moderated some of their original demands. Instead of complete amnesty for all jailed demonstrators, they were released on bail; instead of immediate desegregation and hiring of black employees, these reforms were to be implemented gradually, within specified timetables. Attorney General Robert Kennedy praised the settlement as 'a tremendous step forward for Birmingham, for Alabama, and for the South generally'.[29]

On Saturday, 11 May, King returned to Atlanta for the weekend. He wanted to be with his family, and to preach at the Ebenezer Baptist Church. Meanwhile, white racists in Birmingham sought to undermine the settlement. That evening, following a Ku-Klux-Klan rally in a local park, disgruntled whites bombed SCLC headquarters at the Gaston Motel and the home of A. D. King. In response, angry young blacks flooded the downtown Birmingham streets, hurling rocks and battling with police. The mob eventually totalled about 2500. Rushing back to the city on Sunday, King's presence in the streets helped to quell further rioting. More than 50 persons had been hospitalized, and many feared that the Birmingham settlement would be annulled.

Tensions subsided only after President Kennedy publicly praised the justness of the Birmingham protest, and declared that the federal government would guarantee the settlement. The President ordered 3000 federal troops to the outskirts of the city, and prepared to federalize the Alabama National Guard. On 13 May, King and SCLC staff members toured the Birmingham taverns, poolrooms and restaurants, preaching nonviolence to those blacks, not part of the movement, who had rioted on Saturday night. Within a week, the protesters received more victories. On 20 May, the United States Supreme Court ruled that Alabama's segregation laws were unconstitutional, consequently nullifying the convictions of those protesters who had been arrested in Birmingham. Three days later, the Alabama Supreme Court ruled unanimously that Boutwell's administration was the sole legitimate government in Birmingham, thus expelling Mayor Arthur Hanes, Bull Connor and the other commissioners.

Three weeks later, President Kennedy announced that he was requesting Congress to enact the most comprehensive Civil Rights Bill in history. In a message to Congress in February, the President had proposed moderate civil rights legislation. The Birmingham crisis convinced him that stronger legislative measures were necessary. In a nationally televised address on 11 June, the President proclaimed: 'We are confronted primarily with a moral issue . . . . Now the time has come for this nation to fulfil its promise. The events in Birmingham and elsewhere have so increased the cries for equality that no city or state legislative body can choose to ignore them'.[30] The urgency of Kennedy's message was underscored when, hours later, Medgar Evers, field secretary of the Mississippi NAACP, was assassinated in front of his home in Jackson.

VIII

The Birmingham campaign, a major triumph for the civil rights movement, vindicated the method of militant nonviolent direct action. For over a month, the spotlight was on Birmingham as nonviolent protesters resisted Jim Crow, creating disorder that forced the business community to make significant concessions to the just demands of black citizens, and attracting national support for strong civil rights legislation. As Sidney Smyer, president of the Senior Citizens Committee, said shortly after the settlement was reached: 'Our task has not been pleasant or easy. It was undertaken only after thorough deliberation and under the pressure of growing crisis. It is important that the public understand the steps we have taken were necessary to avoid a dangerous and imminent explosion'.[31] After more than two years of delay, the Kennedy Administration had been induced to intervene actively in support of civil rights. The President was only partly jesting when he remarked to King and other black leaders at a White House meeting shortly after the Birmingham settlement: 'I don't think you should all be totally harsh on Bull Connor. After all, he has done more for civil rights than almost anybody else'.[32]

The Birmingham campaign sparked a new militancy among black Americans. In the summer of 1963, King asserted, blacks wrote their own Emancipation Proclamation, discarding three centuries of psychological slavery, and declaring: '"We can make ourselves free!"'[33] No longer willing to wait, their slogan became an insistent 'Freedom Now'. Inspired by the example of Birmingham, blacks throughout the land, infused with confidence in the nonviolent method, protested for civil rights. The U.S. Department of Justice reported a total of 1412 separate demonstrations during the summer of 1963. In the ten weeks following the Birmingham campaign, there were 758 demonstrations in 186 cities. In the three months after Birmingham, nearly 800 boycotts, marches and sit-ins occurred in some 200 Southern cities and towns. In the North, hundreds of thousands of blacks joined the protest movement, launching rent strikes, job campaigns and school boycotts. Writing on 'The Meaning of Birmingham', Bayard Rustin concluded that the campaign was a turning point in the black struggle for equality. Before Birmingham, he said, blacks had fought for limited civil rights goals, such as desegregation of public accommodations and integrated schools. But now blacks had broadened their goals and were 'demanding social, political and economic changes'.[34]

IX

The wave of nonviolent protests throughout the summer of 1963 reached a dramatic climax with the 'March on Washington for Jobs and Freedom' on 28 August, the largest demonstration in the history of civil rights. The March was conceived by A. Philip Randolph, whose proposal for a similar demonstration in 1941 had prompted President Franklin D. Roosevelt to desegregate the nation's defence plants and to institute the Fair Employment Practices Commission. On 30 May 1957, Randolph had been instrumental in organizing the Prayer Pilgrimage to Washington, in which some 37 000 demonstrators listened to King's eloquent speech calling upon Congress to pass legislation guaranteeing black Americans the right to vote. In 1963, capitalizing upon the national moral outrage aroused by the Birmingham campaign, a March on Washington was planned by black leaders to show mass support for the pending Civil Rights Bill.

On 22 June, President Kennedy met at the White House with the 'Big Six' of the civil rights movement: King, Randolph, Roy Wilkins of the NAACP, James Farmer of CORE, John Lewis of SNCC and Whitney Young of the National Urban League. Also present were Vice President Johnson, Attorney General Robert Kennedy, United Automobile Workers president Walter Reuther and millionaire Stephen Currier, president of the Taconic Foundation. The purpose of the meeting was to discuss the pending Civil Rights Bill and the proposed March on Washington. The President expressed concern that the March was poorly-timed and would be counter-productive. Originally, there had been plans to disrupt the Capitol with massive civil disobedience. But Kennedy warned: 'We want success in Congress, not just a big show at the Capitol'. The President feared that if the March were to become violent, it would be perceived by Congress as a threat, and provide a justification for those who were opposed to the bill. 'Some of these people are looking for an excuse to be against us; and I don't want to give any of them a chance to say "Yes, I'm for the bill, but I am damned if I will vote for it at the point of a gun." '[35]

Although Wilkins shared the President's fears, Randolph nevertheless insisted that it was too late to cancel the March. 'The Negroes are already in the streets', he told the President. 'It is very likely impossible to get them off'. In response to Kennedy's contention that the March was ill-timed, King said: 'Frankly, I have never engaged in any direct-action movement which did not seem ill-timed. Some people thought Birmingham ill-timed'.[36] King also maintained that the March would provide a nonviolent means for blacks throughout the country to channel their legitimate discontent. James Farmer added that black leaders would be in a difficult position if the bill were defeated in Congress after the March was called off. Embittered blacks might resort to violence. By the end of the meeting, President Kennedy, realizing that the March on Washington could not be stopped, had no alternative but to use his influence to ensure that it would not be disruptive.

Elaborate preparations preceded the Washington demonstration. Bayard Rustin was appointed national organizer. Under the directorship of Stephen Currier, the United Civil Rights Leadership Council was set up to coordinate plans for the March. In order to attract sympathy for the Civil Rights Bill, black leaders decided to work with the Kennedy Administration to make it a moderate demonstration. Plans for massive civil disobedience to disrupt Capitol Hill were put aside, and an attempt was made to gain the support of white liberals and church and labour groups throughout the nation. The March would be confined to a mass demonstration in front of the Lincoln Memorial, a site chosen for its symbolic significance. With a push from Kennedy, the civil rights movement had joined the democratic coalition, and the March on Washington had become respectable. On 17 July, the President said that the forthcoming demonstration was within 'the great tradition' of peaceful assembly for 'redress of grievances'.[37]

They came by the thousands to Washington on 28 August. Far exceeding original expectations, an estimated 250 000 demonstrators, including at least 75 000 whites, arrived in the nation's capital by aeroplane, train, bus and car. They gathered for a peaceful parade from the Washington Monument to the Lincoln Memorial. After being entertained by celebrities, the huge crowd listened to a number of speakers, presented by Randolph: Reverend Eugene Carson Blake of the United Council of Churches, Walter Reuther of the UAW, John Lewis of SNCC, Floyd McKissick of CORE, Whitney Young of the Urban League, Matthew Ahmann of the National Catholic Conference, Roy Wilkins of the NAACP, Rabbi Joachim Prinz of the United Jewish Council and, finally, Martin Luther King, Jr., president of the Southern Christian Leadership Conference. In keeping with the spirit of moderation that characterized the demonstration, John Lewis had been pressured by March leaders, especially Randolph, to revise the first version of his speech because it was considered too critical of the Kennedy Administration.

The highlight of the day was the speech of King. Introduced by Randolph as 'the moral leader of our nation', the crowd roared as he approached the rostrum. The previous night, King had worked diligently for hours on the speech, with some assistance from his staff. He decided to begin by calling the nation's attention to the persisting American Dilemma, and to conclude by stating his dream of an America that provided freedom and equality to all citizens, regardless of race. Standing in the shadow of the Lincoln Memorial, King addressed the crowd and the millions of people witnessing the historic event on television or radio.

King reminded his audience that a century ago, President Abraham Lincoln signed the Emancipation Proclamation. Though this historic document originally gave great hope to millions of slaves, the black American was still not free in the twentieth century. The thousands of demonstrators had come to Washington that day, King said, to dramatize this condition and to compel the nation to fulfil its promise. 'When the architects of our republic wrote the magnificent words of the Constitution and the Declaration of Independence', King proclaimed, 'they were signing a promissory note to which every American was to fall heir . . . the promise that all men, yes, black men as well as white men, would be guaranteed the unalienable rights of life, liberty, and the pursuit of happiness'. The crowd shouted in approval as King proceeded to point out that the nation continued to deny the blessings of democracy to black Americans. Now is the time, he insisted, to fulfil the promise of democracy by ending segregation and racial injustice. Black Americans would wait no longer to be granted full citizenship rights. After urging blacks to employ nonviolence in their struggle for justice, 'meeting physical force with soul force', King stopped reading his prepared speech, and began to speak extemporaneously. Borrowing phrases from the Declaration of Independence, the Bible and the patriotic hymn, 'My Country 'Tis Of Thee', he revealed to the nation his dream, 'a dream deeply rooted in the American dream', that all Americans, regardless of race, would one day live together in freedom, justice, equality and brotherhood. As the crowd roared, King concluded with the words of the Negro spiritual: 'Free at last. Free at last. Thank God Almighty, we are free at last'.[38]

The 'I Have a Dream', speech, the most inspiring of his career, etched the image of King as a dreamer indelibly on the national consciousness. But King was not a mere dreamer. He dedicated his life to moving masses of blacks to take practical steps to attain their rights as American citizens. In pursuit of his ideals, King was indefatigable. *Time* magazine reported that in 1963 alone he travelled some 275 000 miles and made more than 350 speeches throughout the United States.[39]

X

Many regarded the March on Washington as the finest moment of the nonviolent civil rights movement, anticipating a bright new day for the black American. Millions watched the event live on television, and it was transmitted internationally via telestar satellite. The evil of Southern racism had been dramatized to the entire world. Journalist David Halberstam described the March as a 'great televised morality play'.[40] According to *New York Times* reporter Russell Baker: 'No one could remember an invading army quite as gentle as the two hundred thousand civil-rights marchers who occupied Washington today'.[41] James Baldwin later epitomized the prevailing optimism among blacks: 'That day, for a moment', he reflected, 'it almost seemed that we stood on a height, and could see our inheritance. Perhaps we could make the kingdom real, perhaps the beloved community would not forever remain that dream one dreamed in agony'.[42] Immediately following the demonstration, March leaders met with President Kennedy, who later issued a public statement praising the 'deep fervor and quiet dignity' that had characterized the protest. The President concluded: 'The nation can properly be proud of the demonstration that has occurred here today'.[43]

The impact on Congress is difficult to measure. As Senator Hubert Humphrey observed: 'All this hasn't changed any votes on the civil-rights bill, but it's a good thing for Washington and the nation and the world'.[44] New York Senator Jacob Javits said that the March 'may or may not change the votes of any member of Congress, but it will certainly establish a mood for the coming civil rights Congressional battle'.[45] King believed that the March mobilized national support for the Civil Rights Bill. The Washington demonstration, he said, 'has already done a great deal to create a coalition of concern about the status of civil rights in this country. It has aroused the conscience of millions of people to work for this legislation'.[46]

Amid the chorus of enthusiasm, there were some discordant voices. Malcolm X attacked the March as 'the Farce on Washington', accusing its leaders of selling out to the racist system.[47] In his well-known 'Message to the Grass Roots' speech, Malcolm explained that, as originally conceived, the black masses were going to protest the inevitable Southern filibuster of the Civil Rights Bill:

They were going to march on Washington, march on the Senate, march on the White House, march on the Congress, and tie it up, bring it to a halt, not let the government proceed . . . . It was a grass roots revolution out there in the street . . . . When they found out that this black steamroller was going to come down on the capital, they called in Wilkins, they called in Randolph, they called in these national Negro leaders that you respect and told them, "Call it off". Kennedy said, "Look, you are letting this thing go too far". And old Tom said, "Boss, I can't stop it, because I didn't start it" . . . . And that old shrewd fox, he said, "If you all aren't in it, I'll put you in it. I'll put you at the head of it. I'll endorse it. I'll welcome it. I'll help it. I'll join it".[48]

Malcolm's denunciation reflected the sentiments of many young black militants. Cleveland Sellers recorded the further disillusionment of SNCC as a result of the March – the shift in strategy from disruption and confrontation, the censoring of John Lewis's speech and the 'take-over' by the white liberal establishment.[49] SNCC's James Forman also expressed resentment: 'We were beginning to see the whole process by which fancy productions like the March on Washington tended to "psych off" local protest and make people feel they had accomplished something – changed something, somehow – when, in fact, nothing had been changed'.[50]

Despite the criticisms of SNCC and others, the March on Washington was a landmark in the black freedom struggle. No demonstration, Bayard Rustin wrote a decade later, 'has influenced the course of social legislation and determined the shape of institutional reform to the degree that the March did'.[51] Just as President Kennedy realized that he could not prevent the March, black leaders realized that the March had to be moderate in order to receive support for the Civil Rights Bill from white liberals, and civic, church and labour groups throughout the nation. This coalition, galvanized by militant nonviolent direct action in Birmingham and throughout the South in 1963, was essential for the defeat of *de jure* segregation. To most observers, passage of the Civil Rights Act of 1964 signified that the nation had taken a giant stride toward resolving the American Dilemma.

5

Interlude: King's Letter to America

I

One of the most significant documents in American history is Martin Luther King, Jr.'s 'Letter from Birmingham Jail'. It has been compared to Lincoln's Gettysburg Address, Emile Zola's letter in defence of Dreyfus and John F. Kennedy's Inauguration Speech. Like these classics, King's Letter is a model of expository prose, and testimony to the power of ideas to transcend time. In the spring of 1963, a dramatic moment had arrived in the civil rights movement, calling for a statement of goals and principles. Having launched the Birmingham campaign, King was arrested on Good Friday, 12 April 1963, and placed in solitary confinement for violating a state court injunction prohibiting protest demonstrations. While imprisoned, King composed the famous Letter, seizing the opportunity to defend his philosophy of nonviolent resistance and present the case of black Americans to the entire nation.

The 'Letter from Birmingham Jail' was a response to a statement published in the *Birmingham News* by eight of the city's leading white clergymen – of the Protestant, Catholic and Jewish faiths – attacking the protest campaign as 'unwise and untimely'.[1] The clergymen praised the community, news media and law enforcement officials for calmly handling the demonstrations, which they regretted were led in part by 'outsiders'. Criticizing the protest as extreme and unjustified, the clergymen appealed to blacks to pursue their demands 'in the courts and in negotiations among local leaders, and not in the street'.[2] As the principal leader of the Birmingham protest movement, and an 'outsider', King was clearly the object of the clergymen's criticism.

With the eyes of the nation riveted on Birmingham, King decided to reply to his critics in the form of an open letter to the American people. There was no thought of waiting until after the turmoil in Birmingham had subsided, when he could return to the comfortable confines of his study. The Letter – a synthesis of ideas King had been developing for several years in speeches and articles – was begun in the margins of the newspaper that printed the ministers' appeal, continued on scraps of paper, and concluded on a writing pad furnished by his attorneys. The completed text, approximately 7000 words in length, was then smuggled out of jail. Polished for publication, the 'Letter from Birmingham Jail' was first issued as a pamphlet. It soon appeared in several national periodicals, and it is estimated that nearly a million copies were circulated in churches throughout the land. 'The Letter from Birmingham Jail' became a chapter in King's book, *Why We Can't Wait*, an account of the Birmingham campaign, published in 1964.

II

As King began the Letter, dated 16 April 1963, he was mindful of the slow and often frustrating progress of the civil rights movement. In 1954, the United States Supreme Court issued its historic decision in *Brown* v. *Board of Education*. Yet, nine years later, the Southern states continued to defy the law forbidding segregation in public schools. In December 1955, King had been thrust suddenly into national prominence as the young Baptist pastor who led a successful year-long boycott against segregated bus transportation in Montgomery. Two years later, he became president of SCLC. In 1960, students throughout the South participated in sit-ins to protest segregated public facilities. The following year, courageous Freedom Riders, mobilized by CORE, risked their lives to integrate bus stations in the South. In 1962, King and SCLC suffered a temporary setback with their campaign to desegregate Albany, Georgia. The same year, James Meredith became the first black student to enrol in the University of Mississippi. In 1963, as the nation prepared to celebrate the centenary of Lincoln's Emancipation Proclamation, King did not want America to forget that racial segregation persisted, and that blacks were still deprived of fundamental human rights. As long as the Southern states continued to oppose the full integration of blacks into American society, the ideals embodied in the Declaration of Independence and the Constitution would remain unfulfilled.

From the outset, King knew that his Letter had to address several important questions: As a resident of Atlanta – an 'outsider' – what right did he have to lead a protest campaign in Birmingham? What is nonviolent direct action? When should nonviolent protest be employed rather than negotiation? How does one justify civil disobedience to laws? Does civil disobedience weaken the social order? Why do blacks pursue 'extremist' methods, disrupting the community by protesting, instead of waiting patiently for their rights? By answering these questions, King hoped to satisfy his critics and attain more support for the civil rights movement.

King begins on a conciliatory note, foreshadowing the tone of his Letter. Since the clergymen were men of 'genuine good will' who 'sincerely set forth' their criticisms, he would attempt to respond to their statement in 'patient and reasonable terms'.[3] He then considers the charge that he is an intruding 'outsider'. This allegation was not new to him, having heard it when he led the protest in Albany, Georgia in 1962. The Freedom Riders were also regarded as outsiders. King reminds his critics that he is president of SCLC, which has affiliates throughout the South. He also informs them that months ago, the Alabama Christian Movement for Human Rights, an SCLC affiliate headed by Reverend Fred Shuttlesworth, had invited him to Birmingham to participate in a nonviolent protest to secure equal rights for blacks. Thus King is in Birmingham by affiliation and invitation.

Yet King gives a more important reason for his presence in Birmingham in the spring of 1963. He feels morally obligated to oppose the city's segregation law: 'I am in Birmingham because injustice is here'.[4] According to King, all Americans who are advocates of justice should be concerned with racial conditions in Birmingham and throughout the South. Employing metaphors of particular significance to fellow clergymen, King compares himself to the Old and New Testament prophets who left their villages to spread the Word of God. He points out that St Paul responded to the 'Macedonian call for aid' and left Tarsus to carry the gospel of Jesus Christ to the Greco-Roman world.[5] The comparison to St Paul is more apt than King suggests. The great Christian apostle composed some of his epistles to his disciples while imprisoned in Rome. King also professed to carry a gospel beyond his home town – the gospel of freedom – which, readers of the Letter should infer, ought to be the aim of all Americans. King's conception of *agape* love – unconditional, redemptive love for all men – led him to believe in the 'interrelatedness of all communities and states'. He therefore proclaims: 'I cannot sit by idly in Atlanta and not be concerned about what happens in Birmingham'. King clinches his argument: 'Injustice anywhere is a threat to justice everywhere'.[6]

III

In setting forth his philosophy of nonviolent direct action clearly and cogently, King shows that the demonstrations in Birmingham were undertaken only after months of unsuccessful negotiations, and preceded by careful planning. He regrets that while the clergy-men deplored the protest, they failed to show a similar concern for the conditions that made the protest necessary. The demonstrations are unfortunate, King concedes, but 'it is even more unfortunate that the city's white power structure left the Negro community with no alternative'.[7] King then outlines the four steps of a nonviolent direct-action campaign:

1. the collection of facts, to determine whether injustices exist;
2. negotiation;
3. self-purification;
4. direct action, including boycotts, sit-ins, marches and civil disobedience.

King regarded direct action as a last resort, undertaken only after sufficient fact-gathering, petitions and attempts at negotiation have failed to secure redress of grievances. Accordingly, the demonstrations in Birmingham began only after the first three steps had been taken.

The first step, the collection of facts, is important because a protest movement cannot win the support of public opinion, or claim that it represents the cause of justice, unless it has gathered proof of serious injustice. Evidence must be carefully obtained, showing, for example, that blacks have been discriminated against in employment, or denied the right to vote or equal access to public facilities. King and SCLC carefully gathered facts before determining the site of a nonviolent direct-action campaign. Birmingham was an ideal target because its record of racial injustice was blatant and well-known.

The Letter explains that in September 1962, after a boycott of Birmingham's segregated downtown stores, Fred Shuttlesworth and the Alabama Christian Movement for Human Rights began negotiations with members of the business community. King viewed negotiation as important, not only to discuss grievances, but also to show that every effort has been made to compromise before undertaking direct action. Unsuccessful negotiations enhance the moral position of the petitioner, justifying his subsequent protest in the eyes of uncommitted third parties. After Birmingham merchants promised to remove their offensive Jim-Crow signs and cooperate in efforts to integrate the city's eating facilities, civil rights leaders agreed to halt the boycott. But the blacks of Birmingham soon faced the grim but familiar reality of broken promises. The majority of the signs remained; the segregationist policies continued.

King explains that, finding negotiations fruitless, the black community of Birmingham had no alternative but to initiate a direct-action campaign. Before the protest, a process of 'self-purification' prepared the participants to adhere to nonviolence, regardless of the provocation. Following the philosophy of Gandhi, King believed that unless protesters are purged of hostility and hatred toward their oppressors, unless they are willing to tolerate both verbal and physical abuse, their movement will degenerate into violence. As King reveals: 'We repeatedly asked ourselves: "Are you able to accept blows without retaliating?" "Are you able to endure the ordeal of jail"'[8] To prepare for the Birmingham campaign, participants were trained in workshops, which included socio-dramas that enabled them to practise the nonviolent method. Throughout the 1960s, CORE and SNCC conducted similar workshops.

IV

King's Letter also refutes the criticism that the Birmingham campaign was ill-timed. First voiced by Attorney General Robert Kennedy, this criticism was echoed in a *Washington Post* editorial and in much of the national press. When Albert Boutwell defeated Bull Connor in the run-off mayoralty election on 2 April, members of the Birmingham community, including several black leaders, were hopeful that King would postpone the protest in order to give the new administration a chance to remedy racial injustices. Nevertheless, having already been postponed twice, demonstrations were launched on 3 April. The racist power structure, King explains, would never agree to a proper time for the granting of civil rights to blacks. Although Boutwell was more benign than Bull Connor, he was a committed segregationist who would not agree to desegregation unless pressured to do so. Invoking a lesson of history, King concludes:

> My friends, I must say to you that we have not made a single gain in civil rights without determined legal and nonviolent pressure. Lamentably, it is an historical fact that privileged groups seldom give up their privileges voluntarily. . . . We know through painful experience that freedom is never voluntarily given by the oppressor; it must be demanded by the oppressed.[9]

King reminds his readers that segregationists have yet to view a protest campaign as 'well-timed'. In view of the massive resistance to desegregation in the South, the impatience of blacks is justified: 'For years now I have heard the word "Wait!". . . . This "Wait" has almost always meant "Never!"' Citing the well-known dictum of Chief Justice Earl Warren, King states that 'justice too long delayed is justice denied'.[10]

King then makes an eloquent plea on behalf of millions of frustrated black Americans, no longer willing to wait for their fundamental civil rights:

> We have waited for more than 340 years for our constitutional and God-given rights. The nations of Asia and Africa are moving with jetlike speed toward gaining political independence, but we still creep at horse-and-buggy pace toward gaining a cup of coffee at a lunch counter. Perhaps it is easy for those who have never felt the stinging darts of segregation to say "Wait." But when you have seen vicious mobs lynch your mothers and fathers at will and drown your sisters and brothers at whim; when you have seen hate-filled policemen curse, kick and even kill your black brothers and sisters; when you see the vast majority of your twenty million Negro brothers smothering in an airtight cage of poverty in the midst of an affluent society; when you suddenly find your tongue twisted and your speech stammering as you seek to explain to your six-year-old daughter why she can't go to the public amusement park that has just been advertised on television, and see tears welling up in her eyes when she is told that Funtown is closed to colored children,

and see ominous clouds of inferiority beginning to form in her little mental sky, and see her beginning to distort her personality by developing an unconscious bitterness toward white people; when you have to concoct an answer for a five-year-old son who is asking: "Daddy, why do white people treat colored people so mean?"; when you take a cross-country drive and find it necessary to sleep night after night in the uncomfortable corners of your automobile because no motel will accept you; when you are humiliated day in and day out by nagging signs reading "white" and "colored"; when your first name becomes "nigger", your middle name becomes "boy" (however old you are) and your last name becomes "John", and your wife and mother are never given the respected title "Mrs."; when you are harried by day and haunted by night by the fact that you are a Negro, living constantly at tiptoe stance, never quite knowing what to expect next, and are plagued with inner fears and outer resentments; when you are forever fighting a degenerating sense of "nobodiness" – then you will understand why we find it difficult to wait. There comes a time when the cup of endurance runs over, and men are no longer willing to be plunged into the abyss of despair.[11]

Blacks throughout the South had begun to demand their constitutional rights. Dissatisfied with the legalist method, which relied upon the slower processes of legislative lobbying and court action, blacks had turned to nonviolent protest to confront segregationist communities, provoke crises, highlight racial injustice, and coerce reforms. 'Nonviolent direct action', King explains, 'seeks to create such a crisis and foster such a tension that a community which has constantly refused to negotiate is forced to confront the issue. It seeks so to dramatize the issue that it can no longer be ignored'.[12] Familiar with Plato's *Apology*, the dramatic account of the trial of Socrates, who characterized himself as a gadfly, rousing the dormant minds and consciences of his fellow Athenians, King describes civil rights protesters as 'nonviolent gadflies', provoking the tension necessary to force the nation to confront the evils of racism.

V

Having refuted the criticisms that he was an 'outside agitator', and that the Birmingham campaign was ill-timed, King proceeds to the heart of his Letter – a defence of nonviolent civil disobedience. With the Birmingham campaign escalating, his defence became more significant, as thousands of protesters marched for freedom, nonviolently defying the injunction against demonstrations and willingly submitting to arrest. Civil disobedience – the deliberate, conscientious and public breaking of a law to protest an injustice – raises a fundamental issue: Are there any limits to the obedience which a citizen owes to the State? Put another way: Is a citizen under an absolute obligation to obey a law that he believes to be unjust? Such questions have long concerned humankind, and continue to preoccupy us today. No state can officially recognize the right of civil disobedience. Since the existence of a civilized community depends upon the rule of law, every citizen of a legitimate government has a *prima facie* obligation to obey the law. Nevertheless, this obligation is sometimes overridden by the duty to obey a higher law, dictated by conscience or some theory of natural rights.

Civil disobedience has an ancient history. The Greek dramatist Sophocles immortalized Antigone, a young heroine who is sentenced to death for defying a law of her king that conflicted with higher divine law. The Old Testament records that Shadrach, Meshach and Abednego were executed for refusing to worship a divine image of Nebuchadnezer. Socrates revered the principle of law, as seen in Plato's *Crito*, but he practised civil disobedience to unjust laws, as revealed in the *Apology*. The early Christians chose death rather than worship the Roman Emperor. Over the centuries, several philosophers, from Aquinas to John Locke, have maintained that laws contrary to the higher natural law or the law of God are invalid. John Milton refused to obey the censorship laws of seventeenth-century England. Quakers in colonial America refused to pay taxes for military purposes because they were morally opposed to war. The American Founding Fathers brought forth a new nation on the basis of the natural right to disobey unjust authority. Thomas Jefferson endorsed the epigram: 'Disobedience to tyrants is obedience to God'. The nineteenth-century American Abolitionists defied fugitive slave laws on the grounds that slavery was opposed to the law of God. Henry David Thoreau practised civil disobedience in Massachusetts, and wrote a classic essay on the subject. In the twentieth century, Mohandas K. Gandhi achieved world-wide fame for his nonviolent resistance to unjust laws, first in South Africa, then in his native India. Since the Second World War, civil disobedience has become increasingly important in the United States. The civil rights movement, and protests against the Vietnam War, nuclear weapons proliferation and apartheid in South Africa have emphasized the individual's right to disobey laws that conflict with moral principles.

Although civil disobedience is founded upon an ancient tradition, the willingness of King to break the law, even though nonviolently, was a source of great concern among his critics. It seemed paradoxical to some that while urging the South to obey the United States Supreme Court's *Brown* decision, King and other civil rights activists disobeyed state segregation laws. The underlying fear was that such civil disobedience would promote anarchy. Many assumed that defiance of any law leads to contempt for law in general. If individual citizens are permitted to choose arbitrarily to obey some laws and disobey others, King's critics argued, the social order will be undermined. He responded by pointing out that his decision to break certain laws was not arbitrary, but founded upon sound moral principles and provoked by serious circumstances. King never denied the obligation to obey laws of the State. 'I would be the first to advocate obeying just laws. One has not only a legal but a moral responsibility to obey just laws'.[13] But he insisted that this obligation is subordinate to the duty to disobey those laws conscience deems unjust. King agrees with St Augustine that 'an unjust law is no law at all'.[14]

A proper understanding of civil disobedience dispels the fear that King's protest campaigns posed a threat to the principle of law and order. Disobedience to unjust laws is not an act of revolution. The fact that King and other civil rights protesters violated the law nonviolently and publicly, willingly accepting the legal penalty for their principled disobedience, shows that they did not intend to overthrow constituted authority. On the contrary, their intention was to work within the democratic system to expose and eradicate racial injustice. When used to publicize injustices, civil disobedience can serve to strengthen a democratic society. While, ideally, reform results from a rational discussion of grievances, history shows that official channels are sometimes unresponsive, and that protest involving disobedience to law is sometimes necessary to awaken slumbering consciences, and to compel legal remedies to injustices. Each act of civil disobedience summons a democracy to self-examination.

Most nonviolent protest during the civil rights movement was entirely within the bounds of the law. The United States Constitution, specifically the First and Fourteenth Amendments, guarantees the rights of free expression and peaceful protest. Public meetings, parades and mass demonstrations, as long as they do not violate the rights of others, are perfectly legal. The March on Washington in 1963, involving thousands of nonviolent demonstrators, was not an act of civil disobedience, but a dramatic example of the exercise of constitutional rights. Civil disobedience did however occur in the South when blacks defied segregation laws and legal attempts by state and local authorities to prohibit peaceful protests. This disobedience was usually undertaken to show that local laws were contrary to the United States Constitution. By violating state and local segregation laws, and the court orders enforcing them, King and his associates were in effect appealing to the superior civil law and authority of the federal government, the Constitution and the decisions of the Supreme Court. The protesters were merely asserting rights that were constitutionally guaranteed. In many instances, such as King's campaigns in Birmingham, St Augustine and Selma, civil rights protesters showed their support for the principle of law and order by not resisting arrest for disobeying those laws they deemed unjust. As King concludes:

> One who breaks an unjust law must do so openly, lovingly, and with a willingness to accept the penalty. I submit that an individual who breaks a law that conscience tells him is unjust, and who willingly accepts the penalty of imprisonment in order to arouse the conscience of the community over its injustice, is in reality expressing the highest respect for the law.[15]

Admitting that one has a moral obligation to disobey an unjust law leads to the difficulty of distinguishing between a just and an unjust law. Here King turns to a source of authority that transcends the State – the rich, centuries-old doctrine of natural law. Natural law refers to moral principles perceived by human reason and independent of the State. In theory, all laws of a sovereign State are legal; but not all laws are just. Disobedience to unjust civil laws may be defended on moral grounds, but by definition it is never legal. One may have a legal right to protest against a particular law, but one never has a legal right to disobey it. Nevertheless, throughout history, civil disobedients have believed that non-cooperation with evil is as much a moral obligation as cooperation with good. Disobedience to unjust civil laws is justified by appealing to a higher law – moral or natural law.

King's ideas on natural law were derived from St Thomas Aquinas, one of the greatest Christian philosophers. According to Aquinas, natural law reflects man's participation in the eternal moral law of God, enjoining man to do good and avoid evil. A civil law that conflicts with the natural law is unjust, and must in conscience be disobeyed. As King summarizes: 'A just law is a man-made code that squares with the moral law of God. An unjust law is a code that is out of harmony with the moral law. To put it in the terms of St Thomas Aquinas: An unjust law is a human law that is not rooted in eternal law and natural law'.[16] Those who tend to regard law and order as sacrosanct are reminded by King that what the Hungarian freedom fighters did to resist aggression from the Soviet Union was 'illegal', and that it was 'illegal' to aid Jews in Hitler's Germany. Furthermore, the Boston Tea Party was a 'massive act of civil disobedience'.[17] King would agree with Thoreau's proposition: 'They are the lovers of law and order who observe the law when the government breaks it'.[18]

The remaining question is: Why are segregation statutes unjust? Here King depends upon Judaeo-Christian ethics, according to which each person is endowed by God with dignity and worth. While a student at Boston University, King was influenced by the philosophical personalism of Edgar S. Brightman and L. Harold DeWolf. Segregation is immoral, King argues, because it deprives a person of his inherent dignity, reducing him to an object. As King affirms:

Any law that uplifts human personality is just. Any law that degrades human personality is unjust. All segregation statutes are unjust because segregation distorts the soul and damages the personality. It gives the segregator a false sense of superiority and the segregated a false sense of inferiority.[19]

King also appeals to modern theologians:

Segregation, to use the terminology of the Jewish philosopher Martin Buber, substitutes an "I–it" relationship for an "I–thou" relationship and ends up relegating persons to the status of things. Hence segregation is not only politically, economically and sociologically unsound, it is morally wrong and sinful. Paul Tillich has said that sin is separation. Is not segregation an existential expression of man's tragic separation, his awful estrangement, his terrible sinfulness?[20]

By anchoring his philosophy in the writings of leading theologians, King makes it clear that segregation statutes are unjust because they are dehumanizing, contrary to natural law and the Judaeo-Christian heritage.

Developing his argument with greater precision, King shows that segregation violates the cherished democratic principle of equality before the law:

An unjust law is a code that a numerical or power majority group compels a minority group to obey but does not make binding on itself. This is *difference* made legal. By the same token, a just law is a code that a majority compels a minority to follow and that it is willing to follow itself. This is *sameness* made legal.[21]

King holds that a law, such as a segregation law, is unjust if imposed upon a minority that, because they have been denied the right to vote, played no role in its enactment. King knew, for instance, that of the 80 000 voters in Birmingham in 1963, only 10 000 were blacks, even though they constituted 40 per cent of the city population.[22] He therefore questioned whether the Alabama legislature that passed the state's segregation laws, was democratically elected. The Jim Crow laws, established by the South during the late nineteenth century and imposed upon a largely disenfranchised minority, contradicted the ideal upon which the United States was founded – government of the people, by the people and for the people.

King also recognizes that a just law may be unjustly applied. While a parade ordinance to maintain law and order is justified, it becomes unjust, he says, when used to support racial segregation and to deny constitutional rights to peaceful assembly and protest. Hundreds of civil rights protesters were arrested in the South for violating laws against disorderly conduct and disturbing the peace, laws necessary and just in themselves, but unjustly administered.

VI

In the last part of his Letter, King expresses profound disappointment with two influential groups in American society that he had hoped would support the cause of racial justice: white moderates and white clergymen. King confesses that he has almost concluded that the great obstacle for blacks in their 'stride toward freedom' is not the blatant racism of the Ku-Klux-Klan and the White Citizens' Councils, but white moderates who, while professing to agree with civil rights goals, are devoted more to 'order' than to justice, regard direct action as extreme and advise blacks to continue to wait for freedom. Yet King points out that law and order exist to establish justice, and that direct action has been instrumental in remedying racial injustice. He notes that his clergymen critics had condemned the Birmingham protest because, even though peaceful, it precipitated violence. But this is like condemning a robbed man, King responds, because his possession of money led to the act of his being robbed. The federal courts affirmed that individuals may pursue their constitutional rights even though the quest might lead to violence. White moderates fail to perceive that the segregationist order is merely a 'negative peace', in which blacks passively accept oppression, rather than a 'positive peace', in which human dignity is promoted. Nonviolent direct action succeeds by disrupting this 'negative peace', exposing the underlying injustice 'to the light of human conscience and the air of national opinion before it can be cured'.[23]

Much of King's success against segregation in the South can be attributed to the fact that he was eventually able to win the support of a great number of white moderates. Their consciences having been stung by the exposure of racist brutality in Birmingham, in addition to the eloquence of King's Letter, many more moderates became sympathetic to the civil rights cause after the March on Washington in August 1963. In seeking their support, King understood the importance of disassociating himself from those who advocated violent means to racial justice. August Meier has argued persuasively that King's influence can largely be explained by his being a 'conservative militant', who combined direct action with moderation and a willingness to compromise when necessary.[24] He was able to attract much support from whites because his nonviolent method provided the civil rights movement with respectability. King's public image was enhanced by his friendship with President

Kennedy, and by his receiving the Nobel Peace Prize in 1964.

White liberals accepted King because – at least until his far-reaching critique of American society and foreign policy during the final year and a half of his life – neither his goals nor his methods were radical. As King explains in his Letter, he represented a middle course between two opposing groups in the black community. On the one side, were those who had resigned themselves to segregation, either because years of oppression had deprived them of the desire for dignity, or because they were among the minority of blacks who had risen to the middle class and succumbed to the privileges of their new status. On the other side, King saw the promoters of 'bitterness and hatred', who came 'perilously close to advocating violence', and regarded the white man as an 'incorrigible devil'.[25] This anger, nourished by the intransigence of white racism, was expressed by various black nationalist groups that preached black supremacy, the largest being the Muslim organization of Elijah Muhammad and his chief minister, Malcolm X. But King always regarded the doctrine of black supremacy as evil as the doctrine of white supremacy. He therefore rejected the black nationalists for having 'absolutely repudiated Christianity' and having 'lost faith in America'.[26]

King insists that all protest must be nonviolent, no matter how severe the injustice: 'Nonviolence demands that the means we use must be as pure as the ends we seek'. He maintains that 'it is wrong to use immoral means to attain moral ends', because the means employed determine the nature of the end produced.[27] If the philosophy of nonviolence had not emerged, King concludes, 'by now many streets of the South would, I am convinced, be flowing with blood'.[28] If whites continue to dismiss the practitioners of nonviolence as 'rabble-rousers' and 'outside agitators', he warns, millions of despairing blacks will turn to black nationalism, leading to 'a frightening racial nightmare'.[29] Drawing upon his knowledge of human psychology, King argues that nonviolent direct action is a constructive means for blacks to vent their justifiable anger, and to act on their own behalf to achieve civil rights without resorting to bloodshed:

> The Negro has many pent-up resentments and latent frustrations, and he must release them. So let him march; let him make prayer pilgrimages to the city hall; let him go on freedom rides – and try to understand why he must do so. If his repressed emotions

are not released in nonviolent ways, they will seek expression through violence; this is not a threat, but a fact of history.[30]

Thus King appeals to white moderates to accept the method of nonviolent direct action, both in Birmingham, and in the struggle for civil rights throughout the nation. Those who oppose the nonviolent method are faced with the prospect of frustrated and disillusioned blacks turning to armed rebellion.

Nevertheless, there remained those who, refusing to see the moderation of King's nonviolent method and the justness of his goals, charged him with extremism. In one of his most eloquent paragraphs, King reminds his critics that history reveals that 'extremism' has often been vindicated:

Though I was initially disappointed at being categorized as an extremist, as I continued to think about the matter I gradually gained a measure of satisfaction from the label. Was not Jesus an extremist for love: "Love your enemies, bless them that curse you, do good to them that hate you, and pray for them which despitefully use you, and persecute you." Was not Amos an extremist for justice: "Let justice roll down like waters and righteousness like an over-flowing stream" Was not Paul an extremist for the Christian gospel: "I bear in my body the marks of the Lord Jesus." Was not Martin Luther an extremist: "Here I stand; I cannot do otherwise, so help me God." And John Bunyan: "I will stay in jail to the end of my days before I make a butchery of my conscience." And Abraham Lincoln: "This nation cannot survive half slave and half free." And Thomas Jefferson: "We hold these truths to be self-evident, that all men are created equal . . ." So the question is not whether we will be extremists, but what kind of extremists we will be. Will we be extremists for hate or for love? Will we be extremists for the preservation of injustice or for the extension of justice?[31]

VII

After appealing to the white moderate, King confronts the other source of his disappointment: the white church and its leadership. Having travelled throughout the South, admiring the beauty of its churches, he found himself asking repeatedly: '"What kind of

people worship here? Who is their God? . . . . Where were they
when Governor Wallace gave the clarion call for defiance and
hatred?"'[32] Despite notable exceptions, King says, most white
clergymen in the South failed to support the quest for civil rights.
He recalls that during the Montgomery bus boycott in 1956, he
had expected white ministers and priests to rally behind him.
Although he was disappointed in Montgomery, King confesses
that he hoped that the white clergy would support him in
Birmingham. Again he was disappointed. He laments that many
Southern white ministers urged their congregations to comply with
segregation ordinances merely because they were the law. In the
midst of grave injustice, many ministers, maintaining what King
regards as an 'un-Biblical' separation between the sacred and the
secular, held that the church should not be concerned with social
issues.[33]

In contrast, King held that the gospel of individual salvation
must be supplemented by the social gospel. He believed firmly
that a religion which is concerned solely with a life after death,
neglecting the social evil that afflicts man in this world, is a
spiritually dead religion. From the beginning, King regarded his
commitment to the struggle for civil rights as inseparable from his
Christian ministry. He warns that unless the church revives the
'sacrificial spirit' of the early Christians, who were champions of
humanity and justice, 'it will lose its authenticity, forfeit the loyalty
of millions, and be dismissed as an irrelevant social club with no
meaning for the twentieth century'.[34]

Even if the white church fails to 'meet the challenge of this
decisive hour' and take the side of racial justice, King is optimistic
about the future of the struggle for civil rights.[35] Wishing to inspire
activists in Birmingham and throughout the nation to continue
their efforts to attain justice and equality for the black American,
he expresses faith that they will ultimately be victorious:

> I have no despair about the future. I have no fear about the
> outcome of our struggle in Birmingham, even if our motives are
> at present misunderstood. We will reach the goal of freedom in
> Birmingham and all over the nation, because the goal of America
> is freedom. Abused and scorned though we may be, our destiny
> is tied up with America's destiny. Before the pilgrims landed at
> Plymouth, we were here. Before the pen of Jefferson etched the
> majestic words of the Declaration of Independence across the

pages of history, we were here. For more than two centuries our forefathers labored in this country without wages; they made cotton king; they built the homes of their masters while suffering gross injustice and shameful humiliation – and yet out of a bottomless vitality they continued to thrive and develop. If the inexpressible cruelties of slavery could not stop us, the opposition we face now will surely fail. We will win our freedom because the sacred heritage of our nation and the eternal will of God are embodied in our echoing demands.[36]

By connecting the victory of the civil rights movement to the destiny of America, King appeals to the conscience of the nation by underscoring what Swedish economist Gunnar Myrdal characterized in 1944 as an 'American Dilemma' – the conflict between the nation's democratic creed of freedom and equality, and its actual practice. According to Myrdal, the 'Negro problem' is not only America's great failure, but also its great opportunity, a moral challenge to the nation to fulfil the promise embodied in the democratic creed.[37] The nonviolent direct-action campaigns of King and SCLC were effective in the South largely because they highlighted the American Dilemma, reminding those indifferent to the civil rights cause that they were perpetuating injustice, and summoning them to fulfil the ideals of democracy. Indeed, a nation that takes pride in its heritage of freedom, and yet denies fundamental human rights to a race that played so great a role in its history, is certainly confronted by a dilemma. A nation that takes pride in itself as a haven for the homeless and the oppressed, and yet permits so many of its citizens to languish in abject poverty, is guilty of shameful hypocrisy. The cry of the black man for freedom and equality echoes throughout American history.

Before closing his Letter, King repeats the American Dilemma theme in a final tribute to all those who have sacrificed for the cause of racial justice. Anticipating his great 'I Have A Dream' speech of August 1963, he links the success of the civil rights movement to the realization of the American dream:

One day the South will recognize its real heroes. They will be the James Merediths, with the noble sense of purpose that enables them to face jeering and hostile mobs, and with the agonizing loneliness that characterizes the life of the pioneer. They will be the old, oppressed, battered Negro women, symbolized in the seventy-two-year-old woman in Montgomery, Alabama, who rose up with a sense of dignity and with her people decided not to ride segregated buses, and who responded with ungrammatical profundity to one who inquired about her weariness: 'My feets is tired, but my soul is at rest.' They will be the young high school and college students, the young ministers of the gospel and a host of their elders, courageously and nonviolently sitting in at lunch counters and willingly going to jail for conscience sake. One day the South will know that when these disinherited children of God sat down at lunch counters they were in reality standing up for what is best in the American dream and for the most sacred values in our Judaeo-Christian heritage, thereby bringing our nation back to those great wells of democracy which were dug deep by the founding fathers in their formulation of the Constitution and the Declaration of Independence.[38]

VIII

When Martin Luther King, Jr. put down his pen on 16 April 1963, he had composed the manifesto of the civil rights movement. The 'Letter from Birmingham Jail' is the most eloquent and powerful statement of his philosophy, method and goals. He had defended his presence in Birmingham as an apostle of nonviolence and justice, and appealed to America to grant rights to its black citizens that were long overdue. He had expounded his philosophy of nonviolence and explained the effectiveness of militant nonviolent protest. He had outlined the steps in a direct action campaign. He had defended the decision of blacks to disobey unjust segregation laws by turning to the centuries-old doctrine of natural law. He had argued that civil disobedience does not create anarchy because the civil disobedient, in seeking to awaken the conscience of the community to injustice, is willing to accept the penalty of imprisonment for disobeying a law he believes to be unjust. He had shown that nonviolent protest offered blacks a means to channel their anger and frustration while confronting the violence of racism. He had prodded the consciences of millions of white moderates and church leaders to come forward in defence of racial justice. He had emphasized the American Dilemma, appealing to democratic values, and showing that the demands of blacks represented not a rejection but an embracing of American society and its institutions. He had explained that blacks would wait no longer for the granting of their fundamental human rights. Finally, he had answered the charge of extremism by showing that his actions in Birmingham were consistent with the great tradition of those who devoted their lives to the cause of liberty, justice and equality. In a historic letter to the nation, Martin Luther King, Jr. had proclaimed that the achievement of civil rights for blacks was essential for the fulfillment of America's cherished ideals.

6

The Struggle Continues, 1964

The historic March on Washington on 28 August 1963 dramatized widespread support for the Civil Rights Bill. But the enthusiasm engendered by the March was short-lived, for black Americans soon faced the grim reality that their long, hard struggle against Southern racism was not over. On 15 September 1963, 18 days after the March, a bomb was tossed into the Sixteenth Street Baptist Church in Birmingham during Sunday school, killing four black girls, aged 11 to 14, and injuring 21 other children. Weeks later, on 22 November, the nation was stunned when President Kennedy was assassinated in Dallas, Texas, leading many blacks to fear for the fate of the pending Civil Rights Bill. King was among the 1200 people invited to attend the President's funeral in Washington. Although Kennedy had initially vacillated on civil rights, the Birmingham campaign had played a major role in prodding him to fulfil his campaign pledge to introduce legislation guaranteeing civil rights. Black Americans were relieved when it became clear that the next Administration would continue Kennedy's efforts. On 27 November, the new President, Lyndon Johnson, declared in his first address to Congress: 'No memorial oration or eulogy could more eloquently honor President Kennedy's memory than the earliest possible passage of the civil rights bill for which he fought so long'.[1]

As the leading spokesman for black Americans, King attracted much support for the Civil Rights Bill. On 4 January 1964, *Time* magazine named him 'Man of the Year' for 1963, the first black American to receive the honour. Featuring King on its cover, the magazine announced that he was chosen not only 'as a man, but also as a representative of his people for whom 1963 was perhaps the most important year in their history'.[2] Although the House of Representatives passed the Civil Rights Bill by a roll-call vote of

290 to 130 on 10 February 1964, strong resistance was anticipated in the Senate. If the bill were not passed, King wrote in the January SCLC *Newsletter*, 'the nation might well fasten its safety belt'.[3] To keep the American Dilemma before the eyes of the nation in the spring of 1964, SCLC chose St Augustine, Florida as the next battlefield. This historic city, 35 miles south of Jacksonville, would be the scene of the final nonviolent campaign against segregated public accommodations in the South.

Debate on the Civil Rights Bill began in the Senate on 9 March, and would continue for the following two months. King and SCLC calculated that if a crisis could be provoked in St Augustine, the resulting publicity might pressure Congress to enact the pending legislation. 'Passage of the civil rights bill', said C. T. Vivian, 'was a primary goal of the SCLC in St Augustine'.[4] The bill was 'so critical for the domestic health of our national community', King declared in the March SCLC *Newsletter*, 'that we must mobilize every force and pressure available to see to it that the civil rights bill before the Senate gets through – *as is*'.[5] A success in St Augustine would also demonstrate once again the viability of nonviolent direct action. In the wake of the Birmingham campaign, nonviolence was challenged by blacks who opposed racism with violence in cities such as Jacksonville, Nashville and Atlanta. According to *New York Times* reporter John Herbers: 'St Augustine is a critical test not only of Dr King's ability to hold the imagination and allegiance of millions of Negroes, but also of the nonviolent method'.[6]

II

In the spring of 1964, St Augustine, the oldest city in the United States, was preparing to celebrate its four-hundredth anniversary the following year. In 1963, President Kennedy appointed a special commission to plan the celebration, and the city hoped to receive federal financial assistance to refurbish its old ruins. Tourism being the city's major source of income, the business community expected the celebration to result in considerable profits. But not all St Augustine residents were looking forward to the festivities. Although blacks constituted 25 per cent of the total population of 15 000, they were deprived of basic civil rights. Not only was the city a haven for the Ku-Klux-Klan and the John Birch Society, but it also had an infamous history of white racist violence. In 1961, police stood by while Klansmen severely beat a group of black students who had staged a sit-in at a local store. Since 1959, Dr R. N. Hayling, a black dentist and head of the local NAACP, had attempted to resist segregation in the city. His efforts were to no avail, as whites responded with violence and intimidation.

In August 1963, the Florida Advisory Committee to the U.S. Commission on Civil Rights held a hearing in St Augustine and issued a report ominously characterizing the city as 'a segregated superbomb. . . . The fuse is short'.[7] That September, Dr Hayling and three other blacks were abducted by Klansmen, beaten unconscious, and nearly burned alive. 'Kill 'em! Castrate 'em!', cried a woman onlooker. After Dr Hayling resigned his NAACP office in bitter frustration, his home was dynamited. In early February 1964, the homes of two black families whose children had integrated public schools were burned. At the same time, Klan members prevented local white businessmen from desegregating their stores by threatening them with physical harm.

As instances of violence multiplied, St Augustine's blacks found no refuge in the law. State and local police authorities, in addition to Mayor Joseph Shelley, regarded violence committed against blacks with indifference. In fact, Sheriff L. O. Davis – an outspoken opponent of desegregation – had gone so far as to enlist an auxiliary force of some 100 volunteer 'special' deputies that included many known Klansmen, and were led by Holsted 'Hoss' Manucy, a convicted felon. Officially named the Ancient City Gun Club, though townspeople knew them as 'Manucy's Raiders', they roamed St Augustine's segregated beaches by day and the town plaza by night, terrorizing black residents. 'My boys are here to fight niggers', Manucy explained. His men patrolled the streets in cars, carrying Confederate flags, and communicated by shortwave radio. After King came to St Augustine, Manucy denounced him as 'an outside nigger and we don't put up with outside niggers in St Augustine. He's a Communist. That's a proven fact'.[8] SCLC's Andrew Young aptly described the racist brutality in the city: 'It's one thing to oppose the Klan. . . . But when you have one man, wearing civilian clothes, beating you while another, wearing a badge, stands waiting to arrest you when the first gets tired, well, that makes you think. St Augustine is really worse than Birmingham. It's the worst I've ever seen'.[9] Although Manucy denied being a member of the Klan, he publicly described it as a 'very good organization'.[10]

The federal government ignored pleas for protection of blacks and civil rights workers in St Augustine. In his annual article for *The Nation*, King underscored the dire need for federal action to bring racial justice and order to the South. In assessing the Albany campaign in 1962, SCLC had concluded that federal support was crucial to nonviolent protests. Thus far, Washington had remained silent on the racial brutality in St Augustine. Although blacks 'marshalled extraordinary courage to employ nonviolent direct action', King lamented, 'they have been left — by the most powerful federal government in the world – almost to their own resources'.[11]

Few people outside of St Augustine took note of the racial injustices there until Easter Sunday, 29 March 1964, when nine members of an interracial group were arrested for trying to integrate the dining room of the Monson Motor Lodge. Among those arrested were 72-year-old Mrs Malcolm Peabody, mother of the governor of Massachusetts, and Mrs John Burgess, wife of the first black Episcopal bishop. The incident made national headlines, publicising black grievances. Meanwhile, Dr Hayling, having resumed the fight for civil rights and become head of the St Augustine SCLC affiliate, visited King in Atlanta. Without King's help, he insisted, the movement to desegregate St Augustine was doomed. On 6 March, Dr Hayling attended an SCLC conference in Orlando, Florida and persuaded C. T. Vivian to visit St Augustine to study the situation. On the strength of Vivian's report, King and SCLC decided to intervene. By the second week of March, shortly after debate on the Civil Rights Bill had begun in the Senate, SCLC staff members Vivian, Hosea Williams, and Bernard Lee arrived in St Augustine to set the stage for a nonviolent direct-action campaign. They were soon joined by Fred Shuttlesworth and James Bevel. Within a short time, local blacks were convinced to participate in workshops on nonviolent techniques.

III

Throughout late March and the first week of April, while King spoke at important fund-raisers across the nation, SCLC launched several nonviolent demonstrations in St Augustine. To make further preparations for the campaign, King dispatched Wyatt Walker to the city. Walker concluded that SCLC could capitalize on St Augustine's economic dependence upon tourism, and its expectation of federal financial assistance for its upcoming anniversary celebration. As in Birmingham, SCLC's strategy was designed to apply economic pressure upon the business community that would force the city authorities to negotiate concessions. If non-violent protesters could disrupt St Augustine, the adverse publicity would cripple its tourist industry, and President Johnson might be persuaded to withhold federal funds.

In May 1964, Hosea Williams, director of the SCLC Field Staff from 1963 until 1970, and one of the most militant members of King's staff, decided that a series of night marches to the historic Slave Market – an obvious symbol of oppression, located ironically in the city's Constitution Plaza – would be effective in dramatizing the plight of St Augustine's black population. According to C. T. Vivian, King consented to night marches as a means to arouse the 'creative tension' necessary to expose the savage white violence and racial injustice in St Augustine to the nation, inducing the federal government to defend the civil rights of black Americans as it had done in Birmingham.[12]

The first night marches occurred without incident. Hosea Williams and Dr Hayling had recruited scores of black youth for the campaign. St Augustine high school students, along with students from Florida Memorial College, were prepared to meet violence with nonviolence. Most older black St Augustinians, fearing their white employers and accustomed to passivity, remained bystanders to the escalating protest. On Tuesday, 26 May, some 400 marchers, led by Andrew Young, left the First Baptist Church at ten at night and proceeded to the Slave Market, where they conducted a prayer ceremony under police protection. The next night, Young led 800 marchers from St Mary's Baptist Church. Arriving at the Slave Market, they found it occupied by about 100 whites, many of them armed. Having been forewarned by Sheriff Davis of the likelihood of white violence, the marchers merely circled the Plaza and headed back to the church unharmed.

Had the white population of St Augustine continued to allow the demonstrators to march unmolested, the protest would have probably died out within a few weeks. But once again, SCLC provoked white racists. On Thursday evening, 28 May, Young led another march, this time from St Paul's A.M.E. Church. Arriving at the Slave Market, the marchers were attacked by whites with iron pipes and chains in the presence of reporters and television cameras. Maintaining their nonviolent discipline, several blacks dropped to their knees to pray, prompting a white hoodlum to exclaim, club in hand: 'Niggers ain't got no God!' After police finally restored order, and many blacks limped back to St Paul's, Sheriff Davis told Young and other black leaders: 'We are declaring martial law. You had no permit for the earlier marches, and no permits will be given for other marches'.[13] SCLC had fomented the 'creative tension' they needed.

The following day, King telegraphed President Johnson, declaring that 'all semblance of law and order has broken down in St Augustine, Florida', and appealing for federal intervention. Although the protest had led to white violence, King informed the President that he was not about to call it off: 'We cannot in good conscience postpone our nonviolent thrust merely because violence has erupted against us, but we sincerely believe that as American citizens our right to peaceably assemble must be guaranteed and not abridged because of the unrestrained lawlessness of the Klan element'.[14] King's plea was rejected, for President Johnson feared that federal intervention in St Augustine would hurt the Democratic Party. Civil rights would be a major issue in the forthcoming 1964 presidential election, and Republican Barry Goldwater was attracting support among Democrats in the Deep South. Meanwhile, Florida Governor Farris Bryant refused to send the National Guard to protect the constitutional rights of St Augustine's black citizens, who became further enraged when the federal government granted the city's request for $350 000 to help finance its four-hundreth anniversary celebration.

On 31 May, Sheriff Davis succeeded in obtaining a local court injunction banning night marches in St Augustine. The same day, as tension continued to build in the city, King arrived, accompanied by a corps of press members, and issued a plea to 'all men of conscience' to join him in the forthcoming demonstrations.[15] He also formally announced the goals of the St Augustine campaign: immediate desegregation of the hotels and motels, restaurants, lunch counters, swimming pools and other public facilities; the hiring of blacks by the fire and police departments; and the creation of a biracial committee, two-thirds of whose members would be chosen by SCLC. The City Commission adamantly refused to discuss these demands.

By obtaining the court order, Sheriff Davis had unwittingly assisted the protest. The day after King's arrival, SCLC lawyers, led by William Kunstler, went to the U.S. District Court in Jacksonville and requested Judge Bryan Simpson to reverse the injunction on the grounds that it violated the First Amendment rights of the protesters to freedom of speech and assembly. Pending the result of a hearing, King agreed to halt the demonstrations. Once again, King and SCLC looked to the federal courts as an ally in the battle for civil rights in the South. Following the Jacksonville hearing, King held a press conference and declared St Augustine 'the most lawless community that we've ever worked in'.[16]

Awaiting Judge Simpson's ruling, King sought to bolster black resistance. SCLC strategy was dependent upon blacks maintaining nonviolent discipline. Addressing a mass meeting, King praised the protesters for their courageous commitment to nonviolence, and urged them to persevere. 'Soon the Klan will see', he predicted, 'that all of their violence will not stop us, for we are on the way to Freedom Land and we don't mean to stop until we get there'.[17] Meanwhile, Hosea Williams also spoke to blacks at the Slave Market, impressing upon them the importance of achieving a nonviolent victory. 'If the black man loses his freedom, no man will be free', he proclaimed. 'We are willing to die so that America shall be free'.[18] Finally, on 9 June, good news arrived from Jacksonville. Although a native Southerner, when Judge Simpson learned that many of Sheriff Davis's 'special' deputies, including Hoss Manucy, were either Klan members or sympathizers, he ruled in favour of King and SCLC, forbidding further interference with the night marches.

But a federal court victory alone would not bring law and order to St Augustine, for white racists continued to employ violence and intimidation. By this time, the national television networks had focused upon Hoss Manucy as the spokesmen for the city's die-hard segregationists. Despite persistent violent white resistance, the black protesters remained undaunted. As King declared at a mass meeting: 'We are determined [that] this city will not celebrate its quadricentennial as a segregated city. There will be no turning back'.[19] Following the strategy of the Albany and Birmingham campaigns, King and SCLC decided that the climactic moment had arrived for his arrest. Having mobilized the black community and generated widespread publicity through non-violent direct action, the stage was set for the campaign to move into high gear. King's arrest would not only increase the 'creative tension' in St Augustine, but also emphasize the necessity of passing the Civil Rights Bill.

On Thursday, 11 June, King, Ralph Abernathy and a small group of protesters went to the Monson Motor Lodge. With reporters and television cameras present, they endeavoured to integrate the restaurant and were arrested for violating Florida's 'unwanted guest' law. Later that evening, some 400 demonstrators, urged earlier by King to 'march tonight as you've never marched before', were attacked by a white mob in the vicinity of the Slave Market.[20] Order was restored only after state troopers arrived and set off tear gas bombs. While in jail, King continued to pressure President Johnson, sending him another telegram stating that St Augustine had just undergone the 'most complete breakdown of law and order since Oxford, Mississippi', and pleading with him to dispatch federal marshalls to the city at once.[21] Finally, on 10 June, the Senate filibuster against the Civil Rights Bill was defeated by a 71 to 29 vote. For the first time in its history, the Senate had voted to close off debate on a civil rights filibuster. Passage of the bill was now virtually inevitable.

Buoyed by the prospect of a national legislative victory for civil rights, King left jail on 14 June and travelled to New Haven to receive an honorary degree from Yale University. Ten thousand spectators cheered as King was cited for having 'kindled the nation's sense of outrage' at the injustices inflicted upon black Americans, and for his 'steadfast refusal to countenance violence'.[22] Meanwhile, in St Augustine, J. B. Stoner, an Atlanta attorney and vice-presidential candidate of the right-wing National States Rights Party, had been rousing racist sentiment. Addressing a large crowd at the Slave Market on 12 June, he shouted: 'Tonight, we're going to find out whether white people have any rights!'[23] He continued: 'When the Constitution said all men are created equal, it wasn't talking about niggers. The coons have been parading around St Augustine for a long time!' The white citizens of St Augustine would tolerate this no longer, Stoner insisted. Neither King, whom Stoner accused of being a 'long time associate of Communists', nor the 'Jew-stacked, Communist-loving Supreme Court' would stop them. After his tirade, Stoner led a mob of angry whites – bearing Confederate flags and signs reading 'Kill the Civil Rights Bill' and 'Put George Wallace on the Supreme Court' – to the black section of town. Accompanied by state troopers with police dogs, they entered the black neighbourhood, where they saw a sign reading 'Welcome. Peace and brotherhood to you'.[24]

As racial tensions increased, King returned to St Augustine. By mid-June, the pressure of almost daily demonstrations had begun to take its toll on the business community. On 17 June, city merchants announced their promise to obey the Civil Rights Bill when it was passed. At the same time, a grand jury, appointed on 11 June to explore ways to resolve St Augustine's racial conflict, recommended an immediate halt to all demonstrations for a period of 30 days, followed by negotiations to form a biracial committee. The jury also insisted that King and SCLC leave St Augustine for the 30-day period. While many white city residents were optimistic that these recommendations would restore peace to the community, King and SCLC promptly rejected them, offering a counter-proposal for a one-week moratorium on protests, contingent on the immediate establishment of a biracial committee.

In retrospect, King and SCLC were wise in rejecting the grand jury's recommendations, which would have impeded the momentum of the protest campaign. The Albany Movement had been hampered by an injunction that temporarily halted demonstrations; the Birmingham campaign, on the other hand, succeeded because black marchers applied constant pressure upon the white power structure. King and SCLC had learned that they could not trust promises made by a segregationist community, and the Albany campaign had proved the futility of a mere verbal agreement. They were therefore determined to continue the protest, vowing to depart only after the city established the biracial committee. Moreover, as long as the Civil Rights Bill was still in the Senate, King and SCLC believed it necessary to remain in St Augustine to dramatize the persistence of segregation in the South.

IV

On 19 June 1964, the black freedom movement attained a substantial victory when the Senate, after 83 days of debate, passed the Civil Rights Bill by a vote of 73 to 27, and returned it to the House for final approval. Predictably, there was a mixed reaction. While Senator Strom Thurmond of South Carolina lamented, 'This is a sad day for America', Senator Jacob Javits of New York hailed the passage as 'one of the Senate's finest hours'.[25] King called it a 'lasting tribute to the memory of John F. Kennedy'.[26]

Meanwhile, white racists remained determined to destroy the protest campaign in St Augustine. When an integrated group jumped into the segregated pool of the Monson Motor Lodge on 18 June, the manager responded by tossing muriatic acid into the water. The incident drew national headlines. On 25 June, some 800 Klansmen, led by Hoss Manucy, attacked black demonstrators at the Slave Market, injuring dozens, some severely. At a White Citizens Rally that night, Klan organizer Connie Lynch bellowed: 'If it takes violence to preserve the Constitution, I say all right. I favor violence to preserve the white race anytime, anyplace, anywhere'.[27] The following day, Florida Governor Bryant defied the federal court injunction protecting the right of peaceful protest in St Augustine by re-instating the ban on night marches.

The protest appeared to be deadlocked, until President Johnson realized that he could no longer ignore the deteriorating conditions in the city. After weeks of demonstrations, and repeated pleas for federal intervention, the President telephoned Florida's U.S. Senator George Smathers, requesting that he use his influence to negotiate a settlement. Smathers conveyed the President's message to Herbert Wolfe, a local St Augustine business leader, and Governor Bryant. At Wolfe's suggestion, Mayor Joseph Shelley then convened a group of 25 St Augustine business and civic leaders to discuss the formation of a biracial committee. After Mayor Shelley argued that it would represent a surrender to the demands of King, the group rejected the committee, and communicated their decision to Governor Bryant on 29 June.

To their surprise, Governor Bryant, responding to pressure from the President, overruled their decision, announcing on 30 June the creation of an emergency biracial committee of four unnamed men to 'restore communications' between the black and white communities, which would fulfil one of the goals of the St Augustine campaign.[28] 'This is merely the first step in the long journey toward freedom and justice in St Augustine', King said, 'but it is a creative and important first step, for it at last opens the channels of communication'.[29] King might have been aware that, in truth, no committee had been formed; nor did the Governor intend to create one. Nevertheless, the declaration of the settlement served both sides. SCLC would be able to leave St Augustine with an apparent local victory, and the city authorities would be free of further protests. Passage of the Civil Rights Bill would accomplish the major goal of the campaign – the desegregation of St Augustine's public facilities. Anticipating passage of the bill, some 80 of the city's hotels, motels and restaurants had already agreed to desegregate their facilities. Moreover, State Attorney Dan Warren assured King that St Augustine blacks would be protected from further white racist violence.

Having achieved all that was possible in St Augustine through nonviolent direct action, King suspended demonstrations on 30 June and departed with SCLC for Atlanta on 1 July. By this time, SCLC had undergone a significant staff change. Wyatt Walker resigned as executive secretary to become vice president of Education Heritage, which planned to publish a multi-volume series on the history and culture of black America. Walker's administrative ability and leadership would be missed by SCLC. Nevertheless, King said that because the Heritage project was so critical to the future of the black community, Walker would depart with his 'full blessings'.[30] Walker would be succeeded by the talented and articulate Andrew Young.

On 2 July, the House approved the Civil Rights Bill as amended by the Senate, by a roll-call vote of 289 to 126. That evening, King joined other civil rights leaders at the White House to witness the signing of the historic Civil Rights Act of 1964 into law by President Johnson. The act outlawed segregation in public accommodations, authorized the Attorney General to initiate suits on behalf of private individuals, established a federal Equal Employment Opportunity Commission to investigate discrimination in hiring, and barred discrimination in federally-funded programmes. Although stronger than the legislation originally proposed by President Kennedy in 1963, the act was not completely satisfactory, for it did not include a strong voting rights clause. Nor did it attack the social and economic roots of racial injustice throughout America. Nevertheless, the act was another milestone in the black freedom struggle.

A number of factors contributed to the enactment of the Civil Rights Act. Militant nonviolent direct action – the Birmingham campaign, the wave of nonviolent protests in the summer of 1963 and the St Augustine campaign – was the catalyst that mobilized national support for the legislation. The act was testimony to the heroic efforts of King and scores of civil rights leaders and organizations, in addition to the masses of nonviolent protesters, who were dedicated to the struggle against racism in America. In

Washington, strong bipartisan backing for the bill in Congress, and active assistance from President Johnson, overcame the Senate filibuster by Southern Democrats. Moreover, the Leadership Conference on Civil Rights – consisting of literally thousands of persons who were members of civil rights, labour and church groups – lobbied for the bill in Congress. The act, a monument to the efficacy of militant nonviolent direct action, sounded the death knell for *de jure* segregation in the South. On 4 July, the headline of the Columbia, South Carolina, *State* read 'SOUTHERN SEGREGATION FALLS SILENTLY, WITHOUT VIOLENCE'.[31]

But the white racists of St Augustine refused to surrender without a final, violent effort to maintain segregation, evoking memories of resistance to civil rights victories in Montgomery and Birmingham. After initial compliance with the Civil Rights Act, St Augustine businessmen bowed to intimidation from the Klan and again barred blacks from integrating public facilities. On 4 July, Klansmen paraded through the St Augustine business district to protest the signing of the act. Blacks who sought integrated services were beaten. King returned briefly to St Augustine on 17 July, urging nonviolence, for black retaliatory violence, he warned, might encourage resistance to desegregation throughout the South. White racist brutality ended when SCLC lawyers, armed with the Civil Rights Act, succeeded in securing a federal court order enjoining St Augustine hotels, motels and restaurants to desegregate their facilities. The injunction named specific individuals, including Hoss Manucy, prohibiting them from harming blacks. Thus, when it appeared that the St Augustine campaign had been stalemated, the Civil Rights Act of 1964 enabled King and SCLC to salvage modest gains.

V

Some might question whether the St Augustine campaign was necessary, since the limited gains were not achieved during the nonviolent protest marches, but after the Civil Rights Act went into effect. Nevertheless, SCLC's ulterior aim in St Augustine had been to exert a national impact that would lead to passage of the Civil Rights Bill. The strategy of King and SCLC was to designate a target city for local nonviolent protests that would ultimately influence the federal government and the American public. The

denial of constitutional rights in Albany, Birmingham, St Augustine
and Selma was not merely a local problem, but also a national one,
for until black citizens achieved freedom and equality, America's
ideals would remain unfulfilled. As King explained in his 1964
president's report to SCLC, the St Augustine campaign was
undertaken 'to remind the nation of the reason the Civil Rights
Bill came into existence in the first place'.[32]

SCLC was willing to accept limited victories in cities like St
Augustine as long as progress was made toward achieving national
legislation. Blacks throughout the South would benefit most from
laws passed by Congress, supported by the federal courts and
enforced by the federal executive. White racist violence, provoked
by nonviolent protest in St Augustine, focused attention once again
upon black grievances, stimulated a federal court injunction in
support of civil rights protesters, and provided publicity that
facilitated enactment of the 1964 Civil Rights Act. According to
Hosea Williams: 'The Civil Rights Act was written in Birmingham
and passed in St. Augustine'.[33] As King concluded, the St Augustine campaign was a lever to influence reform that affected blacks
throughout the nation. 'Some communities', he observed, 'had to
bear the cross'.[34]

Moreover, at a time when many blacks in the Northern ghettos
were beginning to sympathize with the violent rhetoric of persons
like Malcolm X, the St Augustine campaign proved once again that
nonviolence was an effective means to combat racial injustice. In
the judgement of Pat Watters, a reporter for the Southern Regional
Council, compared to the violence in the nation's ghettos, 'the
achievement of Negro nonviolence in St Augustine (and still,
generally, over the South), and the debt the nation owes it, is thus
ever more evident in its grandeur'.[35] Reflecting on the campaign
in 1970, *New York Times* reporter John Herbers thought that it
'provided a case study of the nonviolent technique at its best'.
'Years later', Herbers mused, 'the St. Augustine campaign remains
in the memory a thing of beauty, hard and clean, with none of the
nagging doubts about who was right and who was wrong'.[36]

VI

On 20 July, King and SCLC were in Mississippi to assist SNCC
and CORE in a concerted effort to register black voters, known as

the Freedom Project. The project originated with the autumn 1963 Freedom Vote, a mock election organized by SNCC's Robert Moses, recipient of a masters degree in philosophy from Harvard University, and one of the most dedicated and courageous civil rights activists of the 1960s. Moses was programme director of the Council of Federated Organizations (COFO), a coalition of SNCC, CORE, NAACP, and SCLC, created in 1962 to coordinate efforts for a Mississippi voter registration drive. The Magnolia State had an infamous record of denying civil rights with brutal efficiency. For years, blacks had been deprived of the franchise by means of poll taxes, literacy tests and white racist intimidation. In 1964, only 6.7 per cent of the 400 000 blacks of voting age were registered to vote in Mississippi.[37] National attention again focused upon racial injustice in the South during the fall of 1963 when some 100 white students from Yale and Stanford laboured for two weeks in Mississippi to prepare disenfranchised blacks for the mock election, in which they chose their own governor. The success of the Freedom Vote, in which over 90 000 blacks cast ballots, inspired COFO to form a new political party in the spring of 1964, the Mississippi Freedom Democrats, and to invite hundreds more students, most of them white, to spend the summer in rural Mississippi to ready blacks for the forthcoming national election in November. Historian James W. Silver characterized the student volunteers in the Summer Freedom Project as 'a super-Peace Corps willing to move constantly in the shadow of violence and death for nothing more nor less than the implementation of the promise of democracy and equality in the Declaration of Independence'.[38]

Robert Moses and most of the SNCC leadership had concluded that the ballot rather than King-style demonstrations would be most effective in gaining civil rights for the black masses in the South. The immediate goals of the Freedom Project were to register black voters, establish Freedom Schools to teach them the essentials of the democratic process, and to organize the Mississippi Freedom Democratic Party (MFDP) to challenge the all-white Mississippi Democratic delegation at the National Convention in August, 1964 – a presidential election year. The project also aimed to keep before the American conscience the deplorable racial conditions in the Deep South, and to prod the federal government to enforce civil rights laws. The project organizers calculated that the nation would show greater concern for the safety of white college student volunteers, many from prominent Northern families, than for COFO black activists.

King supported the Freedom Project, speaking at Philadelphia, Meridian, Jackson and Vicksburg, as well as visiting rural areas of Mississippi. For years, he had stressed the importance of the ballot in securing civil rights. But the ballot alone would not substantially improve the living standards of millions of poor blacks. King therefore used the occasions of his Mississippi speeches to muster support for his Bill of Rights for the Disadvantaged – to serve as the basis for a government-sponsored anti-poverty programme – which he planned to submit to the Democratic Convention in August. President Johnson had recently inaugurated a $1 billion War on Poverty, establishing the Office of Economic Opportunity, which King considered to be only a first step.

Nevertheless, the Freedom Project, born amid great hope, became a major disillusionment. Mississippi whites responded with a reign of terror that summer, during which 35 black churches were burned and 30 buildings were bombed; 35 people were shot, 6 murdered, 80 severely beaten, and more than a thousand arrested.[39] Despite the repeated pleas of civil rights activists, the federal government failed to intervene to protect American citizens who were working to bring about racial justice. The Mississippi violence received little national attention until 21 June, when three young project volunteers – James Chaney, Andrew Goodman and Michael Schwerner – were reported missing in Neshoba County. Chaney was a Mississippi black civil rights worker, Goodman and Schwerner were white members of CORE from New York City. Victims of racist violence, their bodies were found buried in an earthen dam near Philadelphia, Mississippi on 4 August. Political analyst Theodore H. White aptly described the anarchic conditions that prevailed in Mississippi during the summer of 1964: 'One must grasp firmly in mind this root fact: that there is no law to govern the relations between the races in Mississippi. The state is an illegal society, flouting and mocking Federal laws whenever it so chooses; and for about 40 per cent of its citizens – the blacks – there is no protection of court, police, law or mercy'.[40]

The climax of the Freedom Project occurred in late August at the Democratic National Convention in Atlantic City, New Jersey. Early that month, the Mississippi Freedom Democratic Party held its convention, electing 68 delegates, all but four of them black, to travel to Atlantic City to challenge the credentials of the regular all-white Mississippi delegation. The Freedom Democrats would take their case to the national party. Since blacks were illegally excluded from the electoral process in Mississippi, the Freedom Democrats hoped to be recognized as the state's legitimate Democratic Party. They expected the support of both the national Democrats and President Johnson as evidence of their commitment to protect the voting rights of Mississippi blacks. Unlike the all-white regular Mississippi Democratic delegates, many of whom opposed the presidential candidacy of Johnson in favour of Republican Barry Goldwater, the Freedom Democrats pledged to endorse the national party's candidates.

The convention reached an emotional peak on 22 August when Fannie Lou Hamer, a Mississippi share-cropper, gave a nationally televised testimony before the Credentials Committee, relating how she had been fired from her job, beaten and shot at, merely for attempting to exercise her democratic right to vote. 'Is this America, the land of the free and the home of the brave', she cried, 'where we are threatened daily because we want to live as decent human beings?'[41] Infuriated by Hamer's speech, President Johnson, who had been viewing the convention on television from Washington, hastily called a press conference to pre-empt live coverage of the convention. Nevertheless, news programmes throughout the country featured Hamer's speech that evening.

Hamer's testimony shocked the conscience of the nation, and moved the party Credentials Committee to offer a compromise that was supported by President Johnson, who was anxious to prevent a floor fight that might provoke a walkout of the Southern delegations. On 23 August, the Credentials Committee suggested that the Freedom Democrats be seated in the convention as 'honoured guests', but be denied voting rights in favour of the regular Mississippi delegation, who would be compelled to take an oath to support the party ticket. More significantly, at future Democratic conventions, no delegations would be allowed from states that discriminated against black voters. When the Freedom Democrats rejected this compromise as insufficient, the President dispatched Senator Hubert Humphrey, the leading Democratic contender for the vice-presidential nomination, to Atlantic City with another offer. The second compromise proposal would seat all regular delegates who took the loyalty oath, and permit two Freedom Democrats – Aaron Henry, president of the Mississippi NAACP, and Edwin King, white chaplain at Tougaloo College –

to sit in the convention as delegates-at-large with full voting rights. The remainder of the Freedom Democrats would be seated as 'honored guests', without voting rights. The national Democratic Party would bend no further, fearing that if the Freedom Democrat delegates were each given voting rights, a precedent would be set whereby in future conventions delegates elected outside the normal legal process would feel justified in attempting to compel recognition of their right to vote.

Civil rights leaders, including King, Farmer, Wilkins and Rustin, in addition to many white liberal allies, favoured the compromise, reasoning that blacks could not afford to lose the support of the President and the Democratic Party. They also saw the compromise as a fortunate victory for Freedom Democrats, whose legal case seemed insupportable. Anthony Lewis of the *New York Times* hailed the proferred compromise as 'a long step toward ending racism in Southern Democratic politics'.[42] King met with the Freedom Democrat delegates and reminded them that politics was the art of the possible. 'Indeed there are segregationists in this party', he told them, 'but indeed the Democratic party is the best we have and we must work to make it better. . . . I'm not going to counsel you to accept or reject. That is your decision. But I want you to know that I have talked to Hubert Humphrey. He promised me there would be a new day for Mississippi if you accept this proposal'.[43] Attorney Joseph Rauh, counsel for the Freedom Democrats, also supported the proposal. So did delegate Aaron Henry. Nevertheless, the Freedom Democrats, resisting pressure from both the federal government and civil rights leaders, voted to reject the second compromise, which they viewed as evidence of liberal hypocrisy and pervasive racism within the Democratic Party. They chose instead to bolt the convention, charging a 'sellout' by the white liberal establishment. According to Mrs Hamer: 'We didn't come all this way for no two seats'.[44]

The repudiation of the Mississippi Freedom Democratic Party in Atlantic City enhanced the disillusionment of SNCC, now alienated from the President, the Democratic Party, Northern white liberals and Martin Luther King, Jr. 'The treatment of the Freedom Democrats', one historian observed, 'snapped the frayed ties that bound SNCC to liberal values, to integration and nonviolence, and to seeking solutions through the political process'.[45] SNCC interpreted President Johnson's behind-the-scenes dealing during the Freedom Democrat challenge as a betrayal of the civil rights movement. As Theodore White concluded: 'There was no moment when the Convention machinery of Johnson . . . might not have imposed a solution'.[46] The Administration, SNCC charged, had subordinated morality to politics. Prisoners of their own moral idealism, SNCC had come to perceive acceptance of any compromise as a surrender to racism. 'Almost any other organization', judged one analyst, 'recognizing the slowness with which so vast and decentralized an institution as the Democratic Party shifts its commitments, would have seen the proffered compromise as a victory'.[47]

The disillusionment of SNCC had serious consequences for the civil rights movement. Although the cry for 'Black Power' was two years away, the anger and frustration that engendered it already existed. Many SNCC field workers, having experienced daily the devastating effects of poverty in Mississippi and other states in the Deep South, saw more clearly that the problems of racism and poverty were interrelated. As the 1964 Democratic National Convention indicated, white America was unwilling to pay the price for black equality. According to SNCC's James Forman, who had urged the Freedom Democrats to reject the Democratic Party's compromise, Atlantic City dashed the last vestige of hope 'that the federal government would change the situation in the Deep South', transforming many people 'from idealistic reformers to full-time revolutionaries'.[48] Three years after the Convention, Stokely Carmichael and Charles Hamilton viewed it as the turning point in the black liberation movement. 'The major moral of that experience', they concluded, 'was not merely that the national conscience was generally unreliable but that, very specifically, black people in Mississippi and throughout this country could not rely on their so-called allies'.[49] SNCC's Cleveland Sellers aptly summed up the prevailing mood: 'Things could never be the same. . . . After Atlantic City, our struggle was not for civil rights, but for liberation'.[50]

VII

Despite the continuing friction between SNCC and SCLC, by the end of 1964 King was at the height of his prestige as leader of the black revolution. The year before, a *Newsweek* magazine poll in July showed that he had an 88 per cent approval rating among the black rank-and-file, and 95 per cent among the black leadership.[51]

After the passage of the Civil Rights Act of 1964, King's national stature was even greater. In October, black America rejoiced when he was chosen to receive the Nobel Peace Prize. At age 35, King was the youngest recipient in the history of the award, and the third black man.

At the same time, trouble was brewing for King and SCLC. When FBI head J. Edgar Hoover learned that King would receive the award, he was furious. King had aroused Hoover's anger by publicly criticizing the Bureau for inadequately protecting civil rights activists in the South. Speaking at a press conference on 18 November 1964, Hoover attacked King as 'the most notorious liar in the country . . . one of the lowest characters in the country'. King responded with a telegram to Hoover, expressing dismay over the assault upon his integrity. 'What motivated such an irresponsible accusation', King said, 'is a mystery to me'. He also issued a public statement, alleging that Hoover must be working under extreme pressure: 'He has apparently faltered under the awesome burden, complexities and responsibilities of his office'.[52]

King had no idea of the depth of Hoover's enmity toward him. Convinced that SCLC had been infiltrated by communists, the Bureau Chief was determined to do everything in his power to stymie its operations. In June 1963, President Kennedy, acting on information received from the FBI, advised King to sever his relationships with two men identified by the Bureau as communists: Stanley Levison, a white New York attorney, and Jack O'Dell, associated with SCLC's New York office. The President insisted that King's connection with them would jeopardize the civil rights movement. King agreed to dismiss O'Dell, a black man whose work as an American Communist Party organizer in the early 1950s was known, but, after publicly breaking with Levison, King resumed their relationship, first through an intermediary, then openly. Levison had been a clandestine benefactor of the Communist Party from 1946 through 1955, when he became disenchanted and withdrew. He had been a close advisor to King, often assisting him in the writing of speeches and books, since the Montgomery bus boycott in 1956. The FBI had no evidence that Levison had retained any affiliation with the party. Throughout the rest of his life, King would be subjected to relentless FBI surveillance, including wire-tapping his phones, a move approved by Attorney General Robert Kennedy. In an effort to undermine King's public image, Hoover sought to secure evidence that King was a Communist instrument, and involved in numerous marital infidelities. On one occasion, the FBI mailed Coretta King a tape recording, allegedly containing evidence of her husband's sexual indiscretions. According to a Senate report in 1976, the FBI tried 'to destroy Dr Martin Luther King'.[53]

King refused to allow Hoover's malicious intentions to deter him from his cause. Journeying to Oslo, Norway, to receive the Nobel Prize on 10 December, he saluted the masses of blacks who were fundamental to the civil rights struggle in America. 'I accept the Nobel Prize for Peace', he declared, 'at a moment when twenty-two million Negroes are engaged in a creative battle to end the long night of racial injustice'.[54] He contributed the $54 000 prize money to the civil rights movement.

Returning to the United States, another project engaged King's attention. Convinced that the franchise was essential for blacks to progress in the Deep South, he sought a means to pressure the federal government to enact major legislation to protect the right to vote. What the Freedom Summer Project failed to achieve, perhaps nonviolent direct action would. Another Birmingham was necessary. While SNCC continued to focus upon black voter registration in rural Mississippi, King and SCLC sought a Southern city in which to dramatize the issue of voting rights. By Christmas, 1964, plans had been completed for the next target: Selma, Alabama – SCLC's final campaign in the South.

7

Selma and the Voting Rights Act of 1965

I

'The die is cast', said Burke Marshall, head of the Civil Rights Division of the Justice Department, to Selma, Alabama's new Public Safety Director, Wilson Baker, in late November 1964. 'They're coming to Selma in January. They've already put too much work in on the project to turn back now'.[1] Marshall relayed the answer he had received from Martin Luther King, Jr. after telephoning him in Atlanta. Baker had journeyed to Washington to plead with Marshall and Attorney General Robert Kennedy to convince King to cancel SCLC's planned voting rights campaign in Selma. Toward the end of December, King and SCLC would accept a formal invitation from the Committee of Fifteen, representing all factions within Selma's black community, to lead a drive to secure the right to vote. Black suffrage had been a major goal for King since 1957, when he led the Prayer Pilgrimage to Washington to demand the ballot. In 1960, SCLC inaugurated the Crusade for Citizenship, a voter registration drive in the South. Although the Civil Rights Act of 1964 dealt a lethal blow to segregation, it did not guarantee the constitutional right to vote. Having perfected the method of militant nonviolent direct action to a fine art, King and SCLC were now resolved to force the nation to confront the issue of suffrage for black Americans. Armed with the ballot, blacks would have the political power to influence further civil rights legislation.

As the year 1965 opened, Selma, like Birmingham two years before, was an ideal stage for a dramatic confrontation with the racist order. Situated in the heart of the Black Belt, and the county seat of Dallas County, Selma was a city of about 13 000 whites and 14 500 blacks. Although blacks constituted over half the population in 1965, fewer than two per cent of them were registered to vote. In nearby Lowndes and Wilcox counties, not one black voter was on the registration rolls. SNCC had been active in Selma since

1963, organizing local blacks and leading voter registration drives, but virtually no progress had been made. Blacks had been denied a fundamental democratic right by means of literacy tests, poll taxes and violent white resistance. One analyst has described the deplorable voting conditions in Selma, typical throughout the Deep South: 'Voter registration in Selma took place only two days per week. An applicant was required to fill in more than fifty blanks, write from dictation a part of the constitution, read four passages from the constitution and answer four questions on them, and sign an oath of loyalty to the United States and Alabama'.[2] Selma also had the dubious distinction of being the hometown of Bull Connor, and the birthplace of the first racist White Citizens' Council. Moreover, the town's Sheriff, James Clark, known for his brutal treatment of civil rights workers over the past few years, was as much a symbol of Southern white racism as Birmingham's Connor.

The city government of Selma was determined to prevent racial disturbances. In 1965, the new mayor, Joseph Smitherman, was anxious to preserve stability in order to attract Northern industry to the city. To curtail the recklessness of Sheriff Clark, the Mayor instituted the position of Public Safety Director, and appointed Wilson Baker to the office. Invested with the highest police authority in Selma, Baker hoped to defeat the upcoming SCLC campaign by emulating the nonviolent tactics of Albany, Georgia's Chief Laurie Pritchett. Baker was thus on a collision course with King and SCLC, who were planning to foment a crisis in Selma to arouse national support for legislation guaranteeing the right to vote. As SNCC's John Lewis recalled: 'Dr. King kept saying that the goal was to get Selma to write a Voting Rights Act of 1965 as Birmingham had written the Civil Rights Act of 1964'.[3]

Soon after Christmas 1964, SCLC drew up a six-page strategy plan for the next nonviolent battlefield. Selma would become, in the words of SCLC's Bernard Lee, 'a theater for an act to be played'.[4] John Lewis later concurred: 'It was like a drama . . . with all the various people and forces there just waiting to play a role'.[5] At the opportune time, King would once again submit to arrest and issue a brief published statement from his jail cell to attract national sympathy for the protest.

II

On 2 January 1965, King arrived in Selma and announced an SCLC voter-registration drive in an address to a crowd of 700 people at Brown's Chapel African Methodist Episcopal Church, located in the heart of the town's black section. Selma had been chosen, he told them, 'because it had become a symbol of bitter-end resistance to the civil rights movement in the Deep South'.[6] SCLC aimed to highlight the deprivation of black voting rights not only in Selma, but throughout the South. As King proclaimed: 'We are going to start a march on the ballot boxes by the thousands. If they refuse to register us we will appeal to Governor Wallace. If he doesn't listen, we will dramatize the situation to arouse the federal government by marching by the thousands to the places of registration'. If this proved unsuccessful, the protesters would 'appeal to the conscience of the Congress' by another massive March on Washington. King concluded by stressing that blacks would not play the role of humble supplicants: 'We're not on our knees begging for the ballot. We are demanding the ballot'.[7]

Having launched the campaign, King travelled to the West coast to address religious and civic groups to gain support. Throughout the next two weeks, SCLC, joined by SNCC, led almost daily marches to the county courthouse in downtown Selma, within the jurisdiction of Sheriff Clark. When the first group of demonstrators arrived, they found the Sheriff blocking the entrance. 'You are here to cause trouble', he shouted, before saying to their leader, Hosea Williams: 'You are an agitator and that is the lowest form of humanity'.[8] Dozens of marchers were arrested and charged with unlawful assembly. On 18 January, King returned to Selma and became the first black man to register at the century-old Albert Hotel. As he did so, he was punched and kicked by a white man who was promptly arrested. The same day, King and SNCC's John Lewis led some 400 blacks in a march to the courthouse. Blacks also obtained service at seven previously segregated restaurants. Following a mass meeting that evening at Brown's Chapel, King's staff expressed 'disappointment' because Sheriff Clark had not yet been provoked into treating the marchers with his usual brutality.[9] Persisting in their efforts to elicit violence from Clark and his deputies, King and SCLC scheduled a march to the courthouse the next day. If still unsuccessful in provoking Clark, the focus of the campaign would be shifted to the nearby towns of Marion and

Camden. Mass arrests alone would not bring about reform; Selma needed a crisis.

On Tuesday, 19 January, the campaign reached a turning point. A group of marchers led by local civil rights activist Amelia Boynton were slow to obey an order to clear the pavement in front of the courthouse. Sheriff Clark, who thus far had been restrained by Public Safety Director Baker, grabbed Mrs Boynton by the collar and pushed her half a block into a police car. The following morning, newspapers, among them the *New York Times* and the *Washington Post*, featured a photograph of the incident. The campaign had finally achieved national attention. Wishing to emphasize the incident to the press, King described it as 'one of the most brutal and unlawful acts I have seen an officer commit'.[10] SCLC then decided to escalate the protest. On 21 January, three successive waves of marchers demonstrated at the courthouse and were arrested by Clark for unlawful assembly. Two days later, over a hundred black teachers, ignoring threats that they would be fired by the local school board, protested Boynton's arrest by marching to the courthouse. On Monday, 25 January, as a group of demonstrators stood on the pavement outside the courthouse, 53-year-old Annie Lee Cooper responded to a shove from Clark by punching him in the face. As the Sheriff dropped to his knees, three deputies subdued Mrs Cooper, enabling Clark to strike her on the head with his club. A picture of the incident was circulated in the nation's press. By the end of January, over 2000 blacks were jailed in Selma.

As the campaign gathered momentum, the strategic time had come for King to go to jail. To avoid arrest for violating Selma's parade ordinance, until this time King and SCLC had divided street demonstrations into groups of fewer than 20 people, so as not to constitute a parade. But on Monday, 1 February, King and Ralph Abernathy led a united group of 250 blacks and 15 whites from Brown's Chapel to the Selma courthouse, where they were all arrested for parading without a permit. While the other demonstrators were released on bail the same day, King and Abernathy chose to remain imprisoned. As expected, King's arrest captured worldwide headlines. Later that day, some 500 school children were arrested for picketing the courthouse, and several hundred more children were arrested for demonstrating during the ensuing week.

On 3 February, while King was in jail, militant black Muslim leader Malcolm X arrived in Selma at the invitation of SNCC. Addressing a crowd at Brown's Chapel, he said the demonstrations would be fruitless, and stressed the necessity of meeting violence with violence. Although Malcolm's inflammatory speech worried members of SCLC, ironically, he believed that the talk of violence might prove useful to the campaign. As Malcolm later confided to Coretta King: 'I want Dr. King to know that I didn't come to Selma to make his life difficult. I really did come thinking that I could make it easier. If the white people realize what the alternative is, perhaps they will be more willing to hear Dr. King'.[11] In less than three weeks, on 21 February, Malcolm X was assassinated while addressing a crowd at New York City's Audubon Ballroom.

The events in Selma began to exert an impact upon Washington. New York's Senator Jacob Javits described the hundreds of arrests of Selma citizens seeking 'the most basic right guaranteed by the Constitution' – the right to vote – as 'shocking'.[12] King sent a telegram to House Judiciary Committee chairman Emanuel Celler, declaring that 'events of the past month here in Selma have raised serious questions as to the adequacy of present voting rights legislation'. In response to King's telegram, a group of House members announced that they would journey to Selma on Friday, 5 February, to investigate whether stronger legislation was indeed necessary. On Thursday, 4 February, the Selma campaign received unexpected publicity from the White House when President Lyndon Johnson referred to the protest during a press conference: 'I hope that all Americans will join with me in expressing their concern over the loss of any American's right to vote. Nothing is more fundamental to American citizenship and to our freedom as a nation and a people. I intend to see that that right is secured for all our citizens'.[13]

With national attention drawn to Selma, blacks continued to fill the jails. King was determined to create a crisis in the city. After a one-day halt in demonstrations, he wrote a note to Andrew Young: 'Please don't be soft. We have the offensive. It was a mistake not to march today. In a crisis we must have a sense of drama'.[14] On Friday, 5 February, the day that House members arrived in Selma, King's brief 'Letter from a Selma Jail' appeared as an advertisement in the *New York Times*. As he had done in Birmingham, King hoped to stir the conscience of the entire country: 'THIS IS SELMA, ALABAMA', the Letter declared. 'THERE ARE MORE NEGROES

IN JAIL WITH ME THAN THERE ARE ON THE VOTING ROLLS'.[15] Later that day, King posted bail and announced that he would travel to Washington to enlist President Johnson's support for new voting rights legislation.

At a meeting on 9 February, the President reassured King of his commitment to civil rights, and informed him that appropriate legislation was being drafted. In his televised 4 January 1965 State of the Union address, Johnson had emphasized the importance of enforcing existing civil rights laws, and urged the elimination of 'every remaining obstacle to the right and opportunity to vote'.[16] The same month, Johnson instructed Justice Department lawyers to begin drafting a constitutional amendment that would prohibit states from barring qualified persons from voting. But the protest in Selma had convinced the Johnson Administration that stronger legislation would be more effective than a constitutional amendment in guaranteeing suffrage. Hence, a Voting Rights Bill was drawn up that would prohibit literacy tests, and provide for federal registrars to protect the right to vote. During his visit to Washington in February, King also conferred with Vice President Hubert Humphrey, who expressed doubts that Congress would enact additional civil rights legislation so soon after the 1964 Civil Rights Act. Nevertheless, the Vice President conceded that Congress might do so 'if the pressure were unrelenting'.[17]

Meanwhile, Sheriff Clark was resolved to undermine the Selma protest. He proudly displayed a giant button in his lapel that read 'NEVER', a defiant response to the blacks' cry for 'FREEDOM NOW'. On 16 February, C. T. Vivian of SCLC led a group of 25 protesters to the steps of Selma courthouse. Ordered to disperse by Sheriff Clark, they refused and began singing freedom songs. Vivian proceeded to taunt Clark, insisting that blacks had a constitutional right to register to vote. Ignoring the reporters and television cameras present, the Sheriff punched Vivian in the mouth, knocking him to the ground. The bleeding Vivian was immediately arrested. The nonviolent tactics of SCLC had again succeeded in provoking the opponent and publicly exposing the undercurrent of white racist violence. 'If C. T. had not taken that blow,' Andrew Young recollected, 'we might not have had a Voting Rights Act'.[18] As *Time* magazine observed, whenever the Selma movement began to flag, Sheriff Clark would rekindle the protest with a fresh atrocity.[19] Like Connor in Birmingham, Clark played the role of the villain in a modern morality play. *The Nation* gave much credit to King, praising him as 'the finest tactician the South has produced since Robert E. Lee'.[20]

Returning to Selma from Washington, King found that the campaign had begun to falter in his absence. 'Selma still isn't right', he declared at a mass meeting on 17 February. Despite weeks of protest and more than 3000 arrests, few blacks had been added to the voting rolls. The demonstrations must therefore become more militant. 'We must engage in broader civil disobedience measures', King declared, 'to bring the attention of the nation on Dallas County'.[21] As SCLC prepared to augment the Selma campaign, white racism struck again. On 18 February, a 26-year-old black man named Jimmie Lee Jackson was shot by state troopers while he attempted to defend his mother during a protest in Marion, Alabama – only 30 miles from Selma. Jackson's death eight days later attracted additional sympathy for the Selma campaign. On Sunday, 28 February, King was in Marion to deliver a eulogy before 400 mourners at a service for Jackson. The following day, he was in Selma to lead a group of some 350 marchers to the courthouse. 'We are going to bring a voting bill into being in the streets of Selma, Alabama', he proclaimed.[22]

The campaign needed another dramatic moment. On Friday, 5 March, King made the startling announcement that he would lead a 54-mile march from Selma to the Alabama state capitol in Montgomery on Sunday to petition Governor Wallace to enforce black voting rights. This plan was conceived by SCLC's James Bevel, who had suggested introducing children into the Birmingham campaign. The march, which would take from five to six days, was intended to further dramatize the disfranchisement of blacks throughout the South. Anticipating a confrontation with Alabama state authorities and white racists, King warned those assembled at Brown's Chapel: 'I can't promise you that it won't get you beaten. I can't promise you that it won't get your house bombed . . . . But we must stand up for what is right'.[23] The next day, Governor Wallace officially prohibited the march and ordered state troopers, headed by Colonel Al Lingo, to take 'whatever means are available' to stop it.[24] 'Such a march cannot and will not be tolerated', the Governor insisted.[25]

III

Although King called the Sunday march, he would not lead it, having decided at the last minute to return to Atlanta. The reason why is not entirely clear. Some speculated that he was reacting to threats upon his life. Others pointed out that since Governor Wallace had banned the march, the demonstrators would simply be arrested; with no possibility of going all the way to Montgomery on Sunday, there seemed little need for King's presence. Besides, King could not risk going to jail again because he had to be free to raise financial support and bail money for the campaign. Some believed that he intended to postpone the march until Monday in order to conduct church services at the Ebenezer Baptist Church in Atlanta that Palm Sunday.

Back in Selma, Hosea Williams and James Bevel had assembled hundreds of blacks at Brown's Chapel on Sunday. Williams then telephoned King in Atlanta and received permission to stage a token march that day up to, but not crossing, the Edmund Pettus Bridge, which spans the Alabama River and leads to U.S. Highway 80 – the road to Montgomery. Responding to the enthusiasm of the crowd at Brown's Chapel, Williams disobeyed King and informed Bevel, Andrew Young, and SNCC chairman John Lewis that he had been given permission to proceed all the way to Montgomery. As Joseph Lowery recollected, Williams' plan to carry out the Sunday march 'wasn't a decision made by the group. As it turned out, it played an important role in history. But it wasn't a planned agreed-upon strategy'.[26]

SCLC would be joined in the march by some members of SNCC, despite the fact that tensions between the two groups had been aggravated in recent years. James Forman and other young SNCC militants resented that after they had laid the foundations for the Selma campaign, preparing local blacks for months, King and SCLC were once again receiving most of the credit. Although SNCC laboured long and hard in the Deep South, organizing and educating local blacks while risking their lives in daily confrontation with the worst white racism, their courageous efforts had been largely unheralded. SNCC lamented that King and his staff stirred local crises and left town either without substantial achievements, or before gains could be solidified and implemented. SCLC's C. T. Vivian later conceded: '[Our] only failure was the lack of capacity to back up our activities after we left'.[27] Moreover, members of SNCC, especially Forman, continued to insist that dependence upon charismatic figures such as King made it difficult for blacks to develop the local leaders necessary in their struggle for civil rights. SNCC was also unwilling to forget that King had been among those leaders who had urged the Mississippi Freedom Democrats to accept the compromise at the 1964 Democratic National Convention in Atlantic City. Neverthless, SNCC members, including chairman John Lewis, hopeful that the Selma protest would stimulate national legislation, put their resentment of SCLC aside, at least temporarily. Although SNCC voted not to endorse the march officially, the organization decided to permit members to participate independently.

On Sunday afternoon, with newsmen and television cameras present, SCLC's Hosea Williams and SNCC's John Lewis led over 500 marchers from the red brick Brown's Chapel. Walking two abreast, they proceeded down Sylvan Street and turned right onto Water Street. Reaching Broad Street, they made a left, passing a company of Sheriff Clark's armed possemen, and headed across the Edmund Pettus Bridge. On the far side of the bridge, the marchers saw some 500 helmeted Alabama state troopers equipped with gas masks and standing shoulder to shoulder. Along with the troopers were three dozen more of Sheriff Clark's possemen, 15 on horseback. About a hundred white spectators watched from the sides of the highway. Colonel Lingo and Sheriff Clark watched from a car nearby.

Ignoring his agreement with King, Williams led the marchers beyond the foot of the Edmund Pettus Bridge, about half way across, until Major John Cloud ordered them to halt, shouting through a megaphone: 'This is an unlawful assembly. You are ordered to disperse and go back to your church or to your homes'.[28] The Major rejected Williams' request for a conference, and gave the marchers two minutes to turn around. Before the two minutes had elapsed, the troopers charged the marchers, setting off tear gas, and beating them with clubs, cattle prods and bull whips. As white spectators cheered from the sidelines, troopers forced the marchers to retreat back across the bridge to the Selma side, where they were attacked by Sheriff Clark's possemen, who chased them toward Brown's Chapel and a nearby housing project. 'Get those niggers!', shouted Clark.[29] An estimated 100 marchers were injured, and 16 were hospitalized. John Lewis suffered a concussion. Before entering the hospital, he denounced the federal government: 'I don't see how President Johnson can send troops to Vietnam, and can't send troops to Selma, Alabama. Next time we march, we may have to keep going when we get to Montgomery. We may have to go on to Washington'.[30] The following day, newspapers told the story of the aborted march, calling the event 'Bloody Sunday'. Overnight, Selma had aroused national indignation.

In Atlanta, shocked at the violence on the Edmund Pettus Bridge, King vowed to lead another march – this time all the way to Montgomery – on Tuesday, 9 March, and to seek a federal injunction to prevent interference by Governor Wallace and state police. Though furious at Hosea Williams for his brinkmanship, he concealed his anger publicly, confessing that when he made 'a last minute agreement' to allow Williams to lead the march, he had no idea that violence would erupt; he had expected that the marchers would merely be arrested.[31] John Lewis later corroborated King's statement: 'We never thought anything would happen like it did. We thought we would just be arrested'.[32] The unexpected white violence that Sunday not only stirred the nation's conscience, but also exerted pressure upon the federal government to act. At the same time, King summoned clergymen, black and white, throughout the country to join him in the Tuesday march.

IV

On Monday, 8 March, SCLC lawyers entered the United States Federal Court in Montgomery to apply for an injunction to protect the march scheduled for the next day. Judge Frank Johnson, one of the nation's strongest advocates of civil rights, presided over the court. In 1956, he had been a member of the special three-judge panel that declared the city's bus segregation unconstitutional. In 1961, he had issued an injunction protecting the Freedom Riders from the Klan. Nevertheless, Judge Johnson's decision on 8 March disappointed SCLC. Because some of the defendants (Wallace *et al*) had not been notified of the application for the injunction, the judge denied SCLC's request for an immediate restraining order and scheduled a hearing with representatives from both sides on Thursday, 11 March. He also enjoined SCLC from marching on Tuesday, pending the results of Thursday's hearing.

Judge Johnson's Monday ruling placed King on the horns of a dilemma. His first inclination was to postpone the demonstration in deference to the federal court, but he soon had second thoughts. Although his attorneys anticipated a favourable ruling after

Thursday's hearing, the question was whether King could afford
to call off the Tuesday demonstration on short notice without
disrupting the momentum of the protest campaign and alienating
many supporters. King had not forgotten that the Albany campaign
had been impeded by his obedience to a federal injunction. SNCC
militants, scorning what they regarded as his conciliatory methods,
also pressured King to proceed with the Tuesday demonstration.
SNCC's Cleveland Sellers later explained: 'We were angry. And
we wanted to show Governor Wallace, the Alabama State Highway
Patrol, Sheriff Clark, Selma's whites, the federal government and
poor Southern blacks in other Selmas that we didn't intend to take
any more shit. We would ram the march down the throat of anyone
who tried to stop us. We were ready to go that afternoon'.[33]

Clearly, if King had postponed Tuesday's demonstration, he
would have risked dividing the Selma movement. He could not
ignore SNCC's charge that he had fled the battlefield on 'Bloody
Sunday'. He recalled his distress: 'I shall never forget my agony of
conscience for not being there, when I heard of the dastardly act
perpetrated against nonviolent demonstrators that Sunday. As a
result, I felt I had to lead a march'.[34] By Monday, 8 March, hundreds
of clergymen from throughout the country had responded to
King's plea and converged on Selma, expecting to march. Civil
rights leaders James Farmer of CORE and Birmingham's Fred
Shuttlesworth also arrived. With the eyes of the world fixed on
Selma, the pressure for a march was overwhelming. As Andrew
Young later observed: 'There just had to be a march, some kind of
nonviolent demonstration to get the expression out'.[35]

At the same time, King was subjected to countervailing pressures
to obey the federal injunction and postpone the demonstration.
He knew that without the protection of the federal government
and the support of the federal courts, a march through a line of
troopers might lead to a repetition of Sunday's bloody confrontation. Although white racist violence had assisted SCLC protests in
the past, King could not risk the lives of so many demonstrators.
Moreover, President Johnson was greatly alarmed, and asked
publicly that the march be cancelled. John Doar of the Justice
Department telephoned King and implored him to obey the
injunction. 'This is a federal court order', Doar insisted, 'issued by
a strong and solid judge who has enforced Negro rights time after
time. The Department of Justice will have no choice but to protect
the integrity of the federal courts'.[36] King thus had to weigh the

possible consequences of defying the federal judiciary, which had played an integral role in the black freedom struggle. Over the years, the NAACP had accumulated an impressive series of victories in the federal courts, chipping away at the foundations of legal segregation in the South. Furthermore, Congress had recently enacted the Civil Rights Act of 1964, and was now considering the Voting Rights Bill. King thus could not afford to alienate either the federal judiciary, the President, or Congress.

On Monday, 8 March, King convened with the SCLC and SNCC staffs to determine the wisest course of action. After several hours of intense discussion, King made his decision, announcing to his aides at 4 a.m.: 'It's better to die on the highway than make a butchery of my conscience'.[37] Within an hour, he received a telephone call from Attorney General Nicholas Katzenbach, pleading with him to wait until the injunction was overturned in the court. 'Mr. Attorney General', King replied impatiently, 'you have not been a black man in America for three hundred years'.[38] Katzenbach later recalled that King, despite his apparent determination, seemed to be searching for a way out of his dilemma. Responding to the swelling crisis, President Johnson dispatched to Selma, Leroy Collins, former governor of Florida and head of the newly-created Community Relations Service, to work out a compromise. Failing to convince King to cancel the demonstration, Collins told him that he would attempt to at least prevent the state troopers from repeating the violence of 'Bloody Sunday'. He would try to persuade Colonel Lingo and Sheriff Clark not to harm the marchers if they merely crossed the Edmund Pettus Bridge and turned back when ordered to do so. This gave King the option of leading a symbolic march that would not violate the injunction since the demonstrators would remain within the city limits of Selma. King informed only his closest aides of the possibility of a last minute decision not to go all the way to Montgomery on Tuesday.

V

On Tuesday morning, 9 March, King addressed a large enthusiastic crowd at Brown's Chapel. 'We've gone too far to turn back now. . . . Nothing can stop us', he insisted.[39] Within a few hours, the march was ready to begin. King imparted some final words of inspiration: 'We have the right to walk the highways, and we have the right to walk to Montgomery if our feet will get us there'.[40] A total of 1500 marchers set out, more than half of them white. At the head, linked arm to arm, were King, CORE's James Farmer, SNCC's James Forman, Birmingham's Fred Shuttlesworth, Methodist Bishop John Wesley Lord and Howard Schomer, president of the Chicago Theological Seminary. Among the marchers were some 450 religious leaders – priests, ministers, rabbis – and a contingent of Catholic nuns. King had not yet received word from Collins whether Al Lingo and Sheriff Clark had agreed to the compromise. As the march proceeded, Collins pulled up in a car and said, according to King, that 'everything would be all right'.[41] Not until this point could King assume that Collins had convinced the Alabama authorities to agree to a merely symbolic march past the point where the demonstrators had been brutalized on 'Bloody Sunday'. Collins also gave King a piece of paper designating the route the march should follow. King had only a matter of minutes to reconsider his decision to go all the way to Montgomery. Also weighing on his mind was the responsibility he would have to bear if the marchers were assaulted by state troopers.

Singing 'Aint Gonna Let Nobody Turn Me Round', and 'We Shall Overcome', the marchers walked down Sylvan Street past rows of a dilapidated black housing project, up Water Street, then along the river bank to the Edmund Pettus Bridge. They were met at the foot of the bridge by a U.S. marshall who read to them excerpts from the federal injunction. King responded that he was aware of the order, but that he would proceed with what he thought was a lawful exercise of his constitutional rights. The marshall stepped aside, and the marchers started across the bridge. Several hundred yards ahead on U.S. Highway 80 stood Major Cloud and his armed state troopers. As the marchers reached within 50 feet of the police barricades, Cloud addressed King through a megaphone, ordering him to stop the demonstration. King replied: 'We have a right to march. There is also a right to march to Montgomery'. After Cloud repeated his order, King asked if they could pray. 'You can have your prayer', Cloud replied, 'and then you must return to your church'.[42] The marchers dropped to their knees. Unexpectedly, as the marchers arose, Major Cloud ordered the barricades to be lifted and the troopers to step aside. This move might have been calculated to trap King into proceeding with the march, thus violating the federal injunction. As the troopers cleared the way toward Montgomery, King hesitated a few seconds before making his controversial decision. 'Go back', he shouted. 'Turn around and go back'.[43] Surprised and confused, the marchers turned around and went back across the Edmund Pettus Bridge into Selma.

Realizing that some consolation was necessary, King later declared at Brown's Chapel: 'We have had the greatest demonstration for freedom today that we have ever had in the South'.[44] By proceeding past the point where they were attacked on 'Bloody Sunday', he said, the protesters had established their right to march. Nevertheless, the decision to cut short the march aroused bitter resentment among members of SNCC, particularly James Forman, who accused King of betraying the campaign. The prior agreement with Collins soon became public. As King admitted to reporters: 'We agreed that we would not break through the lines. . . . In all frankness, we knew we would not get to Montgomery. We knew we would not get past the troopers'.[45] In courtroom testimony involving the injunction on 11 March, Judge Johnson asked King: 'Is it correct to say that when you started across the bridge, you knew at the time that you did not intend to march to Montgomery?' 'Yes it is', King replied. 'There was a tacit agreement at the bridge that we would go no further'.[46]

Confronted by a dilemma that Tuesday, King had steered perilously between Scylla and Charybdis. He chose the middle course between not marching at all, which would have divided the Selma movement, and attempting to march through a phalanx of armed police, which might have led to a bloodbath. As Andrew Young later explained: 'If we had run into that police line, they would have beaten us up with court approval'.[47] Even if the police had allowed the marchers to pass, King would have violated the federal injunction. Moreover, snipers might have fired upon the marchers along the route of U.S. Highway 80. Critics would have called King reckless for endangering the lives of hundreds of demonstrators. King therefore accepted a compromise, leading the demonstrators only as far as the police barricade, dramatizing the racial injustice in Selma while avoiding the violence of 'Bloody Sunday'. King's legal staff anticipated that the injunction would be lifted after the Thursday hearing, thus making a federally-protected march to Montgomery possible within a few days. King thus made the wisest decision when he truncated Tuesday's march. As Burke Marshall, former head of the Justice Department's Civil

Rights Division, later acknowledged, King showed 'tremendous courage' in walking 'the line between the two contending forces, making his protest without having defied the federal courts'.[48]

VI

The controversy over King's decision was pushed into the background on Tuesday night when white racist violence again aided the movement. As three white clergymen left a black-owned restaurant in Selma, they were attacked by a group of four white thugs. Unitarian minister James Reeb, who had worked in the black ghetto in Boston, was struck on the head with a club. Taken to a Birmingham hospital, he never regained consciousness, and died two days later. The murder of Reverend Reeb alerted the country once more to the viciousness of white racism. Demands for federal intervention from governors, state legislatures, labour unions, and religious groups flooded the White House; and university campuses ignited in protest. Hours before Reeb's murder on 9 March, Michigan Governor George Romney had led a demonstration of 10000 people in Detroit to support the Selma protest. On Friday, 12 March, more than 4000 religious leaders from across the country converged upon Washington to petition Congress to pass voting rights legislation and to protest presidential inaction. Clergymen picketed the White House, and one of its corridors was disrupted by a sit-in staged by black activists. On 14 March, 15000 demonstrators paraded silently through Harlem in New York City. Protesters blocked traffic in Chicago, Washington and Los Angeles. With the exception of the March on Washington in August 1963, at no time in the history of the black freedom struggle in the South was national sympathy for civil rights so strong. Meanwhile, in Alabama, SNCC, led by James Forman, moved its base of operation from Selma to the state capital in Montgomery, where it intended to launch more militant protests.

Responding to the growing national outrage, President Johnson announced at a press conference on 13 March that he was sending a Voting Rights Bill to Congress. The *New York Times* praised it as 'a sweeping, bipartisan bill to erase all discrimination against citizens seeking to register and vote'.[49] On Monday, 15 March, some 2000 mourners attended a memorial service for Reverend Reeb at the Selma courthouse, and listened to a eulogy delivered by King. That evening, the President addressed a joint session of Congress on national television, calling for speedy passage of the Voting Rights Bill. In one of the most eloquent pleas for human rights ever delivered by a President of the United States, Johnson summoned the nation to fulfil its promise that all men, regardless of race or colour, shall live together in freedom and dignity. Enactment of the legislation would, he explained, 'strike down restrictions to voting in all elections – Federal, state and local – which have been used to deny Negroes the right to vote'. Interrupted repeatedly by ovations from Congress, Johnson emphasized that passage of the Voting Rights Bill would not conclude the civil rights struggle. 'What happened in Selma', he declared, 'is part of a far larger movement which reaches into every section and State in America. It is the effort of American Negroes to secure for themselves the full blessings of American life. Their cause must be our cause too, because it is not just Negroes but really it is all of us, who must overcome the crippling legacy of bigotry and injustice'. Pausing momentarily, the President then emphatically invoked the anthem of the civil rights movement: 'And We Shall Overcome'.[50]

Although King praised the proposed legislation, he announced that the Selma marches would not cease until the bill became law. 'Demonstrations', he declared in an article for *The Nation*, 'experience has shown, are part of the process of stimulating legislation and law enforcement. The federal government reacts to events more quickly when a situation cries out for its intervention'.[51] Meanwhile, on 16 March, James Forman led a group of 600 students in a protest at the Montgomery county courthouse. After police on horseback attacked the protesters, injuring eight, an angry Forman called a mass meeting that night at the Beulah Baptist Church in Montgomery. Realizing that a breakdown in nonviolent discipline might jeopardize passage of the Voting Rights Bill, King rushed to Montgomery. Addressing a group of over 1000, Forman challenged President Johnson to carry out the promise of his speech the night before, and called for massive direct action in Montgomery that would 'tie up every street and bus and commit every act of civil disobedience ever seen'.[52] Ascending the rostrum after Forman, King stressed the necessity of nonviolence, and proposed a peaceful demonstration at the courthouse. After he and Forman led a group of 1600 marchers to the courthouse on Wednesday, 17 March, King declared that blacks would no longer allow racist brutality to remain unexposed: 'We're going to make them do it in the glaring light of television'.[53]

The same day, 17 March, four and a half days of hearings on the injunction suit of *Hosea Williams* v. *George C. Wallace* concluded in the federal district court in Montgomery. The basic issue was whether the First Amendment right to protest outweighed the need for law and order and the reasonable limitation on interference with highway traffic. Besides the threat to the safety of the demonstrators, the court considered whether the state of Alabama had a right to forbid the march to Montgomery, and, if the march were permitted, whether the state was required to supply adequate protection.[54] Witnesses for both sides testified before Judge Johnson, and King, Sheriff Clark and Colonel Lingo were subjected to careful interrogation. Johnson's deliberations were greatly influenced by a detailed plan of action, submitted by lawyers for SCLC, outlining elaborate arrangements for a peaceful, five-day march to the state capital, proceeding along the sides of U.S. Highway 80 so as not to interfere with traffic. The plan provided for mobile kitchen facilities, medical units, clean-up squads and along-the-road campsites. It was obvious that SCLC had undertaken extraordinary planning to ensure the success of the march.

On Friday, 19 March, Judge Johnson lifted the injunction, arguing that an analysis of the facts revealed 'an almost continuous pattern . . . of harassment, intimidation, coercion, threatening conduct, and, sometimes, brutal mistreatment towards these plaintiffs . . . who were engaged in their demonstrations for the purpose of encouraging Negroes to attempt to register to vote and to protest discriminatory voter registration practices in Alabama'.[55] Because Alabama state and local authorities had deprived blacks from exercising their rights as citizens to vote and to protest peacefully, the federal court sanctioned the march. Addressing the contention that the marchers would violate the right of other citizens to use the public highway, Judge Johnson drew a 'constitutional boundary line', arguing that although the march reached the outer limits of what was constitutionally permitted, the 'extent of the right to assemble, demonstrate and march peaceably along the highways and streets in an orderly manner should be commensurate with the enormity of the wrongs that are being protested and petitioned against. In this case the wrongs are enormous. The extent of the right to demonstrate against these wrongs should be determined accordingly'.[56] In rendering his decision, the judge ordered Governor Wallace and the Alabama police to protect the marchers, and concurred that President Johnson had the power to supplement such protection with federal troops.

At this point, Governor Wallace played an important role in King's strategy. The Johnson Administration's view of federalism prevented it from intervening with federal military force in a state unless such action was requested by the state governor on the grounds that law and order could no longer be maintained. After Judge Johnson lifted the injunction, King set 21 March as the date for the Selma-to-Montgomery march. Wallace then provided the President with the necessary pretext for federal intervention by declaring that Alabama could not afford the financial burden of protecting the marchers, and requesting that the federal government provide 'sufficient civil authorities' to enforce the ruling of the federal court. The President responded by federalizing units of the Alabama National Guard and dispatching 250 federal marshalls, military police and FBI agents 'to assure the rights of American citizens pursuant to a federal court order to walk peaceably and safely without injury or loss of life from Selma to Montgomery, Alabama'.[57] The crisis-provoking strategy of King and SCLC had again coerced the federal government to respond to mounting national indignation by enforcing civil rights in the Deep South.

VII

On Sunday, 21 March, the historic five day, 54-mile march from Selma to Montgomery began. It was endorsed not only by the federal government, but also by white liberals and major religious and labour organizations throughout the country. Thousands flooded into Selma to see the civil rights crusaders off. Standing before Brown's Chapel, King addressed over 3000 interracial marchers: 'You will be the people that will light a new chapter in the history books of our nation', he declared. As the crowd's enthusiasm grew, King concluded with an inspirational flourish: 'Walk together children, don't you get weary and it will lead us to the Promised Land. And Alabama will be a new Alabama, and America will be a new America'.[58] Soon more than 2000 marchers crossed the Edmund Pettus Bridge, passing Confederate flags and placards reading 'Nigger Lover', 'Bye, Bye, Blackbird', and 'Martin

Luther Coon'. Along the route, the marchers were protected by 3000 federal troops and two U.S. helicopters. Adhering to Judge Johnson's court order, after eight miles all but 300 marchers left the procession. On the third day, King departed for Cleveland to deliver a fund-raising speech, in which he compared the Selma-to-Montgomery march to Gandhi's great 26-day Salt March to the Sea in 1930, a massive act of civil disobedience against the British salt tax in India, covered by the world press. On the fourth day, King rejoined the marchers with his wife Coretta.

On Thursday, 25 March, nearly 25 000 demonstrators from across the nation, black and white, gathered outside Montgomery to accompany the 300 marchers on the final segment of their pilgrimage. With King in the lead, accompanied by Ralph Bunche, they completed the last three miles in a triumphal procession to the State Capitol. Diagonally across from the Capitol was the Dexter Avenue Baptist Church, where King had begun his mission nearly ten years before. The civil rights movement was on the verge of achieving another landmark. The 1965 Montgomery demonstration was the largest ever for civil rights in the Deep South. Among those present were Rosa Parks, Roy Wilkins, Whitney Young and A. Philip Randolph. Governor Wallace refused to accept the marchers' petition for the enforcement of voting rights, and spent the day viewing the spectacle from his office window. The climax of the day came when Martin Luther King, Jr. stood before the beautiful domed Capitol building to address the crowd. 'We are on the move now', he told the demonstrators and millions of television viewers, 'and no wave of racism can stop us. . . . We are moving to the land of freedom. Let us therefore continue our triumph and march to the realization of the American dream'.[59]

That night, tragedy shattered the optimism of the previous hours. Mrs Viola Liuzzo, a white volunteer from Detroit, and mother of five, was shot to death by Klansmen on U.S. Highway 80 while driving from Selma to Montgomery to pick up returning marchers. The incident was another grim reminder that the spectre of racism still haunted the South. The following day, an irate President Johnson went on television to denounce the Klan, and called for prompt passage of the pending Voting Rights Bill.

With the American conscience aroused, Congress could not ignore the President's plea. After weeks of debate, the Senate and the House overwhelmingly passed the bill. On 6 August, in the presence of King and other civil rights leaders, President Johnson signed the Voting Rights Act of 1965 into law. The historic event was broadcast over nationwide television from the Capitol rotunda in Washington. The act barred literacy tests as a prerequisite to voting, and authorized the appointment of federal examiners to register black voters in the South whenever the right to vote was obstructed. John Lewis characterized the act as a 'milestone and every bit as momentous and significant . . . as the Emancipation Proclamation or the 1954 Supreme Court decision'. President Johnson called the legislation 'one of the most monumental laws in the entire history of American freedom'.[60]

VIII

Militant nonviolent direct action in Selma attained for black American citizens the fundamental democratic right to vote. Assessing the Selma campaign before reporters, King hailed it as 'the most powerful and dramatic civil rights protest that has ever taken place in the South'.[61] If blacks could be taught to exercise the ballot, they would make great strides toward freedom. The black vote had played a significant role in the landslide Democratic victory in 1964, and in Democratic triumphs in several Southern states. Using the vote strategically, blacks might oust the reactionary Southern Democrats from office, and 'place in Congress true representatives of the people who would legislate for the Medicare, housing, and schools and jobs required by all men of any color'.[62] As the number of black voters rose in the South from 1 million in 1964 to 3.1 million in 1968, the Voting Rights Act would contribute to the transformation of the South, altering the balance of political power, and have a profound effect on the politics of the entire nation.

The Selma campaign marked the culmination of the civil rights movement in the South. During the next few years, a combination of domestic and foreign developments conspired to divide the movement and replace civil rights as the county's paramount concern. In March 1965, the month of Selma, President Johnson made the fateful decisions to send the first American combat troops to Southeast Asia, and to bomb North Vietnam. The war soon became a national obsession, polarizing American society, and derailing the President's goal of building the Great Society.

King was among the first national leaders to perceive that the Vietnam War would sabotage the Johnson Administration's much heralded anti-poverty program. As early as 1965, King opposed the war as unjust. The recipient of the Nobel Peace Prize the year before, he felt a moral responsibility to condemn what he regarded as a dangerous threat to world peace. Addressing a statewide rally of SCLC's Virginia affiliates in Petersburg in July 1965, he declared: 'I'm not going to sit by and see war escalated without saying anything about it. . . . It is worthless to talk about integrating if there is no world to integrate in. . . . The war in Vietnam must be stopped'.[63] Not only was the war morally wrong, King insisted, but it also depleted economic resources that should be used to rebuild the ghettos and eradicate poverty in America. In August, King repeated his plea for a negotiated settlement of the Vietnam conflict in a speech before 4000 people at the Birmingham Municipal Auditorium.

In the ensuing months, as riots broke out in the northern ghettos, and as blacks began to demand full equality, the civil rights movement lost much of its legitimacy in the eyes of white Americans, and the liberal consensus that had supported King in previous years dispersed.

8

Interlude: The Paradox of Nonviolence

I

Throughout his public career, King was criticized because the nonviolent protests he led often generated violence. In the wake of the Birmingham campaign, journalist Reese Cleghorn wrote that King knew well that 'the "peaceful demonstrations" he organized would bring, at the very least, tough repressive measures by the police'.[1] When *Time* magazine chose King as 'Man of the Year' for 1963, its feature article contained the following observation: 'King preaches endlessly about nonviolence, but his protest movements often lead to violence'.[2] When King was awarded the Nobel Peace Prize in December 1964, *U.S. News & World Report*, in an article entitled 'Man of Conflict Wins a Peace Prize', remarked that many Americans believed it 'extraordinary that this prize should go to a man whose fame is based upon his battle for civil rights for Negroes – and whose activities often lead to violence'.[3] A 1965 article in the conservative *National Review*, entitled 'The Violence of Nonviolence', charged that King's campaigns, depending upon 'the provocation of violence', constituted a 'violent assault upon representative, constitutional government'.[4] Three years later, shortly after King announced plans for the Poor People's Campaign, the *National Review* assailed what it called King's 'insurrectionary methods', and solemnly warned of impending 'anarchy'.[5] Such criticism persisted even after King's death. In 1968, Lionel Lokos observed: 'It has often been remarked that while Martin Luther King himself was, virtually, Nonviolence on a Pedestal, violence somehow never seemed far behind him'.[6]

On a number of occasions, King admitted that SCLC deliberately provoked violence in racist communities. In a revealing article for the *Saturday Review*, written during the Selma protest in 1965, he outlined the strategy of a successful nonviolent direct-action campaign:

1. Nonviolent demonstrators go into the streets to exercise their constitutional rights.
2. Racists resist by unleashing violence against them.
3. Americans of conscience in the name of decency demand federal intervention and legislation.
4. The Administration, under mass pressure, initiates measures of immediate intervention and remedial legislation.[7]

Critics of King viewed the above scenario as an example of self-incrimination. But they failed to understand the paradoxical nature of nonviolence, which draws its strength as a technique from the violent reactions of opponents. The strategy of nonviolence operates by what has been termed a moral form of *jiu-jitsu*. Skilfully applied, nonviolent action throws the opponent off balance, causing his violence to rebound against him, weakening his moral position.[8] In order for this moral *jiu-jitsu* to work, opponents must be provoked to commit their violence openly so that it may be widely exposed. As SCLC's campaigns in Birmingham and Selma proved, whenever racists responded to nonviolence with violence in the presence of the media, they undermined their support among uncommitted third parties and added legitimacy to the protesters' cause.

Critics also misunderstood nonviolence to be passive and submissive. On the contrary, it is an active and often disruptive method of resisting injustice and bringing about social change. As Gandhi explained, nonviolence 'does not mean meek submission to the will of the evil-doer, but it means the pitting of one's whole soul against the will of the tyrant. Working under this law of our being, it is possible for a single individual to defy the whole might of an unjust empire'.[9] Moreover, nonviolence is often coercive, applying physical and moral pressure to force opponents to bargain. As James Farmer of CORE observed: 'Where we cannot influence the heart of the evil-doer, we can force an end to the evil practice'.[10] According to Gene Sharp, a leading historian and theorist of nonviolence: 'Where nonviolent coercion operates, change is achieved against the opponent's will and without his agreement, the sources of his power having been so undercut by nonviolent means that he no longer has control'.[11]

At the outset of his career, King was inclined to stress the importance of converting racists by reason and persuasion.

Through nonviolence, he believed, blacks could eventually change the hearts of their racist oppressors. But the student sit-ins of 1960 and the Freedom Rides of 1961 – which forced Southern racists to comply with federal law – taught King that nonviolent direct action must rely more upon conflict and coercion, even at the price of provoking violence from white racists. As King wrote in his 'Letter from Birmingham Jail': 'We have not made a single gain in civil rights without determined legal and nonviolent pressure'.[12] The campaigns of SCLC exerted political, economic and moral pressure upon segregationist communities in the South, disrupting order, bringing business to a halt, filling the jails and exposing racial injustice. Moreover, nonviolent direct action was the catalyst that compelled the federal government to act and the federal courts to render decisions in support of civil rights.

Through experience, King perceived that love and reconciliation would not succeed in overturning segregation without the power of nonviolent direct action. In the words of Reinhold Niebuhr: 'Powerless goodness ends upon the cross'.[13] Without power, love is ineffective, and without love, power is liable to become abusive and violent. As King explained: 'Power at its best is love implementing the demands of justice'.[14] When employed on a mass scale, nonviolence is the most potent method for an oppressed people to overcome their oppression. 'There is more power in socially organized masses on the march', King said, 'than there is in guns in the hands of a few desperate men. . . . Our powerful weapons are the voices, the feet, and the bodies of dedicated, united people, moving without rest toward a just goal'.[15]

The aggressive nature of nonviolent direct action is reflected in the martial vocabulary employed by its theorists. Like war, nonviolence is a means of combat, involving strategy and tactics. James Farmer, a pioneer of the nonviolent method in America, referred to its practitioners as 'soldiers', exercising discipline and courage.[16] King spoke of the nonviolent protester as brandishing 'the sword that heals'.[17] Gandhi's disciple Krishnalal Shridharani, author of *War Without Violence*, observed that nonviolence has 'more in common with war than with pacifism'.[18] The influential book, *The Power of Non-violence*, by Richard Gregg, includes a chapter entitled, 'An Effective Substitute for War'.[19] Gregg also originated the phrase 'moral jiu-jitsu', referring to the power of nonviolence to unbalance an opponent.[20] Nonviolent direct action, to adopt a phrase used by American philosopher William James, is 'the moral equivalent of war', providing a means to channel anger and frustration into constructive action.[21] Although comparable to military warfare, theorists agree that nonviolent protest, requiring its practitioners to endure rather than inflict physical harm, demands greater courage.

While critics often seized upon the violence provoked by the coercive nature of King's method, they gave scant attention to the violence inflicted upon the victims of racist oppression. In almost every instance, the oppressor rather than the peaceful protester committed the violence. Racists contended that the protesters should be blamed because their actions precipitated violence and disturbed law and order. Until the protesters arrived, the racists argued, peace reigned in the community. But the absence of overt conflict does not necessarily indicate the presence of justice. The violence provoked by nonviolence indicted not the protesters, but those who sought to uphold the unjust racist system by any means necessary. In effect, the white oppressor said to the black: 'For the sake of law and order, you must submit to a social system even though you believe it to be unjust. If you protest, however nonviolently, I will retaliate with violence and blame you for provoking me'. On the other hand, when blacks did not protest, their passivity was interpreted as acceptance of their subservient condition.

For generations, black Americans had been subjugated by the violence intrinsic to the racist social fabric. Beneath the calm facade of a peaceful segregationist community lay the more subtle and pervasive violence of institutional racism. When not overtly subduing its victims with dogs and clubs, a racist society depends upon a latent form of violence, hidden under the guise of law and order. As long as the black American was resigned to his oppression, he remained a victim of a psychological form of violence that stripped him of his dignity as a human being. James Baldwin, in the poignant letter to his nephew in 1963, the hundredth anniversary of the Emancipation Proclamation, described the sense of inferiority that had been instilled in black Americans: 'You were born into a society which spelled out with brutal clarity, and in as many ways as possible, that you were a worthless human being. You were not expected to aspire to excellence: you were expected to make peace with mediocrity'.[22]

Denied fundamental civil rights, decent housing and adequate education, the spirit of generations of blacks was broken by the covert violence of the racist system. But when blacks confronted racism with nonviolent protest, this hidden violence was exposed. By resisting racial injustice, King explained, the black American would 'force his oppressor to commit his brutality openly – in the light of day – with the rest of the world looking on'.[23] Protests call attention to the existence of social evils that would otherwise continue to be ignored. Each nonviolent protester becomes a target, magnetizing the hatred of white racists and exposing them to public view through the media. As Andrew Young noted, SCLC's strategy made racists attack peaceful protesters 'on Main Street, at noon, in front of CBS, NBC and ABC television cameras'.[24] Clearly, to blame the protesters for the violence induced by their nonviolent resistance to injustice is a prime example of distorting reality by blaming the victims.

II

We have seen that, until the emergence of King and the era of nonviolent protest in the 1950s, blacks had not been organized to fight racial injustice on a mass scale. The dominant vehicle for winning civil rights had been the slow-moving legalism advocated by the NAACP, involving legislation and court action. After it became apparent that the South would continue to defy federal laws and the federal courts in order to maintain its system of *de jure* segregation, increasing numbers of blacks saw the necessity of taking more militant action in pursuit of their basic constitutional rights. Deprived of the political power of the vote in the South, blacks would employ the power of nonviolent direct action, refusing to cooperate with the segregationist system, and directly intervening to disrupt its operation. Henry David Thoreau understood the extraordinary power of a minority when it disobeys unjust laws: 'A minority is powerless while it conforms to the majority . . . but it is irresistible when it clogs by its whole weight'.[25]

The history of the United States illustrates that the federal government had long been derelict in its duty to protect the rights of black citizens. Although civil rights laws were enacted in 1957 and 1960, promising greater equality to blacks, this legislation was either poorly enforced or ignored in the South. During the 1950s and early 1960s, the FBI and the Justice Department stood by while federal laws were defied, and civil rights workers were physically abu$ed, jailed, and sometimes murdered. Too often, civil rights laws were enforced only after the federal government was compelled to do so by a crisis provoked by the coercive power of nonviolent masses on the march. As Charles V. Hamilton observed: 'The history and experience of black Americans . . . is one in which, in very many instances, the political process does not in fact begin until a crisis has been initiated. . . . A politics of crisis is a prominent part of the black political experience'.[26] A number of significant instances have already been noted. Although the *Brown* decision outlawed segregation in public schools, not until a crisis was provoked in Little Rock, Arkansas, in 1957, did President Eisenhower dispatch federal troops to enforce a federal district court order to desegregate the city's Central High School. Although the Supreme Court ruled against segregation in interstate travel, first in 1946 in *Morgan* v. *Virginia*, and again in 1960 in *Boynton* v. *Virginia*, only after violence was committed against Freedom Riders in 1961 did the Kennedy Administration intervene and the Interstate Commerce Commission issue a decree supporting the court decisions. In 1962, President Kennedy was compelled to send federal troops to Oxford, Mississippi when whites rioted in an effort to defy a federal district court order and prevent James Meredith from registering at the University of Mississippi.

Drawing upon the experience of previous years, by 1963 King and SCLC had become masters at fomenting political crises in Southern cities. King often spoke of the redemptive value of voluntary suffering. He knew that in any confrontation, public sympathy usually gravitates to the victims. Hence SCLC carefully chose its target cities – Birmingham, St Augustine and Selma – and capitalized on the well-known brutality of racist opponents – Bull Connor, Hoss Manucy and Jim Clark. Each campaign city became the stage for a morality play in which the nation could easily separate the heroes from the villains. The Children's Crusade in Birmingham, the brutal beatings at the Slave Market in St Augustine and the violence on the Edmund Pettus Bridge in Selma made lasting impressions on the consciences of people of good will throughout the nation. In many cases, the mere threat of increased white violence compelled the more rational segregationist authorities to negotiate with blacks, moderating demands and making valuable concessions. Asked in an interview why President Kennedy proposed comprehensive civil rights legislation in 1963, Roy Wilkins responded: 'He did it because a crisis was created that demanded the attention of the nation on the highest level. . . . I think there is no doubt that . . . what Martin Luther King and his associates did in Birmingham made the nation realize that at last the crisis had arrived'.[27]

In summary, King and SCLC achieved major victories against segregation in the South because they skilfully created dramatic crises by provoking racists to respond to peaceful protest with violence, attracted media attention to the plight of black Americans, drew support from hitherto complacent third parties, and compelled local authorities to bargain and the federal government to intervene. The leadership of King was essential to the implementation of this strategy. An analysis of his protest campaigns shows that while he often appeared to be the lamb, his nonviolent strategy embodied much of the power of the lion and the cleverness of the fox.

III

Citizens of a nation dedicated to the ideals of liberty, justice and equality were disturbed by the fact that a severe local crisis was usually required before the federal government would intervene in the states and localities to defend basic rights. Despite express constitutional guarantees, blacks in the South were frequently beaten and arrested for picketing and demonstrating peacefully, and systematically deprived of the right to vote. The primary responsibility for the enforcement of the Constitution and the laws of the nation lies with the executive branch of the federal government. The President has the duty to 'preserve, protect, and defend the Constitution of the United States' (Article II), which is 'the supreme law of the land' (Article VI). Nevertheless, the executive branch, as we have noted, had a history of reluctance in fulfilling its responsibility.

Under the United States Constitution, all citizens, regardless of race, colour, or creed, are guaranteed the First Amendment rights to speak freely, assemble peacefully and petition the government for a redress of grievances. The Fourteenth Amendment guarantees the right to equal protection of the laws, and prohibits any state from depriving a citizen of life, liberty or property without due process of law. The Fifteenth Amendment protects the right of all citizens to vote. A democracy seeks to balance two concerns. On the one hand, law and order must be preserved to safe-guard the rights of citizens. On the other hand, citizens must be free to act peacefully to protect their rights. They must be free to dissent, organize and demonstrate, This raises the question of whether citizens should be prevented from taking constitutionally protected actions which might provoke violence from others. If the mere possibility of violence is sufficient to sanction the denial of the constitutional right to protest, all an oppressor must do to preserve an unjust order is to indicate beforehand that his response to protest will be violent. Must citizens surrender their right to protest because of the threat of disorder? If this were the case, *de jure* segregation would have never been overthrown in the South. The extent of the right to protest must be directly proportionate to the extent of the injustices that are protested against.

The issue of enforcing civil rights in the South posed a difficult dilemma for the Kennedy and Johnson Administrations because of their view of the American federal system of government. The great architects of the U.S. Constitution perceived that since power tends to corrupt, endangering liberty, the best form of government is one that separates power between a central federal government and individual state governments. Under the federal system, the states' rights doctrine dictates that the police power to maintain law and order is reserved first to the local authorities. The South had long exploited the states' rights doctrine as a means of protecting its racist policies. The federal government assumed the power to intervene in the states – either by court injunction, arrests or federalizing a state National Guard – only when a federal court order was violated, such as at Little Rock in 1957 and at Oxford, Mississippi in 1962, or when a state could no longer control violence, such as during the Freedom Rides in 1961 and during the Selma-to-Montgomery march in 1965. But entrusting protection entirely to the state and local authorities, except in cases of intense crisis, was inadequate, for often these same authorities in the South were the most flagrant violators of civil rights, and allowed whites to commit violence against blacks with impunity.

King and SCLC were counselled on the complexities of federalism by their legal advisors, including members of the NAACP Legal Defence Fund, Inc., seasoned veterans in the struggle for black equality. King and other civil rights activists learned to take advantage of the dual system of federal-state law provided by the federal system. Civil disobedience to state segregation laws was justified by an appeal to higher civil law, as embodied in federal laws, Supreme Court decisions and the Constitution. Beyond this, civil disobedients – as King explains in his 'Letter from Birmingham Jail' – could also take refuge in the natural law as superior to the laws of the state. From the late 1950s to the early 1960s, the incessant demand of activists that the federal government pursue a more aggressive policy in enforcing civil rights in the South presented a formidable challenge to the traditional assumptions and rules of federal-state relations.

The federal government sought to justify its reluctance to intervene in the states to enforce civil rights. The fullest articulation of the Kennedy Administration's position was presented by Burke Marshall – Assistant Attorney General and head of the Civil Rights Division of the Justice Department – in a series of lectures delivered at Columbia University in the spring of 1964, and published as *Federalism and Civil Rights*. In the foreword to the book, Attorney General Robert Kennedy explained that as a check upon the powers of the federal government, the authors of the United States Constitution had constructed a system that left considerable power to the states for the maintenance of law and order. While Kennedy acknowledged the increasing demand for federal protection of blacks and civil rights workers in the South, 'at the same time,' he insisted, 'there is reluctance to start down the path that would lead inevitably to the creation of a national police force'.[28]

Marshall echoed Robert Kennedy's fear that effective federal intervention to enforce civil rights would necessitate the institution of a national police force, with dangerous consequences for the federal system. John Doar, Assistant Attorney General for Civil Rights, presented the case succinctly: 'Maintaining law and order is a state responsibility', he explained to a group of civil rights activists.[29] In an April 1964 address at Boston College, Deputy Attorney General Nicholas Katzenbach said that civil rights workers would have to rely upon state and local law enforcement officials to protect their rights, and that 'to do anything else would be making major changes in the Federal system'.[30] Professor Alexander Bickel of the Yale Law School declared that a national police force would be 'destructive of the values of a free society'.[31] In short, supporters of the Kennedy Administration's policy contended that more active federal intervention on behalf of civil rights would endanger the delicate balance between the national and the state powers that the Founding Fathers deemed essential for the preservation of liberty. Interviewed by Anthony Lewis in 1964, Robert Kennedy expressed grave misgivings when asked whether the federal government should assume primary responsibility for law enforcement in the states: 'I just wouldn't want that much authority in the hands of either the FBI, or the Department of Justice, or the President of the United States'.[32]

For years, civil rights advocates had pleaded with the federal government to investigate and prosecute cases of the unlawful deprivation of constitutional rights in the South. According to Marshall, were the federal government to initiate civil rights suits on behalf of private citizens, it would exceed the legitimate limits of its power. The federal system assumes that constitutional rights are 'individual and personal, to be asserted by private citizens as they choose, in court, speaking through their chosen counsel'.[33] He argued, moreover, that in order to secure an injunction to protect a citizen's rights, the Justice Department must have specific statutory authority, such as that granted under the Civil Rights Acts of 1957 and 1960 for cases involving voting rights.

The federal government's conservative interpretation of its police powers did not go unchallenged. Legal authorities argued that whenever civil rights were denied in the South, the temporary federal assumption of police powers was justified because Southern officials had violated the Constitution, thereby placing themselves outside the federal system. In 1963, the Notre Dame Conference on Congressional Civil Rights Legislation concluded:

> To contain and disarm lawlessness, a clear federal presence is required at the first outbreaks. We think the Attorney General has the power, in the face of determined lawlessness supported by an acquiescent or conspiratorial community, to send federal marshals and agents of the Federal Bureau of Investigation for on-the-spot protection of the exercise of federal rights. . . . This condition does not pose an issue of federalism. Federalism is a system of divided power among governments, and governments are instruments whose purpose is to establish an order of law. In these outlaw communities where citizenship rights are flagrantly destroyed, there is no law to respect.[34]

On 30 June 1964, 27 professors from five of the nation's leading law schools – Columbia, Harvard, New York University, Pennsylvania and Yale – issued a statement designed to establish a firm legal basis for greater federal intervention in defence of civil rights.[35] Citing as precedent the *Debs* case of 1895, in which the Supreme Court ruled that the federal government may enforce the law when necessary by injunctions in any part of the nation, they argued that the Justice Department could seek such court orders to protect the civil rights of individuals in the South without specific statutory authority.[36] Furthermore, they cited Title 10, Section 333 of the United States Code, which reads in part:

The President, by using the militia or the armed forces, or both, *or by any other means* shall take such measures as he considers necessary to suppress, in a State, any domestic violence, unlawful combination or conspiracy, if it –
(1) so hinders the execution of the laws of that State, and of the United States within the State, that any part or class of its people is deprived of a right, privilege, immunity, or protection named in the Constitution and secured by law, and the constituted authorities of that State are unable, fail, or refuse to protect that right, privilege, or immunity, or to give that protection; or
(2) opposes or obstructs the execution of the laws of the United States or impedes the course of justice under those laws. . . .[37]

The foregoing section of the U.S. Code was cited by the Department of Justice when federal forces intervened to protect the Freedom Riders in Montgomery, Alabama, in 1961, and when, the following year, federal troops enforced the enrollment of James Meredith in the University of Mississippi. The section was also employed by the Kennedy Administration to justify sending troops to the outskirts of Birmingham in 1963. Moreover, the Supremacy Clause of the U.S. Constitution (Article VI) empowers the federal government to intervene whenever a state fails to protect constitutionally guaranteed rights. Federal action to protect the right to vote, or the right to demonstrate peacefully, need not have entailed a broad assumption of local police powers. 'The real failure [of the federal government]', Pat Watters and Reese Cleghorn argued, 'was the failure to act with full decisiveness with the powers and forces that existed: to enforce existing federal statutes, and to defend, by *some direct means*, the exercise of undisputed federal rights'.[38] As the Southern Regional Council pointed out in a 1964 report: 'The question of federal police intervention in Mississippi, and the extent and kind of it, is . . . not one of *power to act*, but of policy'.[39] The Kennedy Administration clearly had ample authority to intervene in support of federal statutes and civil rights all along; it simply decided that it was not politically expedient to do so.

As far as a national police force was concerned, civil rights lawyers pointed out that in effect one already existed in the FBI, which was authorized to investigate and arrest criminals who violated federal laws.[40] If the FBI can make on the spot arrests of those guilty of bank robbery, narcotics violations and espionage, why can it not arrest those guilty of violating federal civil rights laws? If the President could dispatch federal marshalls to protect freedom riders, why could he not send marshalls to protect those who attempted to exercise the right to vote? A persuasive argument for greater federal intervention was offered by historian Howard Zinn, who maintained that the original purpose of the Fourteenth Amendment was to place the authority to enforce civil rights in the hands of the federal government instead of the states, which had consistently defied them.[41] Hence, the federal government had jurisdiction over violations of the Fourteenth Amendment, and its refusal to protect civil rights within the states was an abdication of its legal authority and a violation of the Constitution it was entrusted to uphold.

Despite the cogent arguments of civil rights lawyers, the federal government persisted in its policy of sacrificing civil rights to an unjust social order until severe crises arose. Were it not for mass nonviolent direct action, provoking white racist violence, arousing the conscience of the American public, and compelling the federal government to take decisive action, the system of *de jure* segregation would not have been defeated in the South by 1965. In the ensuing years, as the civil rights movement became national, King took his nonviolent legions to the North in pursuit of goals that, if achieved, would radically alter American society. But the Northern cities would present a more difficult challenge than those of the South, and the nonviolent method would no longer have the same effect.

9

A New Direction: Chicago, 1966

I

Having defeated *de jure* segregation in the South and achieved most of their legislative goals by the end of 1965, the major civil rights organizations became divided as they sought a new direction for the black freedom struggle. At an SCLC conference in August 1965, James Bevel declared: 'There is no more civil rights movement. President Johnson signed it out of existence when he signed the Voting Rights Bill'.[1] The long-awaited victories of the recent past now seemed insufficient. Although the legal barriers to equality had been abolished, the majority of black Americans did not have the economic resources to take full advantage of the opportunities now available to them. The Civil Rights Act of 1964 and the Voting Rights Act of 1965 did little to change the oppressive living conditions in the ghettos of the North, where millions of impoverished blacks were plagued by *de facto* segregation, unemployment, inadequate housing and schools, family deterioration and police brutality. The advances of the previous decade had not resolved the American Dilemma; in fact, its resolution would require deeper social and economic changes than most white Americans were willing to tolerate. Public opinion polls in 1966 indicated that increasing numbers of whites were opposed to the recent progress of the black American. A Gallup Poll taken in November showed that 52 per cent of whites – the highest percentage since 1962 – believed that the Johnson Administration was pushing racial integration too fast. A Louis Harris Poll taken at the same time indicated that 75 per cent of whites thought that blacks were progressing too rapidly.[2] As King observed: 'The paths of Negro–white unity that had been converging crossed at Selma, and like a giant X began to diverge'.[3]

The nation's urban problems were shockingly dramatized in August 1965, when Watts, the black ghetto of Los Angeles, erupted

149

in the most severe race riot in the country's history, leaving 34 dead, 1032 injured, and a total destruction estimated in excess of $40 million. The riot signalled a series of 'long hot summers' of ghetto violence that appeared to fulfil James Baldwin's ominous 1963 prophecy – in his best-selling book, *The Fire Next Time* – that black Americans 'may never be able to rise to power, but they are very well placed indeed to precipitate chaos and ring down the curtain on the American dream'.[4] Watts confirmed the view of many civil rights activists that in order for blacks to be fully integrated into American society, the freedom movement must enter a new phase, concentrating upon economic and social reforms to improve the lives of millions of ghetto residents.

A new direction for the civil rights movement was indicated by Bayard Rustin in the February 1965 issue of *Commentary*: 'The civil rights movement is evolving from a protest movement into a full-fledged *social movement*', he proclaimed. 'It is now concerned not merely with removing the barriers to full *opportunity* but with achieving the fact of *equality*'.[5] The achievement of substantial equality for blacks would entail revolutionary change in American society – 'a great expansion of the public sector of the economy', 'radical programs for full employment, the abolition of slums, the reconstruction of our educational system, new definitions of work and leisure. Adding up the cost of such programs, we can only conclude that we are talking about a refashioning of our political economy'.[6] The following month, the controversial Moynihan Report, entitled *The Negro Family: The Case for National Action*, was issued. Written by Assistant Secretary of Labor Daniel Patrick Moynihan, the report drew attention to 'the tangle of pathology' in the nation's ghettos, and concluded that the deterioration of the black family was the root of the perpetuating cycle of unemployment, illegitimate births and urban crime that plagued black America.[7] Like Rustin, Moynihan observed that while the first phase of the black revolution had established equal opportunity, the next phase must focus on attaining complete equality.[8] The report concluded by calling for a national effort to establish a stable black family structure.[9]

The new focus of the black freedom struggle was brought to the attention of the entire nation by President Lyndon Johnson. After his landslide victory in the presidential election in 1964, the President launched a War on Poverty Program. In a nationally televised address to Congress on 15 March 1965, Johnson acknowledged that equal opportunity alone would be insufficient to improve the living conditions of impoverished Americans. Henceforth, the nation must go beyond the goal of opening the gates to opportunity; in order to 'give all our people – black and white – the help that they need to walk through those gates'.[10] Johnson amplified his thoughts in an historic commencement address at Howard University in Washington, D.C. on 4 June. The President argued that blacks must be granted preferential treatment in order to compensate for generations of inherited disadvantages. 'The next and more profound stage of the battle for civil rights', he concluded, must concentrate upon achieving equality of living conditions: 'Not equality as a right and a theory, but equality as a fact and a result'. To discover ways in which blacks might 'move beyond opportunity to achievement', Johnson announced that he would convene a White House Conference, 'To Fulfill These Rights', inviting scholars, experts, black leaders and government officials.[11] The Howard University speech was enthusiastically received by civil rights leaders, who viewed it as a sign that the federal government was set to promote full equality for black Americans. As one reporter recalled: 'Not since Lincoln signed the Emancipation Proclamation had Negroes been offered such hope'.[12]

King was among the first black leaders to perceive that the freedom movement must expand its goals beyond civil rights. In the concluding chapter of *Why We Can't Wait*, published in 1964, he argued that in order to make the black American's freedom substantial, equal opportunity must be combined with 'the practical, realistic aid which will help him to seize it'.[13] To compensate for past injustices, King urged Congress to enact a $12 billion Bill of Rights for the Disadvantaged, as the basis for a massive federal anti-poverty programme to benefit the nation's poor, black and white. In an article for the *Saturday Review*, entitled 'Next Stop: The North' – written shortly after Watts in 1965 – King announced that the movement must now direct its attention to urban poverty. 'The cohesive, potentially explosive Negro community in the North', he observed, 'has a short fuse and a long train of abuses'.[14] Unless blacks of the North rejected violence in favour of nonviolent protest to reform the ghettos, the Watts riot would be repeated throughout the nation. If employed on a mass scale, King believed, nonviolent direct action could transform the North as it had transformed the South: 'If one hundred thousand Negroes march in a major city to a strategic location, they will make municipal operations difficult to conduct; they will exceed the capacity of even the most reckless mayor to use force against them'.[15]

As King's article had revealed, SCLC soon turned to the problems of the nation's ghettos. The first stop was Chicago – a citadel of *de facto* segregation in the North.

II

The seeds for a black protest movement in Chicago had been planted before King and SCLC arrived in 1966. For three years, the Coordinating Council of Community Organizations (CCCO) – a coalition of 34 civil rights, religious and civic groups headed by activist Al Raby – had been engaged in a nonviolent protest to end *de facto* segregation in Chicago's public schools. Rather than integrate the classrooms, school Superintendent Benjamin Willis had resorted to herding black children into trailers. In an attempt to force the dismissal of Willis, the CCCO organized a series of school boycotts and mass demonstrations. At the invitation of Raby, King visited Chicago briefly to bolster the campaign, generating much publicity as he toured the city's ghettos, delivered numerous speeches and led a march of 30 000 demonstrators to City Hall on 26 July 1965.

When the CCCO protest began to falter soon after King departed, Raby went to Birmingham for SCLC's annual convention in August, and appealed for help in organizing a massive boycott of Chicago's segregated public schools. For several months, King and SCLC had been searching for a city to launch their movement in the North. Although Philadelphia, Washington, New York, Cleveland and Detroit were also considered, Chicago was finally selected because the CCCO was the largest civil rights coalition in the North. Moreover, Chicago, one of the most racially segregated cities in the nation, appeared to be an excellent target for SCLC's first Northern campaign. The great mid-western metropolis – the third largest city in the United States – featured some of the worst ghetto problems that, if properly dramatized, might stir the federal government to take action to eradicate urban poverty. Of the city's total population of three and a half million, almost one million were black, the vast majority living in slums on the South and West sides. 'There are more Negroes in Chicago', King observed, 'than in the whole state of Mississippi'.[16] Beyond the ghettos were the suburbs, home of many white racists.

From the outset, some of King's supporters, including members of SCLC, questioned whether the movement could succeed in Chicago, transporting nonviolent protest from the church-oriented South to the despair-ridden ghettos of the urban North. Street demonstrations, disruptive in a Southern town, could be readily absorbed and neutralized in a Northern city of millions. Chicago provided no Bull Connors or Jim Clarks, easily provoked to violence; instead, there was the clever Mayor Richard J. Daley, operator of one of the most powerful political machines in the country.

Mayor Daley was no friend to blacks. In 1963, he was booed off the podium of an NAACP convention after boldly declaring that no ghettos existed in Chicago. The Daley Democratic machine controlled most of the city's politicians and civic leaders, black and white. Chicago had a long history of political corruption. As journalist Paul Good observed in 1966: 'Virtually everyone you talk to acknowledges that Chicago remains the crookedest city in the country. The stench rising from hoodlumism permeates vast areas of politics, labour and industry, and fosters a cynicism about anything (a civil rights movement, for example) that does not depend on pull, payoffs or raw muscle to achieve its ends'.[17] SNCC's Charles Sherrod told King frankly that SCLC was 'out of their depth' in Chicago.[18] When King admitted that he did not intend to topple Mayor Daley from power, Bayard Rustin advised him to forget about a Chicago campaign, for he would 'come away with nothing meaningful'.[19]

Unlike the South, where King and SCLC drew much strength from black church leaders, Chicago's black ministers, succumbing to the Daley machine, seemed indifferent to civil rights. The vast majority of the city's black politicians were also controlled by the white power structure. Congressman William L. Dawson, the most powerful black political leader in the history of Chicago, was boss of the black sub-machine within the overall Democratic machine. A skilful politician, Dawson dominated the wards of Chicago's South Side, with an estimated population of 600 000 blacks. The vast majority of blacks who did vote in Chicago supported Daley; in fact, during his political career, the Mayor received an average of 77.4 per cent of the black vote.[20]

King could not even expect much support from Chicago's black ghetto residents. SCLC would find it far more difficult to penetrate apathy in the slums of the North than in the small towns of the South. As early as 1963, James Baldwin said in an interview that while King 'has great moral authority in the South, he has none whatever in the North. Poor Martin has gone through God knows what kind of hell to awaken the American conscience, but Martin has reached the end of his rope'.[21] Dependent upon the Democratic machine for public welfare, the ghetto poor were in no position to challenge the system. 'The Negroes of Chicago have a greater feeling of powerlessness than I ever saw', SCLC's Hosea Williams lamented. 'They don't participate in the governmental process because they're beaten down psychologically. We are used to working with people who want to be free'.[22] Instead of entering the North, Williams advised, SCLC should remain in the South and concentrate on its voter registration drive. 'Chicago is not our turf', he warned.[23]

Despite these strong reservations, King refused to ignore the problems of the Northern ghettos. Having overcome so many obstacles in the South, he was determined to lead SCLC in the new direction that he believed the black freedom movement must take. Chicago would be 'the test case for the SCLC and for the freedom movement in the North', King said.[24] 'If we can break the system in Chicago, it can be broken anywhere in the country'.[25]

III

The Chicago campaign entailed more preparation than ever before. By October 1965, a group of SCLC staff members, including James Bevel, Andrew Young, Bernard Lee, Walter Fauntroy and James Orange, arrived to begin organizing a full-scale offensive. On 7 January 1966, at the conclusion of a three-day strategy session, King announced to the press that SCLC would soon begin a nonviolent protest campaign in Chicago, its 'first sustained Northern movement'. The city had been chosen, he said, because its slums were 'the prototype of those chiefly responsible for the Northern urban race problem'.[26] Reforms would be sought not only on the city and state level, but also 'on the federal level [where] we would hope to get the kind of comprehensive legislation which would meet the problems of slum life across this nation'.[27]

On 26 January, about 200 blacks cheered as King moved into a

Lawndale slum tenement at 1550 South Hamlin Avenue, in the heart of Chicago's West Side, with a population of 300 000 blacks crammed into 800 square blocks. James Bevel, veteran of the Birmingham and Selma protests, christened the Lawndale area 'Slumdale'. Comparing conditions there to those imposed upon African nations, he called the ghetto a 'system of internal colonialism'.[28] King planned to reside in the slum at least three days a week for the duration of the campaign, hoping that his presence would dramatize ghetto conditions. The rest of his time would be spent at SCLC headquarters in Atlanta, and on visits to various cities to raise money for the Chicago Movement. Day-to-day supervision of the campaign was entrusted to Bevel, and a campaign headquarters was established at the Warren Avenue Congregational Church in the East Garfield section on Chicago's West Side. When King's slumlord learned of his impending residency, a work crew was dispatched to clean up the apartment and remove several violations of the city building code, prompting the *Chicago Sun-Times* to speculate that if King were merely to keep moving, he might single-handedly clean up the city's slums.

By the time King arrived, Daley had already begun to take action to prevent a Southern-style crisis in Chicago. When King went to City Hall, he was politely received by the Mayor, who assured him that the city's slum eradication programme was under way, and that he was happy to have King's support. When newspapers quoted King as saying that he was prepared to 'break any law for the cause of civil rights' in Chicago, Daley replied: 'I am confident that there will not be any reason for breaking the law'.[29] Meanwhile, Superintendent Willis had been pressured to 'resign', thus depriving the Chicago protest of a galvanizing issue. In consultation with his staff, especially Bevel, King decided to focus the protest on the issue of open housing, selecting as a slogan, 'The Campaign To End Slums'. By 1966, open housing was already a national issue. In his January State of the Union Message, President Johnson called for housing legislation and, three months later, it became part of a major civil rights bill.

The evening of his arrival in Chicago, King spoke at a local church and stressed the urgency of solving the problems in the nation's slums: 'I say to the power structure in Chicago that the same problems that existed, and still exist, in Watts, exist in Chicago today, and if something isn't done in a hurry, we can see a darker night of social disruption'.[30] Needless to say, city politicians were unhappy to see King. Black Congressman William Dawson condemned him as a meddling outside agitator: 'What does he mean coming in here trying to tell our citizens that we are segregated? Chicagoans know what's best for Chicagoans'. Alderman Thomas Keane, head of the City Council, also expressed hostility: 'King is a disrupter of society. He is trying to destroy what we built'.[31] According to Mayor Daley, there was no reason for a protest: 'We believe that we do not have segregation in Chicago', he declared. 'Here we recognize every man, regardless of race, national origin, or creed, and they are entitled to their rights as provided in the United States Constitution and the constitution of Illinois'.[32] But the size and complex social structure of Chicago and other Northern cities made it possible to disguise the more pervasive and subtle forms of *de facto* segregation. Most blacks could neither afford to live in white middle class neighbourhoods, nor did they have sufficient education to compete with whites for employment.

On 29 January, King made headlines by announcing that he would lead a rent strike unless Chicago's slumlords undertook to improve their properties immediately. Soon, 'End Slums' placards sprang up throughout the West Side ghetto. SCLC staff members Bernard Lee and James Bevel began organizing tenants on the city's West Side, while King outlined the goals of the campaign:

1. to expose conditions in the nation's slums;
2. to organize ghetto residents into a union that would compel landlords to provide decent living conditions in their buildings;
3. to mobilize slum dwellers into a nonviolent army to stir America's conscience and induce necessary ghetto reforms.

To complete his campaign preparations, King met with leaders of Chicago's principal youth gangs, persuading them to try the method of nonviolence, and conferred with the Superintendent of Police, warning him that in order to expose the problems of the ghettos, it might be necessary to engage in acts of civil disobedience. To the surprise of many, King also visited Black Muslim leader Elijah Muhammad at his Hyde Park mansion, where they agreed to form a 'common front' to combat the city's problems.

But Mayor Daley was ready for King. When SCLC and CCCO – collectively known as the Chicago Movement – began the campaign, the Daley machine declared that because the city was already making strides in the war against poverty, there was no need for interference from 'outsiders' like King. In the Birmingham and Selma campaigns, SCLC encountered overt and violent opposition that dramatized racial injustices. But the shrewd Mayor, instead of opposing the Chicago Movement on every issue, attempted to undermine it by a series of proposals calculated to attract publicity while making merely cosmetic ghetto improvements. As one observer stated to the *New York Times*: 'He [Daley] has always beaten his enemies by taking their programs and running with them'.[33] Whenever King stated a demand, the Mayor produced a programme allegedly in the works. Whenever King said, 'We shall overcome', the Mayor answered, 'Your goals are ours'. When King threatened to march, the Mayor invited him to join his effort to make Chicago an even greater city. As one analyst aptly remarked, after fighting a few rounds with Daley, King must have thought he was 'fighting a pillow'.[34]

On 10 February, the *Chicago Tribune* featured the following headline: 'Plan New Drive on Slumlords'. Daley ordered 50 housing inspectors to be sent into the West Side ghetto to compel landlords to comply with the building code. A fact sheet was also circulated, indicating the 'progress' recently achieved. On 23 February, King announced that the Chicago Movement was seizing a slum tenement on the West Side. The rent collected from the building's four tenants would be used for renovations. The seizure drew widespread publicity, as newspapers throughout the country featured a picture of King shoveling trash from a slum alley. He justified the seizure, saying to reporters that the 'moral question is far more important than the legal one'.[35] Daley responded that evidence had been collected on the landlord's violations and that litigation was already planned. The tenement seizure was later voided by a court order.

On 18 March, Daley outflanked the Chicago Movement once again. While King was away at a speaking engagement, the Mayor met with a group of 25 clergymen – including Roman Catholic Archbishop John P. Cody – at City Hall. After distributing a fact sheet detailing the 'progress' achieved against housing discrimination, Daley invited the clergymen to return at the end of the month with a list of recommendations. The Mayor was effectively stymying the Movement. A bewildered Andrew Young, SCLC's executive director, conceded: 'The strategy hasn't emerged yet'.

Even King could not conceal his dismay. 'We will make mistakes', he told reporters, 'we are not omniscient or omnipotent . . . and we need a great deal of support'.[36]

On 26 May, Daley initiated another manoeuver, utilizing the media to impair the protest campaign. Newspapers carried a story that some 500 slum apartments would be renovated with a federal loan to the city. The Mayor confidently predicted that Chicago slums would be eradicated by the end of the decade. By June, the Chicago Movement was in danger of collapsing. The pressure upon King and SCLC for a victory in the North became overwhelming. A failure in Chicago might incite black ghetto residents throughout the nation to turn to violence. As Andrew Young admitted: 'We have got to deliver results – nonviolent results in a Northern city – to protect the nonviolent movement'.[37] But the prospect of defeating Daley appeared bleak. The Mayor continued to undermine the Chicago Movement by conveying the impression that instead of resisting a drive to reform the slums, he was leading one.

To complicate matters in Chicago, King was no longer fully absorbed by civil rights issues, for he was becoming increasingly concerned about the Vietnam War. In April 1966, at the annual SCLC convention in Miami, he had called for the withdrawal of United States forces from Southeast Asia. The same month, he accepted the co-chairmanship of Clergy and Laymen Concerned About Vietnam, organized by Dr Benjamin Spock and Yale chaplain William Sloane Coffin. At an anti-war rally in Washington on 16 May, Coffin read the following statement from King: 'The pursuit of widened war has narrowed welfare programs, making the poor, white and Negro, bear the heaviest burdens at the front and at home'.[38] Meanwhile, the war continued to escalate, spreading into Cambodia. Secretary of Defense Robert McNamara confessed to President Johnson that 'there was no reasonable way to bring the war to an end soon'.[39] Warned by advisor Stanley Levison that his opposition to the war might jeopardize financial contributions to SCLC, King was adamant: 'I don't care if we don't get five cents in the mail. I am going to keep preaching my message'.[40] In the ensuing months, King would emerge as a leader of the anti-war movement.

On 1 and 2 June, King was in Washington to attend the White House Conference, 'To Fulfill These Rights', originated by President Johnson with his Howard University speech the year before. The purpose of the conference was to discover means to integrate blacks into American society on a more equal basis. Some 2500 persons participated, including representatives of business, labour, industry, government and civil rights groups. The President used the conference to publicize his Administration's contributions to civil rights. Angered by King's public stand against the Vietnam War, Johnson excluded him from playing a major part. Many black leaders, believing that the economic plight of blacks at home was more urgent than foreign policy, avoided confronting the President on the issue of Vietnam. When Floyd McKissick of CORE introduced a resolution condemning the war, it was overwhelmingly defeated. As Whitney Young stated to the White House press corps: 'The Negro is more concerned about the rat at night and the job in the morning than he is about the war in Vietnam'.[41] The conference concluded that only a massive national effort could solve the grave problems in the nation's ghettos. A. Philip Randolph proposed a $185 billion Freedom Budget, supported by King, to finance a ten-year war against poverty in America.

IV

While King and SCLC were in Atlanta searching for means to vitalize the Chicago campaign, an incident in Mississippi returned the focus of the civil rights movement temporarily to the South. On Sunday afternoon, 5 June 1966, James Meredith, famous for having integrated the University of Mississippi in 1962, began a Freedom March from Memphis, Tennessee to Jackson, Mississippi. The purpose of the march, he said, was to show that blacks could no longer be intimidated in the South, and to encourage them to vote. On the second day of his projected 220-mile pilgrimage along Highway 51, barely ten miles into his home state of Mississippi, a white sniper blasted Meredith in the back with a shotgun. When King and his staff heard the first press reports on Monday afternoon, 6 June, they thought Meredith had been killed. After learning from Reverend James Lawson, head of SCLC's Memphis affiliate, that Meredith was not dead, but recovering from multiple superficial buckshot wounds in Memphis Municipal Hospital, SCLC and other civil rights organizations agreed that the Meredith incident might provide another opportunity to gain valuable publicity for the movement.

The following day, 7 June, black leaders rushed to Memphis to visit Meredith in the hospital: King from Atlanta; Floyd McKissick, recently succeeding James Farmer as national director of CORE, from New York. They were joined by a new black leader, Stokely Carmichael, a 24-year-old militant who had recently replaced John Lewis as chairman of SNCC. A native of Trinidad, and educated at New York City's Bronx High School of Science and Howard University, Carmichael had played an important role in the 1964 Mississippi Freedom Project, directing the Freedom School in Greenwood. He was now determined to assert his leadership of SNCC. Over the next few weeks, events would reveal the extent of the divisions brewing within the civil rights movement.

At Memphis Municipal Hospital, King, McKissick and Carmichael conferred with Meredith, who approved their plan to continue his Freedom March. 'It is bigger than any single individual', Meredith admitted. 'It is bigger than me'.[42] King, McKissick and Carmichael agreed to sponsor the march jointly for the purpose of highlighting the evils of racism that pervaded Mississippi and the rest of the Deep South. King was confident that the march – now called the 'Meredith March Against Fear' — would rival the great march from Selma to Montgomery the year before. Meanwhile, Roy Wilkins of the NAACP and Whitney Young of the National Urban League, arrived in Memphis. Both hoped that the march would generate support for the 1966 Civil Rights Bill, which contained important provisions for open housing and the protection of civil rights workers. The Meredith March had become a national event.

On 8 June, after setting up headquarters at James Lawson's Centenary Methodist Church in Memphis, King, McKissick, Carmichael and others travelled to the place where Meredith had been wounded. They linked arms and resumed the Freedom March along U.S. Highway 51, protected by the Mississippi state police. King was committed to completing what Meredith had begun. According to his wife Coretta: 'Martin saw the gunning down of Meredith not just as an effort to stop one man, but to intimidate the whole Movement for equality in Mississippi'.[43]

On the first day of the march, Carmichael shouted to a rally: 'The Negro is going to take what he deserves from the white man'.[44] As the marchers proceeded down the highway, King was dismayed when he heard some young activists from SNCC and CORE attack the main beliefs of the civil rights movement:

integration and nonviolence. 'I'm not for that nonviolence stuff any more', cried one. 'This should be an all-black march', shouted another. Others resented the white participants, accusing them of 'invading' their movement. 'This is our march', they insisted. When the marchers began to sing the civil rights anthem, 'We Shall Overcome', a number of blacks became silent at the words 'black and white together'. When King later inquired why they had refrained from singing this verse, they replied that 'the whole song should be discarded. Not "We Shall Overcome", but "We Shall Overrun"'.[45]

The first night, while plans were being made for using tents along the route for the rest of the pilgrimage, the marchers returned to Memphis and checked into a black-owned motel. The remarks of the young black activists earlier that day disturbed King, and became the subject of an intense discussion between himself, McKissick and Carmichael, joined by Roy Wilkins, Whitney Young and an armed group of young militants known as the Deacons for Defense. The discussion centered upon the inclusion of whites in the march and the feasibility of nonviolence. McKissick denounced nonviolence as useless in racist America, adding that blacks ought to break the legs off the Statue of Liberty and 'throw her into the Mississippi'. Carmichael reiterated his angry sentiment of earlier that day: 'I'm not going to beg the white man for anything I deserve. I'm going to take it'.[46] Wilkins and Young were horrified by what they regarded as irresponsible rhetoric.

King pleaded the case for nonviolence as he had done in the past. Not only did he condemn violence on moral grounds, but he also argued that it was inexpedient, for blacks were without the necessary resources. Moreover, a violent uprising would merely give Mississippi whites an excuse to wipe out scores of blacks. If blacks forsook nonviolence, King alleged, 'Mississippi injustice would not be exposed and the moral issues would be obscured'.[47] When Carmichael voiced the view of black militants who wished to exclude whites from the march, King retorted that to reject whites would be a 'shameful repudiation' of those who had 'suffered, bled and died in the cause of racial justice'.[48] People of conscience, regardless of race, should be recruited for the movement. After King threatened to withdraw unless the march was interracial, Carmichael and McKissick relented, recognizing the importance of King's participation, but differences in points of view would not be reconciled.

The following day, King, McKissick and Carmichael issued a manifesto, characterizing the Freedom March as 'a massive public indictment and protest of the failure of American society, the Government of the United States, and the state of Mississippi to "fulfill these rights"'.[49] The manifesto also appealed to President Johnson to dispatch federal voting examiners to Mississippi to protect the right of blacks to vote, and requested that the federal government endorse A. Philip Randolph's $185 billion Freedom Budget for the benefit of all Americans in need. Wilkins and Young refused to sign the manifesto, alleging that its criticism of the federal government would jeopardize passage of the pending Civil Rights Bill. King signed the manifesto, thus siding with Carmichael and McKissick. Significantly, although he disagreed with the emerging black radicals on the issues of nonviolence and white participation in the movement, he refused to repudiate them.

The march resumed, without Wilkins and Young, who returned to New York City. After several days, the marchers reached Greenwood, Mississippi, where SNCC had its greatest influence in the South, having spearheaded the voter registration drive that evolved into the Mississippi Freedom Summer. Meanwhile, King had to rush to Chicago after a riot erupted in the Puerto Rican section of the city on 12 June, threatening SCLC's nonviolent campaign. Back in Greenwood, Carmichael was arrested for attempting to erect a tent on the grounds of a black school. Released shortly after, he declared to a huge rally: 'This is the twenty-seventh time I have been arrested, and I ain't going to jail no more'.[50] Sensing the mood of the crowd, he continued: 'The only way we gonna stop them white men from whuppin' us is to take over. We been saying freedom for six years and we ain't got nothin'.[51] 'What we gonna start saying now is Black Power!' When SNCC's Willie Ricks ascended the platform and shouted, 'What do you want?', the crowd bellowed: 'Black Power!' Ricks repeated the question again and again, and the crowd broke into a chant: 'Black Power! Black Power!'[52]

The cry marked the birth of a new slogan within the civil rights movement, reflecting the mood of many young blacks whose bitterness against the white establishment had been intensified over the past few years. Though the phrase became nationally known in the summer of 1966, it had been used earlier by Richard Wright, referring to the anti-colonialist movement in Africa after the Second World War; and by Adam Clayton Powell, Jr. Even white analyst Charles E. Silberman, in *Crisis in Black and White* (1964), concluded that 'the principal solution to the problem of Negro personality and identity is the acquisition of power: political, social, and economic'.[53]

The basic ideas of Black Power had been expressed by Malcolm X, first as a minister for the black Muslims, and then, after his separation from the Muslims in 1964, as founder of the Organization of Afro-American Unity. Until his murder in Harlem on 21 February 1965, Malcolm was the nation's foremost spokesman of black pride and separatism, advocating that blacks should control the politics and the economy of their own communities. Malcolm, who has been called the 'ideological father of the Black Power movement', gained national attention by attacking the nonviolent method as impotent, and charging that racism was inherent in capitalism.[54] When *The Autobiography of Malcolm X* was published posthumously in 1965, it became a source of ideas and inspiration to young black militants who had grown disenchanted with the American system.

No one articulated the rage of ghetto blacks in the 1960s better than Malcolm. While King spoke of a nonviolent civil rights revolution, Malcolm proclaimed: 'There's no such thing as a nonviolent revolution'.[55] While King was willing to work within the system, compromising with the white establishment when necessary, Malcolm was adamant: 'Revolution is bloody, revolution is hostile, revolution knows no compromise, revolution overturns and destroys everything that gets in its way'.[56] While King participated in the March on Washington, Malcolm denounced it as 'a sellout'.[57] While King called upon the nation to fulfil the promise embodied in the American Dream, Malcolm declared: 'I don't see any American dream; I see an American nightmare'.[58] While King defended nonviolence on the grounds that the means must be as moral as the goals, Malcolm insisted: 'Our goal is complete freedom, complete justice, complete equality, by any means necessary'.[59]

When Black Power became a major issue during the Meredith March, the media seized upon the slogan, focusing attention upon its volatile aspects, and propelling young Stokely Carmichael into prominence. To many white Americans, Black Power conjured up images of Watts in flames. King was concerned that the differences which had surfaced during the Meredith March would destroy the unity of the civil rights movement. As proponents of Black Power began to rival those who cried Freedom Now, the nonviolent method and goal of integration were on trial.

Returning to Mississippi from Chicago in June 1966, King saw the urgency of discussing the implications of Black Power before continuing with the Meredith March. He therefore asked Carmichael and McKissick to meet with him at a small Catholic parish house in Yazoo City, Mississippi. King was not opposed to what he considered to be the main goal of Black Power – self-determination for black Americans by means of consolidating their economic and political resources. As he later conceded, there were certain 'positive aspects of Black Power, which are compatible with what we have sought to do in the civil rights movement all along without the slogan'.[60] Nevertheless, he believed that the violent connotation of the Black Power slogan would be counter-productive. Carmichael argued that, like the nation's various ethnic groups, blacks would progress only by attaining economic and political power. Though King agreed, he insisted that Italian, Jewish and Irish immigrants had attained such power in America not by a threatening slogan, but through 'group unity' and 'creative endeavor'. Black Americans would attain 'legitimate' power 'through a program, not merely through a slogan'.[61] When Carmichael and McKissick pointed out the need for a slogan as a rallying cry, King retorted: 'But why have one that would confuse our allies, isolate the Negro community and give many prejudiced whites, who might otherwise be ashamed of their anti-Negro feeling, a ready excuse for self-justification?' King suggested using 'black consciousness' or 'black equality' as alternative slogans without the violent connotation of Black Power.[62]

After five tense hours, the Yazoo conference ended with a compromise. As an outward show of unity, it was agreed that for the remainder of the pilgrimage to Jackson, neither 'Black Power' nor 'Freedom Now' would be chanted. Carmichael admitted that he had deliberately used King to attain 'a national forum', and force him 'to take a stand for Black Power'. King laughed in response: 'I have been used before. One more time won't hurt'.[63] But King was concerned. The nonviolent method had been successful largely because it was able to use the media to throw a spotlight on white racist brutality in the South. Because Carmichael had introduced the issue of Black Power, King told a reporter, 'we didn't get to emphasize the evils of Mississippi and the need for the 1966 Civil Rights Act'.[64] With the media now directing national attention to the new slogan, the civil rights movement would lose much support.

During the final week of the Freedom March, violence erupted. On 22 June, King led a group of about 250 marchers on a detour to Philadelphia, Mississippi, near where civil rights workers James Chaney, Andrew Goodman and Michael Schwerner had been slain two years before. King intended to hold a memorial service for the three civil rights martyrs at the local courthouse. When they arrived, the marchers were attacked by angry whites with clubs. Police, commanded by Sheriff Lawrence Rainey and Chief Deputy Cecil Price – both still under indictment for the murder of the three martyrs – stood by until the marchers resorted to violence in self-defence. Vowing to return to Philadelphia within a few days, King telegraphed President Johnson, appealing for federal marshalls to protect the marchers. The President refused to comply. Instead, King was informed by a presidential aide that the Mississippi highway police would provide the necessary protection. The federal government once more chose to sacrifice civil rights to an unjust social order.

On 23 June, the marchers, numbering by then about 2000, arrived in Canton, Mississippi. After defying an order not to pitch tents on the grounds of a black elementary school, they were attacked by police with clubs and tear gas. King and McKissick managed to lead the battered marchers off to a nearby black church. Veterans of King's campaigns compared the incident to 'Bloody Sunday' in Selma the year before. The silence of the Johnson Administration worried King: 'The government has got to give me some victories if I'm gonna keep people nonviolent', he confided to journalist Paul Good. 'I know I'm gonna stay nonviolent no matter what happens. But a lot of people are getting hurt and bitter, and they can't see it that way any more'.[65] King again wired the White House, appealing for federal intervention, but the President continued his silence. When a delegation of clergymen visited Attorney General Katzenbach to protest the violence in Mississippi, he responded that the marchers were responsible because they had not only refused three alternative campsites, but they had also 'trespassed' on the school grounds. Such rebuffs made the Black Power slogan more appealing.

On 24 June, King returned to Philadelphia with some 300 nonviolent marchers and conducted the memorial service that had been interrupted by violence two days before. When Sheriff Rainey told King that he was forbidden to climb the courthouse steps to pray, he responded boldly: 'You're the one who had Schwerner and the other fellows in jail'. After Rainey boasted that he was, King looked for a moment at the hostile crowd of whites who had gathered around the courthouse. Then, defying the Sheriff's order, he knelt with Ralph Abernathy on the courthouse steps and, before praying, muttered: 'I believe that the murderers are somewhere around me at this moment'.[66] After praying, King and Abernathy led the marchers out of Philadelphia and back to the route of the March.

On Sunday, 27 June, after three weeks on the road, the marchers finally arrived at the State Capitol in Jackson. Hundreds of National Guardsmen surrounded the square for security. King's wife Coretta, along with James Meredith, who had sufficiently recovered from his wounds, joined the procession to the statehouse, while a band played 'When the Saints Go Marching In'. Also present was a group of celebrities, including Marlon Brando, Burt Lancaster and Dick Gregory. The success of the march was evident, for some 10 000 blacks had participated, and about 4000 Mississippi blacks in towns along the route had registered to vote. But few whites were present for the final festivities, and the cry for 'Black Power' dominated. King, Carmichael and McKissick braved the stifling heat to address the crowd, estimated at 15 000. SNCC militants made sure that NAACP leaders were forbidden to speak. Carmichael called upon blacks to 'build a power base . . . so strong that we will bring [whites] to their knees every time they mess with us'.[67] McKissick proclaimed to the cheering blacks: '1966 shall be remembered as the year we left our imposed status as Negroes and became *Black Men*. . . . 1966 is the year of the concept of Black Power'.[68] King told the crowd that he still hoped that his dream would be fulfilled, and that 'one day, right here in this state of Mississippi, justice will become a reality for all'.[69] But King's words, which had moved so many in the past, now seemed to have a hollow ring.

The Meredith Freedom March had exposed a deep rift within the civil rights movement between SCLC, NAACP, and the National Urban League – who advocated nonviolence and integration – and the black radicals of SNCC and CORE – who advocated violence and separatism. As SCLC's Bernard Lee told *The Reporter*: 'We've learned a lesson from this March. We can't work with the SNCC, or for that matter with CORE either'.[70]

Though never clearly defined, Black Power stirred considerable controversy. Roy Wilkins of the NAACP, and Whitney Young of the National Urban League would soon lead their organizations in denouncing the phrase. 'No matter how endlessly they try to explain it', Roy Wilkins told the 1500 delegates present at the annual NAACP convention in Los Angeles on 5 July 1966, 'the term "black power" means anti-white power. . . . It has to mean separatism. . . . It is a reverse Ku Klux Klan. . . . Black power can mean in the end only black death. . . . We of the NAACP will have none of this'.[71] The following day, Vice President Hubert Humphrey addressed the NAACP convention and warned against embracing 'the dogma of the oppressors – the notion that somehow a person's skin color determines his worthiness or unworthiness'. He concluded: 'We must reject calls for racism, whether they come from a throat that is white or one that is black'.[72] In a speech to the annual convention of the National Urban League, held in Philadelphia, from 31 July to 4 August, Executive Director Whitney Young attacked 'Black Power' as meaning 'all things to all men', and reaffirmed the League's commitment to biracial cooperation, 'an absolute necessity . . . to the success of the movement'.[73] According to Bayard Rustin, Black Power was 'positively harmful', isolating the black community with its doctrine of separatism, encouraging the growth of white racism, and undermining the liberal-labour-civil rights coalition necessary to achieve social justice.[74] New York *Post* columnist James Wechsler saw the emergence of Black Power as a 'national tragedy'. Writing in the December issue of *The Progressive*, he lamented: 'The "killers of the dream" are on the offensive . . . the evidence is unescapable that the cause of civil rights is floundering, all the visions of the Freedom Movement are imperiled, and some deeply dedicated men are helping to set the stage for the destruction of the noblest cause of our time'.[75]

V

Following the Jackson rally, a weary King returned to Chicago where, despite weeks of protests, little progress had been made and tension within the city's ghettos continued to grow. SCLC therefore decided to apply more militant nonviolent tactics. King assembled his staff and called for a coalition of blacks, labour unions, churches and liberal groups to make 'demands greater than Chicago is willing to give . . . so that direct action will become necessary'.[76] Only by forcing Daley and the city administration into opposing what were obviously fair demands could Chicago's injustices be effectively dramatized. As in the Birmingham and Selma campaigns, a crisis must be provoked, so that 'the federal government will be forced to act'.[77] King also called for massive civil disobedience to transform Chicago into 'a just and open city'.[78] To inaugurate this new, more militant phase of the campaign, he announced a huge rally for Sunday, 10 July, at Soldiers Field. 'Freedom Sunday', it was hoped, would attract 100 000 protesters.

Freedom Sunday was a disappointment, for only about half of the 85 000 seats in Soldiers Field were filled. As David Lewis points out, the rally was poorly-timed. To cause a confrontation, a massive protest should have taken place not on a Sunday afternoon, but on a weekday, when thousands of nonviolent protesters could have filled the streets, disrupting traffic, business and municipal buildings.[79] With the temperature at 98 degrees, King addressed the crowd, which included some members of Chicago's youth gangs bearing signs that read 'Black Power'. Roman Catholic Archbishop John P. Cody of Chicago, head of the nation's largest archdiocese, sent a message of support calling for open housing and an end to 'the blight and disgrace of our slums'.[80] King explained the need for direct action in Chicago, since 'freedom is never voluntarily granted by the oppressor. It must be demanded by the oppressed'.[81] Nevertheless, he insisted that the protest must remain nonviolent. He urged blacks to 'fill the jails' of Chicago, if necessary, in order to eradicate slums and eliminate discrimination in city housing, schools and employment. At the conclusion of the rally, about 5000 people followed King from Soldiers Field on a three mile march to City Hall to present the Chicago Movement's demands to Mayor Daley.

Arriving at City Hall, King was not surprised to find the Mayor absent. In a symbolic gesture emulating his sixteenth-century namesake, Martin Luther – who ignited the Reformation by nailing his 95 Theses to the door of the Church at Wittenberg – King posted the Movement's demands on the door of City Hall as some 35 000 people cheered. The demands included the adoption by the city of an immediate desegregation programme; an end to discriminatory practices by real estate agents, banks and loan associations; construction of low-cost public housing throughout the city; increased black employment; and a civilian review board to monitor the police department. But the 'primary target', King affirmed, remained open housing.[82] On the following day, he presented the Movement's demands personally to Daley at City Hall, but the Major rejected them, alleging that Chicago had already adopted a 'massive' programme to end slums.

Freedom Sunday had come, the Chicago Movement had attracted much publicity, but no crisis had been provoked. The poor turnout at Soldiers Field indicated that the Movement had not inspired the black masses. Meanwhile, conditions in the city further deteriorated. On Tuesday, 12 July, a riot occurred in the West Side ghetto. When police shut off fire hydrants illegally turned on by black children to escape the heat, roving black teenagers, most of them unemployed gang members, threw stones and Molotov cocktails at police cars, looted white businesses and shot at police from slum buildings. After two days of rioting, during which King and his aides pleaded unsuccessfully with young blacks to adopt nonviolence, two people had been killed, 56 injured and 282 jailed, in addition to much property damage. The violence finally ended on the third day when 4000 National Guardsmen, sent by Governor Kerner on request from Mayor Daley, restored order.

The next day, newspaper headlines read: 'Mayor Blames King'. Daley accused SCLC of inciting young blacks to riot by showing them films of the destruction in Watts the year before. On the contrary, SCLC responded, their intention had been to show that rioting was inexpedient, destroying black neighbourhoods. The youth gangs, inspired by the new Black Power slogan, were a problem to King and SCLC. Ghetto residents were much more difficult to instruct in the discipline of nonviolence than church-oriented Southern blacks. Whenever blacks engaged in violence, the nonviolent movement was deprived of the moral edge that had been instrumental to its success in the South. King met for five hours with leaders of three Chicago youth gangs responsible for the West Side riot – the Cobras, the Vice Lords and the Roman Saints – and convinced them to try nonviolence. They were receptive because King had managed to persuade Daley to improve certain ghetto conditions. At a joint press conference, King and the Mayor announced that spray nozzles would be attached to West Side fire hydrants, swimming pools and other recreational facilities would be constructed, and a citizens committee would be appointed to investigate ways to improve the relationship between police and the black community. Daley had won a brief peace.

But these changes did nothing to eradicate slums and poverty in Chicago. After weeks of sparring with the Daley machine, King and the Chicago Movement shifted to another front, hoping finally to provoke the crisis that would coerce further concessions from the city authorities. Demonstrations would be moved from the ghettos to the white communities – Gage Park, Bogan, Belmont-Cragin, South Deering and Marquette Park – populated by white ethnic (Polish, Irish, Italian and Lithuanian), blue-collar workers who comprised the bulk of the Chicago suburban population. Although unaffected by the downtown marches, whites could not ignore protests in their own neighbourhoods. Responding to criticism that the suburban protests would provoke white violence, King explained that black ghetto residents were already living under an oppressive covert violence that must be revealed to the nation. 'We do not seek to precipitate violence', he insisted. 'However, we are aware that the existence of injustice in society is the existence of violence. We feel we must constantly expose this evil, even if it brings violence upon us'.[83] King and SCLC again faced the difficult challenge of fomenting white racist violence while preventing black retaliatory violence. Their strategy would succeed only if blacks were portrayed by the media as victims rather than perpetrators of violence.

On Friday, 5 August, King led 600 demonstrators out of the ghetto to the Gage Park district of Chicago's Southwest Side. Advance publicity had drawn an angry crowd of over a thousand white spectators, waving Confederate flags and screaming 'Nigger go home!', 'We hate Niggers!' 'We want Martin Luther Coon!' and 'Kill the Niggers!' Within the jeering crowd were American Nazi Party chief George Lincoln Rockwell and some white-robed Klan members. In the presence of journalists and television cameras, enraged whites bombarded the protesters with a volley of rocks. Struck on the side of the head, King stumbled to the ground, but resumed marching after being assisted by his aides. 'I've been in many demonstrations all across the South', he later told the press, 'but I can say that I have never seen – even in Mississippi and Alabama – mobs as hostile and hate-filled as I've seen in Chicago'.[84] Over the next two weeks, more marches to the white suburbs occurred as the Chicago Movement continued to escalate the protest. On Sunday, 7 August, Al Raby, James Bevel and Jesse Jackson led a march to the Belmont-Cragin district on the city's

Northwest Side. A crowd of between 3000 and 5000, shouting 'White Power!', stoned the marchers until some 600 policemen managed to restore order. That evening, Chicagoans were shocked when they saw scenes on television of police clubbing whites who had attempted to halt the march. The Movement had succeeded in exposing the city's white racism and housing injustices.

In turning their focus to open housing, King and SCLC had ventured into the most controversial area of civil rights. Whites feared that a strong open-housing law would pave the way for a mass exodus of blacks to the suburbs, causing property values to plummet and living conditions to deteriorate. In the South, the nonviolent movement was assisted by the fact that its demands were manifestly in accord with the United States Constitution and the American ideals of individual liberty and equal rights. But when the black protest movement expanded its goals to include not only constitutional rights, but also the economic and social conditions that make the full exercise of freedom possible, it lost much support. Northern white liberals and moderates, who had supported integrated public schools and facilities, in addition to black suffrage, refused to accept that blacks also had rights to decent housing, jobs and health care. The demands of black Americans conflicted with the self-interest of white Americans. 'Many people who marched on Washington in 1963 for Negro dignity', Bayard Rustin observed, 'are not prepared to have their taxes raised to make economic dignity possible'.[85]

Nevertheless, blacks could not be integrated into American society on the basis of full equality unless the nation was willing to pay a substantial price: the redistribution of political and economic power. As King pointed out in his 1966 annual report on the progress of civil rights for *The Nation*, the low wages of blacks and depressed ghetto living conditions were a 'structural part of the economy'. As blacks impinge upon 'financial privilege' and progress toward a 'fundamental alteration of their lives', stubborn resistance is inevitable, since 'the reality of equality will require extensive adjustments in the way of life of the white majority'.[86]

VI

Confronted by the prospect of increasingly dangerous demonstrations, Mayor Daley desperately sought a means to crush the campaign. If police continued their usual brutality toward black protesters, the city risked a bloodbath; on the other hand, if the police restrained the angry whites who attempted to prevent the marches, the Mayor might suffer in the forthcoming November elections. On 17 August, a ten-hour meeting at the St James Episcopal Church between the Chicago Movement and representatives of the city, along with real estate officials, failed to reach an open-housing accord. The next day, King travelled to Washington to participate in a 'Meet the Press' television panel discussion with James Meredith, Stokely Carmichael and Carl Rowan. Questioned about the continuing open-housing demonstrations in Chicago, King responded: 'People all over will adjust to living next door to a Negro once they know it has to be done'.[87]

The morning of 19 August, Daley announced on television that the city would apply at the Cook County Circuit Court for a temporary injunction against the marches. According to lawyers for the city, they constituted a 'clear and present danger' of riot. Following a hearing, Judge Cornelius J. Harrington ruled against the Chicago Movement. Marches, to consist of no more than 500 protesters, were limited to one per day; and no marches were permitted at night or during the hours between 7.30 and 9 a.m. and 4.40 and 6 p.m. Moreover, police must be informed of the time and place of each demonstration at least 24 hours in advance. Marches were therefore prohibited during the Chicago rush-hour, when they would be most effective. King responded by calling the injunction 'unjust, illegal, and unconstitutional'.[88] After first declaring that the Movement would defy the order, putting thousands of nonviolent protesters in the streets, King subsequently followed the advice of his attorneys to fight the injunction in court.

Stalemated by the injunction, the Chicago campaign seemed doomed. 'We're not hopeful', expressed a worried Andrew Young. 'We haven't been able to put on enough pressure yet. In Birmingham and Selma we almost needed martial law before we got anywhere'.[89] To save the campaign, some means was needed to mount a final, all-out nonviolent offensive within the legal limits set by the court order. On 21 August, King announced that he would lead a massive march the following Sunday into the all-white suburb of Cicero, a town of 70 000 people outside Cook County and hence beyond the jurisdiction of the injunction. The march, one of King's boldest proposals, would be more provocative and dangerous than either the Children's Crusade of the Birmingham campaign or the 1965 march from Selma to Montgomery. Cicero, the former residence of gangster Al Capone, was the most racist community in the Chicago area. In 1951, Governor Adlai Stevenson sent 4000 National Guardsmen to Cicero when whites rioted to prevent a black family from integrating the neighbourhood. In May 1966, black teenager Jerome Huey was beaten to death by white youths after seeking employment there. A march to Cicero would most likely provoke brutal white violence, creating a crisis that neither Mayor Daley nor the federal government could afford to ignore.

As anticipated, the proposed Cicero march alarmed the opposition. Cook County Sheriff Richard B. Ogilvie pleaded with King to call off the march. City Hall and Archbishop Cody also implored King to change his mind, while Governor Kerner placed the National Guard on alert. But, with the nation's attention fixed on Cicero, King was adamant. 'No one is going to turn me around at this point', he proclaimed to a crowd at New Liberty Baptist Church. Having received the support of the CCCO, in addition to the Black Power advocates within SNCC and CORE, King predicted that the demonstration would be the 'biggest ever'.[90]

The prospect of a bloody confrontation in Cicero forced the Daley machine to re-open negotiations, this time in good faith. On 26 August, two days prior to the scheduled Cicero march, King and leaders of the Chicago Movement met at the Palmer House with Daley and members of the Chicago Real Estate Board, the Chicago Housing Authority, and the business community, and reached a 'Summit Agreement'. Among the points unanimously accepted were: the Chicago Real Estate Board would support open-housing legislation; the licences of real estate brokers who violated the fair-housing ordinance would be suspended or revoked; the Commission on Human Relations would require real estate brokers to post a summary of Chicago's policy on open housing, and the city would augment its efforts to monitor housing conditions and support state housing legislation; the Chicago Housing Authority would provide for a beneficial distribution of housing projects; the Department of Urban Renewal would report cases of discrimination to the Commission on Human Relations and assist families in relocating to all areas of the city; savings and bankers' associations would lend mortgage money to qualified families, regardless of race; Chicago's major commercial, industrial, labour and municipal organizations would pledge to promote fair housing. Finally, a permanent body, the Leadership Council for Metropolitan Open Housing, would be established, consisting of the principal leadership organizations in Chicago, to provide education and direction for the fulfilment of the entire agreement. After months of demonstrations, nonviolence appeared to have passed the difficult test in Chicago.

VII

The Summit Agreement initially stirred much enthusiasm. According to the *Chicago Tribune*: 'The total eradication of housing discrimination has been made possible'.[91] The *Christian Century* celebrated the achievement with an article entitled, 'Still King'.[92] *Newsweek* magazine characterized the Chicago campaign as a 'solid vindication of Southern style nonviolent protest in a Northern city'.[93] Even Mayor Daley admitted that the agreement marked a 'great day' for the city, an ironic assessment coming from the man who had sought to undermine the Chicago Movement from the beginning. According to King: 'Never before have such far-reaching and creative commitments been made and programs adopted and pledged to achieve open housing in a community'. Neverthless, he cautioned, the agreement was merely 'an important first step in a 1000 mile journey'.[94] As an act of conciliation, King 'deferred' the Cicero march, but he vowed to return and lead the demonstration if the city failed to implement the agreement.

Yet there were critical voices amid the chorus of praise for the Summit Agreement. After all, some black leaders warned, it was merely a series of verbal 'promises', extracted under extreme duress, and without the force of law. Whether these promises would be fulfilled remained to be seen. Members of SNCC and CORE, distrustful of the white establishment, predictably attacked the agreement as a 'sellout'. Chester Robinson, executive director of the West Side Organization, denounced the agreement as 'a lot of words that give us nothing specific we can undertake. We want it to say: apartments should be painted once a year; community people should have jobs in their community. . . . The situation is just pathetic. We're sick and tired of middle class people telling us what we want. And we're gonna march in Cicero on Sunday. We have the right'.[95] SNCC's Monroe Sharp was emphatic: 'We reject the terms of the agreement that Martin Luther King made. The rank and file Negro is a new breed of cat who rejects this'.[96] In defiance of the agreement, some 200 SNCC and CORE militants made an anticlimactic march to Cicero on 4 September, protected by nearly 3000 National Guardsmen. Greeted by vicious white mobs, the marchers were forced to retreat under a barrage of bottles and rocks.

The criticisms by black militants were not without merit. Even if carried out, the housing agreement promised no substantial change in the lives of the city's nearly one million ghetto residents, who were in desperate need of jobs and quality education, and lacked the economic resources to move to better neighbourhoods. Shortly after the agreement was announced, King assessed it frankly at a 'Victory Rally' in a West Side Baptist church. 'Let's face the fact', he conceded, 'most of us are going to be living in the ghetto five, ten years from now. . . . Morally, we ought to have what we say in the slogan "Freedom Now." But it all doesn't come now. That's a sad fact of life you have to live with'.[97] The nation's slums would not be eradicated simply by marching, but by a massive federal anti-poverty programme. As long as America was involved in the Vietnam War, funds for such a programme would be absorbed and diverted. Whereas in 1963, King proclaimed his dream at the March on Washington and encouraged blacks to demand 'Freedom Now', in 1966, sobered by his Chicago experience, he admitted that fulfilment of the dream would have to be postponed.

Chicago exposed the limitations of the nonviolent method in the North. None of their previous campaigns had prepared King and SCLC for the difficulties they faced in Chicago. Daley proved to be their most formidable opponent, a consummate politician who managed to pose as a ghetto reformer. CCCO president Al Raby later confessed: 'I don't think that Martin or any of us realized what a tough town this is and how strong the Democratic organization is. For us, it had to be a learning experience in understanding the power structure'.[98] According to Louis Lomax: 'Chicago was a failure, not for Martin himself, but for his Christian, nonviolent attack upon complex socio-economic problems. Chicago was the final evidence that *The System* which controls the ghetto would not yield power to the nonviolent and the civilized'.[99]

For seven months, the Chicago Movement had met the Daley machine in dramatic confrontation; but when the dust settled and the initial enthusiasm over the promises embodied in the Summit Agreement dissipated, it became evident that the conditions in Chicago's slums would remain substantially the same. Agreements and compromises alone, without strict legal enforcement, are usually ineffectual. In the months immediately following the campaign, the open-housing agreement collapsed because the Daley administration would not implement it, and the Chicago Movement was unable to force it to do so. As Raby later noted: 'Movements, by their nature, are temporary. They have the capacity to bring people to the table, but they don't have the capacity to institutionally follow and monitor and keep other institutions accountable'.[100] The Chicago open-housing agreement thus became another in the long list of unfulfilled promises to rectify racial injustice in America.

The violence that erupted not only in Chicago, but in other Northern cities as well, contributed to the defeat of the 1966 open-housing bill, designed to eliminate discrimination in the sale or rental of all housing. According to Senate Majority Leader Mike Mansfield, the housing bill was defeated by the 'rioting, marches, shootings and inflammatory statements which have characterized this simmering summer'.[101] As the ghettos reverberated with cries for 'Black Power', white sympathy for the black cause was supplanted by fear. Democratic leaders throughout the nation feared a mass defection of white voters from the party in both the cities and the suburbs. As President Johnson later stated: 'The open housing issue had become a Democratic liability'.[102] Vitiated by amendments, the bill was stalled by a Southern filibuster in the Senate, and died before coming to a floor vote. Political analysts Brink and Harris concluded that 'it was the greatest single defeat suffered by the Negroes in their long, hard climb since 1964'. King aptly characterized the prevailing pessimism: 'It surely heralds darker days for this era of social discontent'.[103]

The disappointing Chicago campaign did produce some positive results. The Daley machine had been coerced to the bargaining table. As King explained: 'The whole power structure was forced by the power of the nonviolent movement to sit down and negotiate and capitulate and make concessions that have never been made before'.[104] Although the housing agreement was little more than a pledge of goodwill, David Lewis pointed out that it was 'considerably more comprehensive . . . than any of Martin's previous accords. . . . If Birmingham was a triumph, then Chicago certainly ought not to have been assessed as a virtual rout'.[105] To deal with the problems of poverty and unemployment highlighted by the campaign, Operation Breadbasket, the economic arm of SCLC, was instituted in Chicago in 1966 under the stewardship of Jesse Jackson. Founded in Atlanta in 1962, Operation Breadbasket had succeeded in several Southern states by boycotting white businesses to compel them to employ blacks. After Jackson achieved much success in attaining jobs for blacks in Chicago by means of the boycott, Operation Breadbasket was established in other cities throughout the nation.

Although Congress again did not pass open-housing legislation in 1967, the Chicago campaign had forced the nation to face the deeply rooted problems of the urban slums, preparing the way for the enactment of the Fair Housing Act of 1968, which was stronger than the bill that had died in Congress 18 months before. The Housing Act of 1968 was passed on 10 April, six days after the assassination of King.

10

King Takes a Radical Stand, 1967–8

I

During the final year and a half of his life, King challenged the nation to undertake radical reforms. Stiffening white resistance to black equality, in addition to the spreading ghetto riots and the escalating Vietnam conflict, had created the greatest crisis in America since the Civil War. King saw these developments as symptoms of a moral sickness afflicting the nation that could be remedied only by radical changes in its political, social and economic structure. In an interview with journalist David Halberstam in 1967, he explained his recent political transformation: 'For years I labored with the idea of reforming the existing institutions of society, a little change here, a little change there. Now I feel quite differently. I think you've got to have a reconstruction of the entire society, a revolution of values'.[1] King spoke of the possible nationalization of certain industries, a guaranteed annual income, a review of foreign investments and programmes to revitalize the cities. In the ensuing months, King would promote radical proposals such as these while the broad coalition of support he had depended upon in the past continued to dwindle. The Chicago campaign and the 'white backlash' clearly revealed that racism was not confined to the South, but was deeply ingrained in all aspects of American life. 'Most Americans', King lamented, 'are unconscious racists'.[2]

The Vietnam War was to a great extent responsible for King's radical stand. By 1967, Vietnam had supplanted civil rights as the major issue confronting the nation, and hundreds of young activists were diverted from the black freedom struggle to protests against the war. Refusing to ignore what he regarded as an injustice and the most serious threat to world peace, King emerged as one of the most prominent spokesmen of the anti-war movement. Though he had publicly opposed the war since 1965, he delivered his first speech devoted entirely to Vietnam at a conference in Los Angeles sponsored by *The Nation* on 25 February 1967. Attacking American foreign policy as 'supporting a new form of colonialism', he argued that 'we are presently moving down a dead-end road that can only lead to national disaster'. He concluded: 'We must combine the fervor of the civil rights movement with the peace movement. We must demonstrate, teach, and preach until the very foundations of our nation are shaken'.[3] At a rally in the Chicago Coliseum on 25 March, King repeated his call to unite the civil rights and peace movements. Within a week, his stand was approved by the directors of SCLC, who condemned the war as 'morally and politically unjust'.[4] In an interview on 2 April with John Herbers of the *New York Times*, King said that if the war continued to escalate, 'it may be necessary to engage in civil disobedience to further arouse the conscience of the nation'.[5]

King's most famous denunciation of the war occurred at Riverside Church in New York City on 4 April 1967, when he was the principal speaker at a convocation sponsored by Clergy and Laymen Concerned About Vietnam. Delivered to a crowd of 3000, King's speech was widely covered by the news media. 'A time comes when silence is betrayal', he began. Alleging that the war was symptomatic of a 'malady within the American spirit', King pulled no punches, charging that the United States government was 'the greatest purveyor of violence in the world today'. He then surveyed the background to the war: the proclamation of Vietnamese independence under the leadership of Ho Chi Minh in 1945; the refusal of the United States to either recognize Vietnam's independence or support its war against French colonialism; the United States' endorsement of the repressive regime of 'one of the most vicious modern dictators', Premier Diem in South Vietnam and the failure of the United States to honour the 1954 Geneva accords, conspiring with Diem to prevent an election that would have established Ho Chi Minh as leader of a united Vietnam. After the fall of Diem, increasing numbers of American troops buttressed a series of corrupt military dictatorships in South Vietnam, encountering staunch resistance from the insurgent National Liberation Front or Viet Cong. Pointing to the devastating effect of the war upon the Vietnamese people – the destruction of their land, villages and families – King observed: 'They must see Americans as strange liberators'.

To end the tragic war and bring justice to a victimized people,

King proposed that the United States declare a unilateral cease-fire, halt the bombing of Vietnam, recognize the right of the National Liberation Front to participate in peace talks and in any future Vietnamese government and establish a date for the withdrawal of all foreign troops from Vietnam, consistent with the Geneva accords. 'Somehow this madness must cease', King implored. 'We must stop now . . . . I speak as an American to the leaders of my own nation. The great initiative in this war is ours. The initiative to stop it must be ours'.

Expanding his indictment of American foreign policy beyond Vietnam, King charged that the United States was 'on the wrong side of a world revolution' against exploitation and oppression in Asia, Africa and South America. The nation was more interested in protecting its foreign investments than in promoting international peace and justice. If America did not radically alter its policies, taking the side of justice, he warned, humanity would continue headlong into war and destruction. In a world threatened by nuclear holocaust, King believed that the decision had to be made: either 'nonviolent coexistence or violent co-annihilation'. He explained that before America could take an international role in defeating the triple evils of 'racism, materialism, and militarism', the nation had to undergo a 'radical revolution of values', substituting a 'person-oriented' society for a 'thing-oriented' society. Such a revolution would undermine the appeal of communism, which he regarded as a symptom of the failure of capitalism. The best defence against communism, King proclaimed, is not violent warfare, but the removal of the poverty and injustice which provide fertile ground for its development.[6]

Later that April, King again criticized America's involvement in the war. At a press conference, he supported those whose conscience opposed military service. 'Honestly, if I had to confront this problem,' he confessed, 'I would be a conscientious objector'.[7] On 15 April, King was in New York City as the principal speaker for the 'Spring Mobilization to End the War in Vietnam', organized by SCLC's James Bevel, in which over 125 000 demonstrators marched from Central Park to the United Nations Plaza. Among the participants were Dr Benjamin Spock, Harry Belafonte, Stokely Carmichael and Floyd McKissick. At the conclusion of the protest, King inspired the huge crowd, attacking the war in a condensed version of his Riverside Church speech. Meanwhile, his wife Coretta, a pacifist since college and a member of the Women's

International League for Peace and Freedom, spoke to 60 000 people at an anti-war rally in San Francisco. In November 1967, King had an opportunity to re-state his arguments in a radio speech recorded for the Canadian Broadcasting Corporation, and later published as part of his book, *The Trumpet of Conscience*.

King's opposition to the war alienated many supporters of civil rights. In 1967, the majority of Americans, white and black, approved of the war. In fact, according to a Harris poll, only 25 per cent of all black Americans favoured King's anti-war stand.[8] Even civil rights leaders rebuked King. Roy Wilkins of the NAACP and Whitney Young of the National Urban League accused him publicly of hindering the cause of racial justice. On 12 April, the NAACP adopted a resolution declaring: 'To attempt to merge the civil rights movement with the peace movement . . . is, in our judgment, a serious tactical mistake. It will serve the cause neither of civil rights nor of peace'.[9] Prominent black Americans, including Massachusetts Senator Edward Brooke, Ralph Bunche of the United Nations and former athlete Jackie Robinson, concurred. But King was relentless. What his critics regarded as two separate issues, racism at home and the war abroad, he considered inseparable. 'I have worked too long now', he said in a television interview on 28 July 1967, 'and too hard to get rid of segregation in public accommodations to turn back to the point of segregating my moral concern. Justice is indivisible'.[10]

King was also severely criticized by the national press. The *Washington Post* condemned the Riverside Church speech as 'a grave injury' to the civil rights struggle, and concluded that King had 'diminished his usefulness to his cause, to his country, and to his people'.[11] A *Life* magazine editorial, entitled 'Dr. King's Disservice to His Cause', contended that King had exceeded his personal right to dissent by proposing a peace plan that was tantamount to 'abject surrender' in Vietnam. A *New York Times* editorial echoed the prevailing criticism, alleging that King's speech was 'a fusing of two public problems that are distinct and separate', and was therefore 'a disservice to both'.[12] In an article for *Reader's Digest*, 'Martin Luther King's Tragic Decision', black journalist Carl Rowan argued that the Riverside Church speech 'put a new strain and new burdens on the civil rights movement'. To the disadvantage of millions of impoverished black Americans, Rowan charged, King had not only lost the support of his friends in Congress, but he had also become '*persona non grata* to Lyndon

Johnson'. Rowan, convinced that King had fallen under Communist influence, also maintained that Americans of all races regarded as 'utterly irresponsible' King's urging young blacks to resist the draft. 'It is a tragic irony', Rowan concluded, 'that there should be any doubt about the Negro's loyalty to his country – especially doubt created by Martin Luther King, who has helped as much as any one man to make America truly the Negro's country, too'.[13]

But King remained true to his moral conviction that injustice anywhere is a threat to justice everywhere. He could not advocate nonviolence and civil rights at home and ignore violence and injustice abroad in Vietnam or any other country, especially when America was involved. A recipient of the Nobel Peace Prize, he felt a moral imperative to resist violence and speak out for the victims of poverty and injustice throughout the world.

II

While King denounced the Vietnam War and began his radical reassessment of America, racial tension increased throughout the nation. The summer of 1967 witnessed violent uprisings in more than a dozen cities as angry ghetto blacks revolted against a system that denied them an equal share in the nation's plenty. The worst violence occurred in Newark, New Jersey and Detroit, Michigan. During five days of rioting and shooting, 23 persons died in Newark. The Detroit riot was even more devastating, injuring more than 2000 persons and killing 43, 33 of them black. Infuriated blacks shouted 'Burn, baby, burn!', and H. Rap Brown, successor to Stokely Carmichael as SNCC chairman in 1967, announced that 'violence is as American as cherry pie'.[14] Brown later threatened: 'If America doesn't come around, we're going to burn America down'.[15]

On 28 July, President Johnson appointed a National Advisory Commission on Civil Disorders, chaired by Illinois Governor Otto Kerner, to investigate the causes of the riots and to propose means of preventing them in the future. The report of the Kerner Commission, issued on 1 March 1968, warned that the United States was 'moving towards two societies, one black, one white, separate and unequal'.[16] With surprising frankness, the commission singled out 'white racism' as the essential cause of 'the explosive mixture which has been accumulating in our cities since the end of World War II'.[17] For generations, the nation had perpetuated a system of racial injustice. 'What white Americans have never fully understood – but what the Negro can never forget – is that white society is deeply implicated in the ghetto. White institutions created it, white institutions maintain it, and white society condones it'.[18]

To eliminate the cause of the urban riots and halt the polarization of American society that threatened to destroy basic democratic values, the commission called for a massive federal programme to provide blacks with employment, education, housing and income supplementation: 'Only a commitment to national action on an unprecedented scale can shape a future compatible with the historical ideals of American society'.[19] One member of the commission, Oklahoma Senator Fred Harris, estimated that the cost of implementing these recommendations would be approximately $32 billion – about the same price as waging war in Vietnam for one year. The report concluded: 'It is time now to end the destruction and the violence, not only in the streets of the ghetto but in the lives of people'.[20] Nevertheless, the Johnson Administration, obsessed with pursuing the Vietnam War, chose not to act on the commission's recommendations, thus abandoning the pledge to eradicate poverty throughout the nation.

Meanwhile, Black Power revolutionaries were augmenting their attack upon America, inciting discontented ghetto blacks to join in a war against white society. Stokely Carmichael was among the most inflammatory, railing against the capitalist system. Travelling to Cuba in the summer of 1967, while American cities were in revolt, he said to a group of Third World revolutionaries: 'We have a common enemy. Our enemy is white Western imperialist society. Our struggle is to overthrow this system . . . . We are moving into open guerrilla warfare in the United States. We have no alternative but to use aggressive violence in order to own the land, houses, and stores inside our communities and control the politics of those communities'.[21] Visiting North Vietnam in August 1967, Carmichael declared at a public meeting in Hanoi: 'We are not reformists; we do not propose to bring about reforms, we do not want to form part of the government of the United States or the American system, we are revolutionaries, we want to change the American system'.[22] Needless to say, such volatile statements were captured by the press. In 1968, Carmichael became allied with the Black Panthers, extreme proponents of Black Power. Founded in Oakland, California in October 1966 by two young blacks, Huey P.

Newton and Bobby Seale, the Black Panther Party sought to combat police brutality in the ghettos by arming blacks for self defence. Applauding the urban riots as rebellions in the war for black liberation, the Panthers advocated a violent overthrow of American capitalism.

III

As the growing anguish of the ghettos and the anti-war protests plunged America deeper into domestic crisis, King sought to answer the challenge of Black Power in his book, *Where Do We Go From Here: Chaos or Community?*, published in 1967. While continuing to repudiate separatism and violence, King sympathized with those Black Power advocates who maintained that the American system was fundamentally flawed, and that resistance to the Vietnam War was part of the struggle against colonialism throughout the Third World. He condemned the most powerful nations of the West for refusing to take a stand against South Africa. He pointed out, moreover, that $700 million of American capital 'props up the system of apartheid', and that United States corporations controlled 'the life and destiny of Latin America'.[23] Reverting to ideas that he had expressed during the Meredith March in 1966, King agreed with the Black Power movement that 'the problem of transforming the ghetto is . . . a problem of power', and that blacks must 'amass political and economic strength' by using the ballot and pooling their financial resources 'to achieve their legitimate goals'.[24] He also endorsed Black Power's emphasis upon instilling racial pride. Instructed on their contributions to history and culture, black Americans would acquire a sense of dignity and worth, enabling them to overcome the cripppling psychological effects of institutional racism. King asserted: 'As long as the mind is enslaved the body can never be free'.[25]

At the same time, King insisted that the 'negative values' of Black Power precluded it from becoming the basic philosophy of the civil rights movement. Black Power was 'a nihilistic philosophy', devoid of a constructive programme and nourished by despair.[26] King regretted that many Black Power advocates quoted neither Gandhi nor Tolstoy as their Bible, but Frantz Fanon's *Wretched of the Earth*. Before his death in 1961 at the age of 31, Fanon, a black psychiatrist born in Martinique, was an articulate supporter of the

Algerian rebels in their war for independence from France. He preached that violence was a psychologically healthy means for colonized peoples to overcome oppression. According to Fanon: 'The colonized man finds his freedom in and through violence . . . . At the level of individuals, violence is a cleansing force. It frees the native from his inferiority complex and from his despair and inaction; it makes him fearless and restores his self-respect'.[27] Translated into English in 1965, Fanon's book inspired young radicals who had forsaken nonviolence and identified the black struggle in the United States with the liberation of oppressed peoples throughout the world.

King was convinced that those black Americans who advocated separatism and retaliatory violence had embarked upon a self-defeating course. While blacks must take pride in themselves and their culture, they cannot escape the fact that their 'destiny is tied up with the destiny of America'.[28] In a multi-racial society such as the United States, blacks cannot achieve their goals in isolation. The vast majority of blacks would continue to remain outside the mainstream of American life if they were to separate themselves politically and economically. Furthermore, King rejected aggressive violence as immoral and ineffective, for it 'destroys community and makes brotherhood impossible'.[29] The advantages of retaliatory violence are illusory. The ghetto riots of the previous few summers had devastated black neighbourhoods without improving the lives of the urban poor. In contrast, King pointed to the solid accomplishments of nonviolent protest, which defeated segregation and secured the right to vote in the South with minimum loss of life. 'Fewer people have been killed in ten years of nonviolent demonstrations across the South', he declared, 'than were killed in one night of rioting in Watts'.[30]

Nevertheless, King agreed that impoverished blacks could not attain substantial equality without radical changes in American society. While King was willing to work within the democratic system to transform the political, economic and social structure of the country, Carmichael and others advocated a violent overthrow of the government and the creation of two separate societies – one black, and one white. Whereas Black Power advocated mere violence and destruction, King called for an interracial coalition of liberal, labour and civil rights organizations to influence the federal government to initiate programmes to improve the living conditions of the poor.

Despite his arguments, King was still unable to convince Black Power militants that integration through nonviolent means should be the goal of the black freedom struggle. He was also disappointed by the critical reception of *Where Do We Go From Here?* within the white liberal community. In the *New York Review of Books*, journalist Andrew Kopkind wrote what amounted to an obituary for a fallen civil rights leader. 'The Movement is dead; the Revolution is unborn', he proclaimed. Confronting what he termed the 'irrelevancy' of King, Kopkind concluded that he 'has been outstripped by his times, overtaken by the events which he may have obliquely helped to produce but could not predict'. While one reviewer found King's analysis of Black Power 'possibly the most reasoned rejection of that concept by any major civil rights leader in the country', another reviewer indicated that King's 'rejection of black power seems more rhetorical than real'.[31]

IV

The events of the previous few years induced King to reflect on the ideas of the Social Gospel movement that he had absorbed at Crozer Theological Seminary. The goal of substantial equality for black Americans was a mainstay of his life. While a student, he was profoundly affected by Walter Rauschenbusch's *Christianity and the Social Crisis* (1907), which led him to conclude that 'any religion which professes to be concerned about the souls of men and is not concerned about the social and economic conditions that scar the soul, is a spiritually moribund religion'.[32] In his first book, *Stride Toward Freedom*, published in 1958, King wrote that from his youth he had been concerned about the gulf in American capitalist society between the rich and the poor, and the need for 'a better distribution of wealth'.[33] With the black freedom struggle having entered its human rights phase, King believed that economic injustice might be overcome by the same powerful nonviolent method that had overthrown legal segregation in the South.

King's final speeches and writings reveal his commitment to radical economic and social change. Addressing the tenth anniversary convention of the Southern Christian Leadership Conference in Atlanta, Georgia, on 16 August 1967, he told the audience that poverty in America raises 'questions about the economic system, about a broader distribution of wealth. When you ask that question, you begin to question the capitalistic economy . . . . We've got to begin to ask questions about the whole society . . . . One day we must come to see that an edifice which produces beggars needs restructuring'. Lest he be misunderstood, King added: 'I'm not talking about Communism. What I'm talking about is far beyond Communism'. SCLC must leave the convention, he concluded, bearing the following message: 'America, you must be born again!'[34] In 'A Testament of Hope', a posthumously published essay, King again argued that blacks had been deprived of equality because 'America is deeply racist and democracy is flawed economically and socially'. The black revolution, he insisted, exposed 'systemic rather than superficial flaws and suggests that radical reconstruction of society itself is the real issue to be faced'.[35]

In essence, King advocated neither capitalism nor communism, but Christian democratic socialism. Communism is flawed, he argued, because it rejects spiritualism, denies individual freedom and 'reduces men to a cog in the wheel of the state'. Capitalism is equally flawed because, when unrestrained, it allows the selfish few to exploit and deprive the many. 'The profit motive, when it is the sole basis of an economic system, encourages a cutthroat competition and selfish ambition that inspire men to be more I-centred than thou-centred'.[36] Neither capitalism nor communism fosters the 'Kingdom of Brotherhood'.[37] In contrast, democratic socialism, motivated by Christian values, can establish economic programmes to provide for the needs of all individuals, regardless of race. At a meeting at Frogmore, South Carolina, on 14 November 1966, King pointed to the example of Sweden, which had instituted free health care, eliminated poverty and unemployment and 'grappled with the problem of more equitable distribution of wealth'. Democratic socialism was also practised in Western Europe. King concluded that America too 'must move toward a democratic socialism'.[38]

King's proposals for substantial government intervention in the economy was not new to America. Ever since the Second World War, the United States has adopted modified socialist measures in the form of the welfare state. But most Americans shun the word 'socialism' because of its Marxist connotations. Indeed, except in private meetings, King himself avoided describing his philosophy as socialist. Nonetheless, the United States has developed a mixed economic system, incorporating private enterprise along with government controls on business and the economy. The New Deal of Franklin D. Roosevelt and the Great Society of Lyndon Johnson were essentially attempts to combine democratic capitalism and socialism. The federal government created jobs and minimum wage laws, public housing, education and various welfare programmes to improve the lives of citizens. Yet neither the New Deal nor the Great Society programmes were able to resolve the American Dilemma, and, notwithstanding the achievements of the civil rights movement, blacks have still not attained equality and millions of Americans, both black and white, continue to live below the poverty level in the world's richest nation.

To stem the tide of ghetto riots and avert a national disaster, King insisted that the federal government must institute a massive programme, costing billions of dollars, to provide employment, quality education, decent housing and adequate health care for all citizens, regardless of race. The Kerner Commission had confirmed King's diagnosis of the ills plaguing American society, and suggested similar remedies as a solution. Because the federal government failed to respond to the overwhelming cry for such far-reaching reforms, King decided that thousands of the poor of all races must be mobilized for another nonviolent March on Washington to compel the 'unwilling authorities to yield to the mandates of justice'.[39]

V

At a meeting of SCLC on 4 December 1967, King announced plans for a mass nonviolent Poor People's Campaign in Washington, D.C. the following spring. 'Our nation is at a crossroads of history', he warned, 'and it is critically important for us, as a nation and a society, to choose a new path and move upon it with resolution and courage. It is impossible to underestimate the crisis we face in America'.[40] King repeated this ominous tone in his final SCLC fund-raising letter: 'We intend, before the summer comes, to initiate a "last chance" project to arouse the American conscience toward constructive democratic change'.[41] In mid-January 1968, King sent some 40 SCLC field workers to various urban and rural areas throughout the country to begin organizing for the largest nonviolent offensive in the nation's history.

In 'Showdown for Nonviolence', an article for *Look* magazine, written shortly after the release of the March 1968 Kerner Report,

King outlined the details of the Washington protest, and sought to impress upon the conscience of America the urgency of acceding to the just demands of the poor: 'We believe that if this campaign succeeds, nonviolence will once again be the dominant instrument for social change – and jobs and income will be put in the hands of the tormented poor. If it fails, nonviolence will be discredited, and the country may be plunged into a holocaust – a tragedy deepened by the awareness that it was avoidable'.[42] With the ghettos aflame, the nation could no longer afford to ignore the problem of poverty. Nonviolent direct action, King argued, provided a constructive alternative to riots. 'It must be militant, massive nonviolence, or riots', he warned.[43]

The Poor People's Campaign called for an initial cadre of 3000 poor blacks, whites, Puerto Ricans, Mexican Americans and Indians – trained in nonviolence – to march on Washington from ten cities and five rural communities throughout the nation. Enormous planning would be involved. Scheduled to begin on 22 April, the protest would also include concurrent nationwide support demonstrations and boycotts of selected industries and urban shopping areas. 'This is a mammoth job', said King. 'Before, we mobilized one city at a time. Now we are mobilizing a nation'.[44] The campaign would be a grass roots populist movement to bring full democracy to America. As David Lewis observed, King's multiracial coalition represented 'a Popular Front of the racially abused, economically deprived, and politically outraged, cutting across race and class'.[45] The immediate purpose of the campaign was to prod Congress to enact King's proposed $12 billion Bill of Rights for the Disadvantaged, guaranteeing an end to housing discrimination, a job for those who were able to work and an income for those who were disabled. Federally-funded job training programmes and ghetto reconstruction would also be demanded. Asked by a reporter whether the interracial protest signified his abandonment of civil rights, King replied: 'But you can say that I am in human rights'.[46]

The opening Washington demonstrations would be confined to First Amendment activity – marches, rallies and speeches. To dramatize the plight of the poor, the protesters would erect a shanty town, called Resurrection City, along the Potomac River. If Congress failed to respond favourably after a few weeks, the number of demonstrators would increase by thousands, escalating militant nonviolence to 'disruptive dimensions'.[47] Though remaining nonviolent, the protesters would engage in massive civil disobedience, bringing the nation's capital to a halt by staging sit-ins in Congress and government buildings, and disrupting traffic. King intended the protest to be 'powerful enough, dramatic enough, morally appealing enough, so that people of goodwill, the churches, labor, liberals, intellectuals, students, poor people themselves begin to put pressure on congressmen to the point that they can no longer elude our demands'.[48]

In 1963, when the movement focused on integrated public accommodations and the Civil Rights Bill had already been intro-duced in Congress, the March on Washington did not have to be disruptive; it was a dramatic expression of a growing national consensus in support of laws prohibiting segregation. In 1968, having moved beyond civil rights to economic rights, King and SCLC were attacking deeply rooted vested interests. 'In a sense', King explained to José Yglesias of the *New York Times*, 'you could say we are engaged in the class struggle'.[49] Now that the movement challenged the entire American system, calling for the redistribution of wealth and income, King believed that massive nonviolent direct action, more disruptive than ever before, was necessary to compel the federal government, and most white Americans, to make the concessions required to bring economic justice to the poor.

King's plan for the Washington campaign was opposed by his advisers, including Bayard Rustin and socialist Michael Harrington, who feared that it would be counter-productive. Rustin stated in a memo: 'Given the mood in Congress, given the increasing backlash across the nation, given the fact that this is an election year, and given the high visibility of a protest movement in the nation's capital, I feel that in this atmosphere any effort to disrupt transpor-tation, government buildings, etc., can only lead to further backlash and repression'.[50] Rustin could not ignore the widespread concern that the protest might escalate into a mass rebellion. Although King insisted that 'if the demonstrations become violent we shall call them off',[51] Rustin warned that the planned disruption would attract 'the most irresponsible and uncontrollable elements', demonstrators who were not committed to nonviolence: 'There is in my mind a very real question as to whether SCLC can maintain control and discipline over the April demonstration, even if the methods used are limited to constitutional and nonviolent tactics'.[52]

When King huddled with SCLC executive staff members at their retreat in Frogmore, South Carolina, on 28 November 1967, more reservations were voiced. James Bevel doubted whether President

Johnson would 'give enough opposition for us to build up steam and momentum'. Unlike Birmingham's Bull Connor, the President could not be expected to assist the protest by overreacting. Bevel also believed that King and SCLC should direct their efforts to the most urgent issue confronting the nation – the Vietnam War. Andrew Young thought that 'with an asinine Congress like this', the campaign would be unlikely to attain its goals.[53] Such scepticism was shared by Jesse Jackson and Hosea Williams. Despite the reservations of his leading advisers and staff members, King remained adamant. The protest must be 'as dramatic, as dislocative, as disruptive, as attention-getting as the riots without destroying life and property'.[54] Realizing that a failure in Washington would discredit both his leadership and the nonviolent method, King frankly admitted that he was 'going for broke' with the Poor People's Campaign. His perseverance prevailed. At a Miami meeting of SCLC ministers in January 1968, he won approval for the campaign from the majority. As usual, King had the support of his life-long friend and confidant, Ralph Abernathy.

Meanwhile, despite the assurances of General William C. Westmoreland, the U.S. commander in Vietnam, it became clear that victory was not in sight. On 31 January 1967, the eve of the Tet festival, North Vietnamese and Viet Cong armed forces launched a massive offensive, simultaneously attacking more than a hundred cities and towns in South Vietnam, including the American Embassy in Saigon. Though most of these targets were recaptured within a short time, the Tet offensive was instrumental in undermining support for the Vietnam War in the United States and in turning the tide of public opinion against President Johnson.

VI

On Sunday, 4 February 1968, King was in Atlanta to deliver a sermon at Ebenezer Baptist Church. When he died, he told the congregation, he wanted the eulogist to mention that 'Martin Luther King, Jr. tried to give his life serving others . . . tried to be right on the war question . . . tried to love and serve humanity. Yes, if you want to say that I was a drum major, say that I was a drum major for justice . . . for peace . . . for righteousness'.[55] On 12 February, King met with his staff in Atlanta for an all-day strategy session, producing a master plan for the upcoming Poor People's Campaign. To recruit volunteers and enlist the necessary financial support for the protest, King embarked on People-to-People tours, travelling thousands of miles in the early weeks of 1968, meeting with leaders of all ethnic groups throughout the nation.

On 12 February, the day of the Atlanta strategy meeting, events began to unfold in Memphis, Tennessee that would lead to tragedy. The sanitation workers union, most of whose members were black, went on strike to protest unjust treatment by the city. The newly-elected mayor, Henry Loeb, refused to recognize the union, rebuffing its requests for a wage increase and improved working conditions. Vowing not to return to work until their demands were met, blacks organized marches from the Memphis Masonic Temple to City Hall, highlighting their cause by carrying signs reading: 'I AM A MAN'.

While the Memphis strike gathered momentum, King's People-to-People pilgrimage brought him back to the scenes of his greatest nonviolent victories. On 15 February, he spoke in Birmingham, where thousands of nonviolent demonstrators had aroused the nation's conscience against racism in 1963; on 16 February, he spoke in Selma, the scene of the voting rights campaign in 1965. 'We can change this nation', he declared at a rally. 'We can bring it up to the point that it will live up to its creeds'.[56] Later that day, he was in Montgomery, the origin of his nonviolent crusade 12 years before. On 23 February, King was in New York City to address an assembly at Carnegie Hall in celebration of the hundredth birthday of the black activist and scholar, W. E. B. Dubois, who had died in 1963. Author James Baldwin and actor Ossie Davis were present at the occasion, which was organized by former SCLC member, Jack O'Dell, now associated with *Freedomways* magazine. Hailing Dubois as 'one of the most remarkable men of our time', and 'a radical all of his life', who 'exemplified black power in achievement', King did not ignore the issue of Dubois's communism. 'It is time to cease muting the fact that Dr. Dubois was a genius who chose to be a Communist'. After referring briefly to the upcoming Washington protest, and the 'unjust' Vietnam War, King asserted that the essence of Dubois's greatness lay in his concern for the oppressed and his dissatisfaction with all forms of injustice. Inspired by Dubois, King concluded: 'Let us be dissatisfied until our brother of the Third World – Asia, Africa, and Latin America – will no longer be the victim of imperialist exploitation, but will be lifted from the long night of poverty, illiteracy, and disease'.[57] King's speech revealed his increasingly outspoken radicalism.

While King mustered support for the Poor People's Campaign, the Memphis strike was transformed into a major racial confrontation. On Wednesday, 21 February, tension worsened in the city after Mayor Loeb issued an ultimatum that all sanitation workers who refused to return to work would be fired. The next day, the Mayor began hiring non-union workers to replace the strikers. On 23 February, the day King was in New York City honouring Dubois, a nonviolent march in Memphis by sanitation workers was brutally repulsed by police with clubs. The following week, a familiar pattern of events began to unfold. James Lawson, head of the local SCLC affiliate, telephoned King and invited him to visit Memphis and address a mass meeting. Lawson was among the leaders of the Community on the Move for Equality (COME), a coalition which was directing the strike. He and his associates hoped that King's presence in Memphis would inspire a Southern-style protest campaign, attracting national attention to the plight of the striking workers. King and SCLC believed that a nonviolent success in Memphis would generate publicity for the Poor People's Campaign, and allay fears that it was doomed to degenerate into violence. Leading a march of the poor in Memphis would be an excellent prelude to the up-coming spring protest in Washington. As Ralph Abernathy explained to Coretta King: 'We're going to Washington by way of Memphis'.[58]

On Monday, 18 March, King arrived in Memphis with his staff and addressed a rally of some 15000 people at the large Masonic Temple. Buoyed by the enthusiasm of the crowd, he promised to return and lead a nonviolent demonstration on Friday, 22 March. Andrew Young, James Bevel, Hosea Williams and James Orange were prepared to participate. King then journeyed to Mississippi to enlist more recruits for the Poor People's Campaign. When Memphis was hit by a blizzard on Friday, leaving a foot of snow on the city streets, the demonstration was postponed until Thursday, 28 March. Meanwhile, King had been deeply disturbed by a memorandum, dated 8 March 1968, written by Mrs Marian Logan, a highly-respected SCLC board member, urging cancellation of the Washington campaign. The memo, sent to each member of the SCLC board, argued that the campaign would not 'move the conscience' of Congress. Logan also expressed grave doubts that the demonstrators would remain nonviolent.[59] After making several telephone calls to convince Mrs Logan to withdraw her objections, King travelled to New York City for a meeting at the apartment of Marian and Arthur Logan on Monday, 25 March. After an all-night effort to gain her support, an exhausted King left unsuccessful.

On Thursday, 28 March, King arrived from New York to lead some 6000 protesters in a march through downtown Memphis toward City Hall. It turned out to be a serious mistake. King and SCLC were unaware of a strong undercurrent of sympathy for Black Power among some of the city youth, who opposed Lawson and the other strike leaders as insufficiently militant. Shortly after the march began, young blacks, many belonging to a group known as the Invaders, started to riot on Beale Street, smashing windows and looting stores. What had been intended to be a peaceful march to City Hall dissolved into mayhem. There is some evidence that the riot was instigated by *agents provocateurs* planted in the march by the FBI.[60] Realizing what was happening, Ralph Abernathy and Bernard Lee pushed King into a passing car and brought him to the Rivermont Holiday Inn on the banks of the Mississippi. The violence – which left one black youth dead, 60 persons injured and 155 stores damaged – continued until the National Guard arrived to restore order. In Washington, President Johnson promised to send federal troops if necessary, and declared: 'We will not let violence and lawlessness take over the country'.[61]

At his hotel room, King was on the brink of despair. The press would focus upon the Memphis riot to illustrate the dangers of the Poor People's Campaign. A few days before, on 25 March, Adam Clayton Powell, Jr. had solemnly pronounced in New York City that 'the day of Martin Luther King has come to an end'. Now Powell referred derisively to 'Martin Loser King'.[62] Many concluded that the Memphis riot signified the death of the nonviolent movement. A *New York Times* editorial urged King to call off the Poor People's Campaign: 'None of the precautions he and his aides are taking to keep the capital demonstration peaceful can provide any dependable insurance against another eruption of the kind that rocked Memphis'.[63] The Memphis *Commercial Appeal* said in an editorial: 'Dr. King's pose as a leader of a non-violent movement has been shattered. He now has the entire nation doubting his word when he insists that his April project . . . can be peaceful'.[64]

After conferring with his staff, King vowed to lead a peaceful march in Memphis the following week. 'Yes, we must come back', he insisted. 'Nonviolence as a concept is now on trial'.[65] The Poor People's Campaign, he told reporters, would not be cancelled. 'We are fully determined to go to Washington. We feel it is an absolute necessity'.[66] But the campaign was doomed to fail unless King could prove in Memphis that the nonviolent method was still effective. As for the riot on 28 March, he explained that he and SCLC had been thrust at the head of a demonstration they had not planned, and that the violence had been unforeseen. SCLC advance men had not tested the situation in Memphis beforehand. 'Our intelligence', King confessed, 'was totally nil'.[67] To avoid a repetition of the riot, he met in his motel room with leaders of the Invaders – Charles Cabbage, Calvin Taylor and Charles Harrington – and convinced them to try the method of nonviolence. At the same time, King had to contend with his staff's opposition to a second Memphis march. On 30 March, at an SCLC executive staff meeting in Atlanta, James Bevel and Jesse Jackson argued that preoccupation with Memphis was interfering with plans for the Poor People's Campaign. But King reiterated his conviction that failure to conduct a nonviolent march in Memphis would jeopardize the Washington protest. Putting aside their strong reservations, Bevel and Jackson, along with James Orange and Andrew Young, prepared for the march, scheduled for Friday, 5 April.

In the midst of the turmoil in Memphis, startling news came from Washington. On 31 March, President Lyndon Johnson announced on national television: 'I shall not seek, and I will not accept, the nomination of my party for another term as your President'.[68] He did not want the office of the presidency harmed by becoming 'involved in the partisan divisions that are developing'.[69] Disappointed by the results of the New Hampshire Democratic primary, in which Senator Eugene McCarthy of Minnesota had made an impressive showing, and expecting to be challenged for the nomination by Robert Kennedy, the President chose to withdraw. Recent national public opinion polls had demonstrated that his popularity had sunk to its lowest level. Having been elected by an overwhelming majority in 1964, at first it seemed to many that his goal to construct the Great Society might be fulfilled. But by 1968, Lyndon Johnson's political career was destroyed; it had been destroyed by the war in Vietnam.

On Wednesday, 3 April, King and members of his staff left Atlanta by aeroplane for Memphis, where they checked into Room

306 of the black-owned Lorraine Motel. On the advice of Bayard Rustin, King agreed to hold off the march until the following Monday, 8 April, thus providing time for labour and civil rights groups from throughout the country to converge on Memphis. It would also allow for more thorough preparation to ensure that the march would be nonviolent. Attempting to crush the protest, Mayor Loeb applied to the federal district court for an injunction against 'nonresidents' marching in the city. King's lawyers informed him that the injunction would probably be granted. 'Whether it is granted or not', King told Abernathy, 'I am going to lead that march'.[70] On 3 April afternoon, the federal court issued a temporary restraining order. King maintained his decision to disobey it; the possibility of further angering the federal government did not concern him. Having antagonized the Johnson Administration by his stand against the Vietnam War, and now planning to lead thousands of the nation's poor in an invasion of Washington, King could no longer depend upon the federal government for support. Meanwhile, SCLC lawyers challenged the injunction in federal court.

The evening of 3 April, a heavy rain fell upon Memphis. King was scheduled to address a mass meeting at the Masonic Temple, but his staff advised him not to go because a poor turnout might again inspire the news media to write about a requiem for nonviolence. Ralph Abernathy went instead. Arriving at the meeting, he was surprised to see 2000 people present, clamouring for their leader, Martin Luther King, Jr. Abernathy immediately telephoned King at the Lorraine Motel, and told him that the crowd was waiting.

Arriving at the Masonic Temple that rainy night, King was greeted by an ovation from the enthusiastic crowd. He would lead Monday's march, he told them, despite the 'unconstitutional' injunction, a denial of 'First Amendment privileges'. The crowd cheered. The march must be orderly and nonviolent, he warned, even at the risk of death or going to jail. He concluded:

We've got some difficult days ahead. But it doesn't matter with me now. Because I've been to the mountaintop. And I don't mind. Like anybody, I would like to live a long life. Longevity has its place. But I'm not concerned about that now. I just want to do God's will. And He's allowed me to go to the mountain. And I've looked over. And I've seen the promised land. I may not get there with you. But I want you to know tonight, that we, as a people will get to the promised land. And I'm happy tonight. I'm not worried about anything. I'm not fearing any man. Mine eyes have seen the glory of the coming of the Lord.[71]

King's speech was later dramatized by the media as a premonition of his own death. For 12 years he had served as a Moses to black Americans. He had led them part of the long and difficult way up the mountain toward freedom and equality; they would have to complete the ascent without him.

On Thursday morning, 4 April, King met with his staff, including Bernard Lee and Jesse Jackson, to review plans for Monday's march. Andrew Young was sent to the district court to testify at a hearing on the injunction. Later that afternoon, King and SCLC rejoiced upon hearing that the injunction had been overturned. The Monday march would be permitted as long as the demonstrators marched only six abreast, and were accompanied by parade marshalls trained in nonviolence.

Shortly before 6 p.m., on 4 April, King, Abernathy and members of SCLC were at the Lorraine Motel preparing to go to dinner. A mass meeting was scheduled for that evening. After dressing, King went onto the balcony outside Room 306. A gunshot rang out. Abernathy rushed from the room to find King lying diagonally across the balcony, mortally wounded. One hour later, King was pronounced dead at Memphis St Joseph's Hospital. The assassination of King aroused anger in blacks throughout the nation. During the week following his death, riots erupted in over a hundred cities, in which 3500 people were injured, 20 000 arrested and 46 killed.

While the nation mourned the slain civil rights leader, Coretta King and Ralph Abernathy led a memorial march through the streets of Memphis on 8 April. The next day, millions watched the televised funeral ceremony held in Atlanta, attended by state dignitaries, celebrities and civil rights activists. A long procession followed the farm wagon drawn by two mules that transported the coffin to the grave. Inscribed on King's tombstone are the words he had chosen from the black spiritual to conclude his famous 'I Have a Dream' speech: 'Free at last! Free at last! Thank God Almighty, I'm Free at last!'

Martin Luther King, Jr., apostle of militant nonviolence, dedicated his life to a black freedom movement that ranks in the annals of history as one of humanity's supreme accomplishments. His ideals continue to inspire those who strive to resolve the American Dilemma.

11

Epilogue

I

Martin Luther King, Jr., apostle of militant nonviolence, has left an enduring legacy. As an eloquent spokesman for the conscience of humanity, King's significance is recognized throughout the world. He is remembered for his inspirational leadership of a nonviolent black freedom struggle that shook the foundations of racism in America, overthrew legal segregation in the South, and guaranteed the basic democratic right to vote. During the 12 years that King dedicated his life to the civil rights movement, blacks made more progress than in any other period in American history, overcoming the damaging psychological effects of generations of oppression, and acquiring a sense of unity and dignity.

From the 1950s to the early 1960s, the black freedom movement launched a two-pronged attack upon Southern racism – legal action, confined to the courthouses and the legislative chambers, spearheaded by the NAACP; and militant nonviolent direct action, filling the streets with masses of nonviolent marchers exercising the right to protest for constitutional goals that even many white Americans supported. King was America's greatest advocate of nonviolence as a philosophy of life and as a method of protest. Like Gandhi in India, he showed that nonviolence is not passive, but a militant, powerful and coercive method to achieve social reform. Determined nonviolent protesters stirred crises in Southern cities by disrupting business, filling the jails and overloading the courts. Massive nonviolent direct action dramatized racist brutality, pressured the federal government to enforce civil rights, and awakened the conscience of the nation to the injustice inherent in 'separate but equal'.

In the Southern phase of their freedom struggle, most blacks were willing to work within the American political system, prodding the nation to fulfil the ideals of freedom and equality professed in the Declaration of Independence and the Constitution. That these ideals had been denied to black citizens raised a moral issue that was creatively exploited by King and other civil rights leaders, appealing to allies throughout the nation – liberals, labour and church groups, intellectuals and the often hesitant federal government. Nonviolent protesters availed themselves of First Amendment rights to plan, organize, publicize, assemble and peacefully march. Civil disobedience, though an important tactic of the movement, was the exception rather than the rule, and protesters showed respect for the principle of law and order by willingly submitting to arrest as a consequence of disobeying unjust segregation laws.

The nonviolent method relied upon the media for much of its success. The nation followed on television and in the press the events of the sit-ins, the Freedom Rides, the Birmingham campaign, the March on Washington and the Selma-to-Montgomery march. Nonviolent protesters in the South – ministers and their congregations, students, women and even children – inspired by leaders such as King, stood in stark contrast to the violent and irresponsible reactions of racists. The media captured the events, portraying them graphically before the conscience of America. Defiant defenders of Jim Crow acted out their villain roles as if performing in a modern morality play. Uninhibited Southern sheriffs, such as Bull Connor and Jim Clark – symbols of racist oppression – were manoeuvered and provoked into leading violent resistance to peaceful protests in their towns; Southern governors – such as John Patterson and George Wallace of Alabama, and Ross Barnett of Mississippi – predictably defied the United States Constitution. While the cameras rolled, and reporters wrote their stories, the American public watched in horror as the Jim Crow South met nonviolent protests for civil rights with inflammatory rhetoric, attack dogs, high-pressure fire hoses, clubs and cattle prods, church bombings, hooded Klansmen, Confederate and Nazi banners and murders of civil rights workers.

King was a consummate master of the media. From the Montgomery bus boycott until his death in 1968, reporters and television cameramen flocked to the protest campaigns he led, bringing national and international exposure to the cause of racial justice. Each campaign city became a stage on which King and SCLC led masses of nonviolent blacks in moral confrontations with the entrenched segregationist order while the nation looked on. Seizing a dramatic moment during his imprisonment in Birmingham in the spring of 1963, King composed the most famous statement of his goals and a defence of the nonviolent method, the 'Letter from Birmingham Jail'. Widely circulated by the media, the Letter moved millions of Americans. Shortly after King's release from jail, SCLC's histrionic strategy sent hundreds of black children marching against segregation in Birmingham like David against Goliath.

By 1965, having overcome what had seemed to be insurmountable obstacles, the civil rights phase of the black freedom struggle had run its course. Jim Crow had been vanquished – nonviolently. Black Americans had taken a giant stride toward freedom, and stood on the threshold of achieving full and equal participation in American society.

II

The next phase of the black freedom struggle – with the goal of substantial equality – proved to be much more difficult. The securing of civil rights had little effect upon the quality of life in the nation's urban slums and rural backwaters. By 1966, it had become evident that blacks wanted not only the integration of public facilities and protection of the right to vote, but also jobs, quality education, decent integrated housing and adequate health care. The expectations of black Americans had been raised beyond civil rights to full equality.

King erred in his belief that the nonviolent method that had succeeded in the South could be readily transferred to the struggle for equality in the North. In the Northern cities, he had to deal with a different constituency, the ghetto black, embittered by abject poverty and less receptive to his charisma and the gospel of nonviolence. The urban metropolises were virtually impervious to street demonstrations and mass rallies. When King and SCLC entered Chicago, they confronted more deeply rooted problems than in the South, in addition to the powerful and corrupt political machine of Mayor Daley. The nation did not respond to the demand for full equality, causing many blacks to lose faith in American democracy and the nonviolent method in the late 1960s. As scores of ghetto blacks turned from nonviolence and integration toward violence and separatism, the media focused upon the angry cry for Black Power.

In the North, King lacked the broad national coalition of support which had sustained his Southern campaigns. As he enlarged his

vision from civil rights to human rights, attempting to join the
black freedom struggle with the anti-war movement, his allies
began to drift away. The nation's fateful involvement in the
Vietnam War fragmented the civil rights movement, destroyed
President Johnson's Great Society programme, and undermined
King's leadership.

During the final year and a half of his life, having concluded
that racism, poverty and the Vietnam War were interrelated, King
launched a radical critique of American capitalism and foreign
policy, advocating democratic socialism. With the ghettos aflame,
and the nonviolent method on trial, he spent his last months
preparing for an interracial march of the poor to Washington to
demand economic justice. The Poor People's Campaign would be
a final, desperate attempt to make human rights a national priority.
The campaign laid the foundations for the 'Rainbow Coalition' of
blacks, Hispanics, native American Indians and other minority
groups that became the basis for the presidential candidacy of Jesse
Jackson in 1984. History has vindicated King's stand on the tragedy
of Vietnam, and, as the world faces the persistent threat of
nuclear devastation, his message has become most urgent: either
nonviolence or non-existence.

As we approach the last decade of the twentieth century,
the human rights phase of the black freedom struggle remains
unfinished. The legal barriers to equality have been to a large
extent overcome, and protest activity has declined as blacks have
increasingly sought to bring about reforms through the electoral
process. Many blacks have been elected to political office, and
several cities, including Atlanta, Birmingham and Chicago have
elected black mayors. Despite these achievements, America
remains divided into two societies – separate and unequal. Blacks
have yet to make the economic gains necessary to derive full
benefit from their civil rights; increasing numbers are falling
below the national poverty level. They still suffer from severe
unemployment, inadequate schools, housing and health care, and
a deteriorating family structure. In fact, black Americans are worse
off now economically than at the time of the 1963 March on
Washington. Unless the United States confronts these grave problems swiftly and effectively, increasing numbers of blacks may lose
confidence in the institutionalized political channels and again
resort to massive protest. Only a concerted national effort can
begin to resolve the American Dilemma. King's dream was that

America, the richest nation of the world, founded upon the noblest ideals, would use its vast resources to provide a decent standard of living for all citizens, regardless of race.

III

Most Americans remember King as a dreamer. He has become identified with the theme that pervades his most famous speech, 'I Have a Dream', delivered at the March on Washington in 1963. History shows that the progress of the human race has depended upon the dreamer. King never ceased advocating the ideal of 'black and white together'. He believed that until individuals of all races in the United States achieve human rights, the American Dilemma will remain unresolved, and America will remain unredeemed. In 1983, Congress voted to establish the third Monday in January as a national holiday commemorating King's birthday. Other than George Washington, no American has been accorded such an honour. Each year, the nation has an opportunity to reflect upon what it has done to fulfil King's dream.

But King was not a mere dreamer, setting ideals for humanity; he was also a doer, a drum major for freedom, justice and equality, leading and inspiring many to take practical steps toward the attainment of these ideals. Often attacked as an 'extremist', King ranks in history with other so-called extremists such as Socrates, Jesus and Gandhi. Martyrs for their ideals, each challenged humanity to transcend itself. That King achieved so much in the short span of 12 years is testimony to the fact that his dream is deeply rooted in reality. The genius of Martin Luther King, Jr. was his ability to perceive that there is something noble in humanity that, once tapped, has the power to transform the world.

Notes and References

PREFACE

1. Mehta, Ved, 'Gandhism Is Not Easily Copied', *New York Times Magazine*, (9 July 1961), pp. 8ff.

1 MONTGOMERY: THE WALKING CITY, 1955–6

1. Martin Luther King, Jr., *Why We Can't Wait*, (New York, 1964), pp. 90–1.
2. William Brink & Louis Harris, *The Negro Revolution in America*, (New York, 1964), p. 103.
3. King, *Stride Toward Freedom: The Montgomery Story*, (New York, 1958, pp. 61–3.
4. Lerone Bennett, Jr., *What Manner of Man: A Biography of Martin Luther King, Jr.*, 3rd ed. rev. (Chicago, 1968), p. 68.
5. King, *Stride Toward Freedom*, p. 137.
6. Bennett, *What Manner of Man*, p. 71. (Bennett's italics).
7. Jim Bishop, *The Days of Martin Luther King, Jr.*, (New York, 1971), pp. 166–7.
8. King, *Stride Toward Freedom*, p. 142.
9. Harvard Sitkoff, *The Struggle for Black Equality, 1954–80*, (New York, 1981), p. 54.
10. Norman W. Walton, 'The Walking City: A History of the Montgomery Boycott', *Negro History Bulletin*, 20 (November 1956), p. 28.
11. King, *Strength to Love*, (Philadelphia, 1963), p. 125.
12. King, *Stride Toward Freedom*, p. 160.
13. Ibid., p. 161.
14. Ibid., p. 164.
15. King, 'Facing the Challenge of a New Age', *Phylon*, 18 (April 1957), p. 30.
16. Walton, 'The Walking City', *Negro History Bulletin*, 20 (April 1957), p. 147.
17. Bishop, *King*, p. 185.
18. Walton, 'The Walking City', p. 150.
19. Harris Wofford, *Of Kennedys and Kings*, (New York, 1980), p. 119.
20. Aldon D. Morris, *The Origins of the Civil Rights Movement: Black Communities Organizing for Change*, (New York, 1984), p. 127.
21. *Time* (18 February 1957), p. 17.
22. Ralph Ellison, *Invisible Man*, (New York: 1972), p. 3.

2 NONVIOLENCE SPREADS IN THE SOUTH, 1957–61

1. Anthony Lewis, *Portrait of a Decade: The Second American Revolution*, (New York, 1964), p. 29.
2. Ibid., p. 30.
3. Francis M. Wilhoit, *The Politics of Massive Resistance*, (New York, 1973), pp. 285–7.
4. Lewis, *Portrait of a Decade*, p. 45.
5. Gene Sharp, *Gandhi as a Political Strategist*, (Boston, 1979), p. 15.
6. August Meier, Elliott Rudwick, & Francis L. Broderick, eds, *Black Protest Thought in the Twentieth Century*, 2nd ed. (Indianapolis, 1971), p. 276.
7. Howell Raines, *My Soul is Rested: Movement Days in the Deep South Remembered*, (New York, 1977), p. 18.
8. James Farmer, *Lay Bare the Heart: An Autobiography of the Civil Rights Movement*, (New York, 1985), pp. 187–8.
9. King, *Stride Toward Freedom*, p. 105.
10. Ibid., p. 96.
11. Adam Fairclough, 'The Southern Christian Leadership Conference and the Second Reconstruction, 1957–1973', *South Atlantic Quarterly*, 80 (Spring 1981), p. 178.
12. Harry S. Ashmore, *Hearts and Minds: The Anatomy of Racism from Roosevelt to Reagan*, (New York, 1982), p. 248.
13. James M. Washington, ed., *A Testament of Hope: The Essential Writings of Martin Luther King, Jr.*, (San Francisco, 1986), pp. 197–200.
14. Bennett, *What Manner of Man*, p. 88.
15. Louis E. Lomax, *The Negro Revolt*, (New York: 1963), p. 106.
16. Washington, *Testament*, p. 21.
17. Sitkoff, *Struggle for Black Equality*, p. 68.
18. Farmer, *Lay Bare the Heart*, p. 192.
19. William R. Miller, *Martin Luther King, Jr.: His Life, Martyrdom, and Meaning for the World*, (New York, 1968), p. 91.
20. Pat Watters, *Down To Now: Reflections on the Southern Civil Rights Movement*, (New York, 1971), p. 79.
21. Cleveland Sellers, *The River of No Return*, (New York, 1973), p. 36.
22. Meier, Rudwick, & Broderick, *Black Protest Thought*, p. 307.
23. James C. Harvey, *Civil Rights During the Kennedy Administration*, (Hattiesburg: Miss., 1971), pp. 6–7.
24. Ibid., p. 9.
25. Ibid.
26. Steven F. Lawson, *Black Ballots: Voting Rights in the South, 1944–1969*, (New York, 1976), p. 253.
27. Harvey, *Civil Rights During the Kennedy Administration*, p. 13.
28. Carl M. Brauer, *John F. Kennedy and the Second Reconstruction*, (New York, 1977), p. 43.
29. Washington, *Testament*, p. 152.
30. Lawson, *Black Ballots*, p. 271.
31. James Farmer, *Freedom – When?* (New York, 1965), p. 69.
32. Sitkoff, *Struggle for Black Equality*, p. 103.

33. Miller, *King*, p. 107.
34. August Meier & Elliott Rudwick, *CORE: A Study in the Civil Rights Movement*, (Chicago, 1975), p. 139.
35. Victor S. Navasky, *Kennedy Justice*, (New York, 1971), p. 73.
36. Bennett, *What Manner of Man*, p. 126.
37. Edwin Guthman, *We Band of Brothers*, (New York, 1971), p. 155.
38. Herbert S. Parmet, *JFK: The Presidency of John F. Kennedy* (New York, 1984), p. 255.
39. Navasky, *Kennedy Justice*, p. 233.
40. Lerone Bennett, Jr., *Before the Mayflower: A History of the Negro in America, 1619–1964*, rev. ed. (Baltimore, 1964), p. 325.

3 THE LESSONS OF ALBANY, GEORGIA, 1961-2

1. Howard Zinn, *The Southern Mystique*, (New York, 1964), p. 154.
2. James Forman, *The Making of Black Revolutionaries*, 2nd ed. (Washington D.C., 1985), p. 253.
3. Morris, *Origins of the Civil Rights Movement*, p. 244.
4. Watters, *Down to Now*, p. 14.
5. Bishop, *King*, pp. 259, 263.
6. Morris, *Origins of the Civil Rights Movement*, p. 243.
7. Forman, *Black Revolutionaries*, p. 254.
8. Clayborne Carson, *In Struggle: SNCC and the Black Awakening of the 1960s*, (Cambridge, Mass., 1981), p. 62.
9. John A. Ricks III, '"De Lawd" Descends and is Crucified: Martin Luther King, Jr. in Albany Georgia', *The Journal of Southwest Georgia History*, II (Fall 1984), p. 6.
10. 'Man of the Year: Never Again Where He Was', *Time*, (3 January 1964), p. 15.
11. Ricks, '"De Lawd" Descends', p. 6.
12. Zinn, *Southern Mystique*, p. 170.
13. 'Man of the Year', *Time*, p. 15.
14. Juan Williams, *Eyes on the Prize: America's Civil Rights Years, 1954–1965*, (New York, 1987), p. 170.
15. David J. Garrow, *Bearing The Cross: Martin Luther King, Jr. And The Southern Christian Leadership Conference*, (New York, 1986), pp. 203–4, 664.
16. Zinn, *Southern Mystique*, p. 173.
17. Ricks, '"De Lawd" Descends', p. 9.
18. Alan F. Westin & Garry Mahoney, *The Trial of Martin Luther King*, (New York, 1974) p. 45.
19. William Kunstler, *Deep in My Heart*, (New York, 1966) p. 102.
20. Ibid., p. 106.
21. Ricks, '"De Lawd" Descends', p. 9
22. Miller, *King*, p. 120.
23. Ricks, '"De Lawd" Descends', p. 10
24. Ibid.
25. Miller, *King*, p. 120.

26. Brauer, *Kennedy*, p. 175.
27. Wm. Roger Witherspoon, *Martin Luther King, Jr . . . . To the Mountain-top*, (Garden City, New York, 1985), p. 103.
28. Reese Cleghorn, 'Epilogue in Albany: Were the Mass Marches Worthwhile?, *The New Republic*, (20 July 1963), p. 16.
29. Reese Cleghorn, 'Martin Luther King, Jr., Apostle of Crisis', in C. Eric Lincoln, *Martin Luther King, Jr.: A Profile*, rev. ed. (New York, 1984), p. 124.
30. Malcolm X, 'Message to the Grass Roots', in *Malcolm X Speaks*, ed. by George Breitman (New York, 1965), p. 13.
31. Bennett, *What Manner of Man*, pp. 130–1.
32. Cleghorn, 'Epilogue in Albany', p. 16.
33. Morris, *Origins of the Civil Rights Movement*, p. 249.
34. Watters, *Down To Now*, p. 233.
35. Witherspoon, *King*, p. 98.
36. Clayborne Carson, 'SNCC and the Albany Movement', *The Journal of Southwest Georgia History* II (Fall 1984), p. 22.
37. Ricks, ' "De Lawd" Descends', p. 13.
38. Bishop, *King*, p. 262.
39. Roy Wilkens, *Standing Fast*, (New York, 1982), p. 286.
40. Carson, *In Struggle*, p. 61.
41. David L. Lewis, *King: A Biography*, 2nd ed. (Chicago, 1978), p. 151.
42. Coretta Scott King, *My Life with Martin Luther King, Jr.*, (New York, 1969), p. 204.
43. Westin & Mahoney, *King*, p. 59.
44. William R. Miller, *Non-Violence: A Christian Interpretation*, (London, 1964) p. 328.
45. King, *Why We Can't Wait*, p. 48.
46. Wyatt T. Walker, 'Albany, Failure or First Step?', *New South*, (June 1963), p. 4.
47. Cleghorn, 'Martin Luther King, Jr., Apostle of Crisis', in Lincoln, *King* p. 125.
48. Garrow, *Bearing the Cross*, p. 221.
49. Morris, *Origins of the Civil Rights Movement*, p. 253.
50. Fairclough, 'Southern Christian Leadership Conference', p. 180.
51. Morris, *Origins of the Civil Rights Movement*, p. 93.
52. Transcript of television show, 'Recollections of Dr. King: A *Like It Is* Special', WABC-TV, New York, Part II, hosted by Gil Noble, (12 January 1986), pp. 43–4.

4 BIRMINGHAM AND THE MARCH ON WASHINGTON, 1963

1. King, *Why We Can't Wait*, p. 43.
2. Wilhoit, *Politics of Massive Resistance*, p. 88.
3. King, *Why We Can't Wait*, p. 37.
4. Ibid., p. 47.
5. *Like It Is*, 'Recollections of Dr King', transcript, Part II, (12 January 1986), p. 20.

6. 'Man of the Year', *Time*, (3 January 1964), p. 16.
7. King, *Why We Can't Wait*, p. 55.
8. Michael Dorman, *We Shall Overcome*, (New York, 1964), p. 146.
9. Ibid., p. 145.
10. Staughton Lynd, ed., *Nonviolence in America: A Documentary History*, (Indianapolis, Ind., 1966), pp. 459–60.
11. Forman, *Black Revolutionaries*, p. 312.
12. Robert Penn Warren, *Who Speaks for the Negro?*, (New York, 1965), p. 226.
13. Miller, *King*, p. 135.
14. King, *Why We Can't Wait*, p. 61.
15. Westin & Mahoney, *King*, p. 51.
16. Ibid., p. 78.
17. Ibid., p. 79. (King's italics).
18. Bennett, *What Manner of Man*, p. 152.
19. Witherspoon, *King*, p. 123.
20. Flip Schulke & Penelope McPhee, *King Remembered*, (New York, 1986), p. 127.
21. King, *Why We Can't Wait*, p. 102.
22. Lester A. Sobel, ed., *Civil Rights, 1960–66*, (New York, 1967), p. 181.
23. Richard Polenberg, *One Nation Divisible*, (New York, 1980), p. 184.
24. Bennett, *What Manner of Man*, p. 152.
25. Sobel, *Civil Rights*, p. 182.
26. King, *Why We Can't Wait*, p. 110.
27. Dorman, *We Shall Overcome*, p. 158.
28. Ibid., pp. 163–4.
29. Ibid., p. 165.
30. Leon Friedman, ed., *The Civil Rights Reader: Basic Documents of the Civil Rights Movement*, rev. ed. (New York, 1968), pp. 65–6.
31. Dorman, *We Shall Overcome*, p. 165.
32. Arthur M. Schlesinger, Jr., *A Thousand Days: John F. Kennedy in the White House*, (Boston, 1965), p. 971.
33. King, *Why We Can't Wait*, p. 121.
34. Meier, Rudwick, & Broderick, *Black Protest Thought*, p. 334.
35. Schlesinger, *Thousand Days*, p. 969.
36. Ibid., p. 969–70.
37. Sobel, *Civil Rights*, p. 170.
38. Washington, *Testament*, p. 217–20.
39. 'Man of the Year', *Time*, (3 January 1964), p. 27.
40. Lincoln, *King*, p. 194.
41. Lewis, *Portrait of a Decade*, p. 254.
42. James Baldwin, *No Name in the Street*, (New York, 1972), p. 140.
43. Lewis, *Portrait of a Decade*, pp. 253–4.
44. Thomas R. Brooks, *Walls Come Tumbling Down* (Englewood Cliffs, New Jersey, 1974), p. 228.
45. Ibid.
46. Ibid.
47. *The Autobiography of Malcolm X*, (New York, 1973), p. 278.
48. *Malcolm X Speaks*, pp. 14–15.

49. Sellers, *River of No Return*, pp. 62–5.
50. Forman, *Black Revolutionaries*, p. 336.
51. Arthur M. Schlesinger, Jr., *Robert Kennedy and His Times*, (Boston, 1978), p. 366.

5   INTERLUDE: KING'S LETTER TO AMERICA

1. King, *Why We Can't Wait*, p. 77.
2. Garrow, *Bearing the Cross*, p. 242.
3. King, *Why We Can't Wait*, p. 77.
4. Ibid., p. 78.
5. Ibid.
6. Ibid., pp. 78–9.
7. Ibid., p. 79.
8. Ibid., p. 80.
9. Ibid., p. 82.
10. Ibid., p. 83.
11. Ibid., pp. 83–4.
12. Ibid., p. 81.
13. Ibid., p. 84.
14. Ibid.
15. Ibid., p. 86.
16. Ibid., p. 85.
17. Ibid., p. 87.
18. David Spitz, 'Democracy and the Problem of Civil Disobedience', *American Political Science Review*, 48 (June 1954), p. 402.
19. King, *Why We Can't Wait*, p. 85.
20. Ibid.
21. Ibid. (King's italics).
22. Ibid., p. 41.
23. Ibid., pp. 87–8.
24. August Meier, 'On the Role of Martin Luther King', *New Politics*, IV (Winter 1965), pp. 52–9; in Lincoln, ed., *King*, pp. 144–56.
25. King, *Why We Can't Wait*, p. 90.
26. Ibid.
27. Ibid., p. 91.
28. Ibid., p. 98.
29. Ibid.
30. Ibid.
31. Ibid., p. 92.
32. Ibid., p. 95.
33. Ibid.
34. Ibid., p. 96.
35. Ibid., p. 97.
36. Ibid., pp. 97–8.
37. Gunnar Myrdal, *An American Dilemma: The Negro Problem and Modern Democracy*, rev. ed. (New York, 1962), pp. 1021–4.
38. King, *Why We Can't Wait*, p. 99.

6 THE STRUGGLE CONTINUES, 1964

1. Lawson, *Black Ballots*, p. 298.
2. Schulke & McPhee, *King Remembered*, p. 162.
3. Miller, *King*, p. 178.
4. David R. Colburn, *Racial Change and Community Crisis: St Augustine, Florida, 1877–1980*, (New York, 1985), p. 63.
5. Ibid. (Italics in original).
6. John Herbers, 'Critical Test for the Nonviolent Way', *New York Times Magazine*, (5 July 1964), p. 5.
7. Pat Watters, 'St Augustine', *New South*, (September 1964), p. 7.
8. Larry Goodwyn, 'Anarchy in St Augustine', *Harper's*, 230 (January 1965), p. 76.
9. Ibid., p. 78.
10. Ibid., p. 76.
11. King, 'Hammer on Civil Rights', in Washington, *Testament*, p. 173.
12. Stephen B. Oates, *Let the Trumpet Sound* (New York, 1982), p. 295.
13. Kunstler, *Deep in My Heart*, pp. 287–8.
14. Colburn, *Racial Change*, p. 84.
15. Bishop, *King*, p. 340.
16. Ibid., p. 342.
17. Miller, *King*, p. 189.
18. Watters, *Down to Now*, p. 289.
19. Bennett, *What Manner of Man*, p. 202.
20. Kunstler, *Deep in My Heart*, p. 298.
21. Oates, *Let the Trumpet Sound*, p. 298.
22. Bennett, *What Manner of Man*, p. 203.
23. Oates, *Let the Trumpet Sound*, p. 298.
24. Miller, *King* p. 191.
25. Benjamin Muse, *The American Negro Revolution: From Nonviolence to Black Power, 1963–1967*, (Bloomington, Indiana, 1968), p. 91.
26. Colburn, *Racial Change*, p. 105.
27. Goodwyn, *'Anarchy in St Augustine'*, p. 79.
28. Colburn, *Racial Change*, pp. 11, 109–10; Garrow, *Bearing the Cross*, pp. 335–7.
29. Kunstler, *Deep in My Heart*, p. 303.
30. Lewis, *King*, pp. 243–4.
31. Muse, *American Negro Revolution*, p. 92.
32. Colburn, *Racial Change*, p. 209.
33. Witherspoon, *King*, p. 159.
34. John Herbers, *The Lost Priority: What Happened to the Civil Rights Movement in America?*, (New York, 1970), p. 70.
35. Watters, *'St Augustine'*, p. 19.
36. Herbers, *Lost Priority*, p. 68.
37. Stokely Carmichael & Charles V. Hamilton, *Black Power: The Politics of Liberation in America*, (New York, 1967), p. 88.
38. James W. Silver, *Mississippi: The Closed Society*, new ed. enl. (New York, 1966), p. 257.
39. Witherspoon, *King*, p. 162.

40. Theodore H. White, *The Making of the President – 1964*, (New York, 1965), p. 188.
41. Sitkoff, *Struggle for Black Equality*, p. 181.
42. Lawson, *Black Ballots*, p. 305.
43. Forman, *Black Revolutionaries*, p. 392.
44. Carson, *In Struggle*, p. 126.
45. Sitkoff, *Struggle for Black Equality*, p. 185.
46. White, *Making of the President*, p. 291.
47. Emily Stoper, 'The Student Nonviolent Coordinating Committee: Rise and Fall of a Redemptive Organization', in Jo Freeman, ed., *Social Movements of the Sixties and Seventies*, (London, 1983), p. 325.
48. Forman, *Black Revolutionaries*, pp. 395–6.
49. Brink & Harris, *The Negro Revolution*, p. 120.
50. Carmichael & Hamilton, *Black Power*, p. 96.
51. Sellers, *Rivers of No Return*, p. 111.
52. David Garrow, *The FBI and Martin Luther King, Jr.*, (New York, 1983), pp. 122–3.
53. Howard Zinn, *The Twentieth Century: A People's History*, (New York, 1984), p. 164.
54. Washington, *Testament*, p. 224.

7   SELMA AND THE VOTING RIGHTS ACT OF 1965

1. Charles E. Fager, *Selma 1965*, (New York, 1974), p. 7.
2. James C. Harvey, *Black Civil Rights During the Johnson Administration*, (Jackson, Mississippi, 1973), p. 29.
3. Schulke & McPhee, *King Remembered*, p. 183.
4. Oates, *Let the Trumpet Sound*, p. 328.
5. *New York Times*, (4 March 1985), p. 14.
6. David J. Garrow, *Protest At Selma: Martin Luther King, Jr., and the Voting Rights Act of 1965*, (New Haven, Conn., 1978), p. 39.
7. Ibid; and Schulke & McPhee, *King Remembered*, pp. 182–3.
8. Lewis, *King*, p. 267.
9. Garrow, *Protest At Selma*, p. 42.
10. Ibid., p. 43.
11. Coretta King, *My Life*, p. 256.
12. Garrow, *Protest At Selma*, p. 49.
13. Ibid., pp. 51–2.
14. Oates, *Let the Trumpet Sound*, p. 342.
15. Garrow, *Protest At Selma*, p. 52.
16. Harvey, *Black Civil Rights During the Johnson Administration*, p. 26.
17. Westin & Mahoney, *King*, p. 167.
18. *Like It Is*, 'Recollections of Dr King', transcript, Part IV, (2 February 1986), p. 12.
19. Oates, *Let the Trumpet Sound*, p. 344.
20. *The Nation*, (15 February 1965), p. 154.
21. Fager, *Selma*, p. 70.
22. Miller, *King*, p. 208.

23. Sitkoff, *Struggle for Black Equality*, p. 189.
24. Oates, *Let the Trumpet Sound*, p. 346.
25. Sitkoff, *Struggle for Black Equality*, p. 189.
26. Witherspoon, *King*, pp. 176–7.
27. Colburn, *Racial Change*, p. 210.
28. Miller, *King*, p. 209.
29. Ibid., p. 210.
30. Fager, *Selma*, p. 96.
31. Lewis, *King*, p. 275.
32. *New York Times*, (4 March 1985), p. 14.
33. Sellers, *River of No Return*, pp. 122–3.
34. 'Behind the Selma March', in Washington, *Testament*, p. 129.
35. Westin & Mahoney, *King*, p. 170.
36. Ibid., p. 172.
37. Bishop, *King*, p. 386.
38. Westin & Mahoney, *King*, p. 173.
39. Sitkoff, *Struggle for Black Equality*, p. 191.
40. Ibid., p. 192.
41. 'Behind the Selma March', in Washington, *Testament*, p. 130.
42. Oates, *Let the Trumpet Sound*, p. 352.
43. Bishop, *King*, p. 388.
44. Ibid.
45. Garrow, *Protest At Selma*, p. 87.
46. Westin & Mahoney, *King*, pp. 175–6.
47. Andrew Young's statement comes from the public television series, *Eyes on the Prize: America's Civil Rights Years*, A Production of Blackside, Inc., (Boston, Massachusetts, 1986), Part Six, 'Selma: The Bridge to Freedom'.
48. Westin & Mahoney, *King*, p. 174.
49. Ibid., p. 175.
50. Friedman, *Civil Rights Reader*, p. 264.
51. 'Let Justice Roll Down', *The Nation*, (15 March 1965), p. 270.
52. Fager, *Selma*, p. 140.
53. Miller, *King*, p. 216.
54. Burke Marshall, 'The Protest Movement and the Law', *Virginia Law Review*, 51 (1965), pp. 785–803.
55. Ibid., p. 788.
56. Frank M. Johnson, 'Civil Disobedience and the Law', *Tulane Law Review*, XLIV, No. 1, (December 1969), p. 4.
57. Eric Goldman, *The Tragedy of Lyndon Johnson*, (New York, 1969), p. 315.
58. Sitkoff, *Struggle for Black Equality*, pp. 194–5
59. Washington, *Testament*, pp. 228–9.
60. Lawson, *Black Ballots*, p. 321.
61. Schulke & McPhee, *King Remembered*, pp. 207, 209.
62. Washington, *Testament*, p. 183.
63. Miller, *King*, p. 225.

8 INTERLUDE: THE PARADOX OF NONVIOLENCE

1. Cleghorn, 'Martin Luther King, Jr., Apostle of Crisis', in Lincoln, *King*, p. 113.
2. 'Man of the Year', *Time*, (3 January 1964), p. 13.
3. 'How Martin Luther King Won the Nobel Peace Prize', *U.S. News & World Report*, (8 February 1965), p. 76.
4. Frank Meyer, 'The Violence of Nonviolence', *National Review*, (20 April 1965), p. 327.
5. Frank Meyer, 'Showdown With Insurrection', *National Review*, (16 January 1968), p. 36.
6. Lionel Lokos, *The Life and Legacy of Martin Luther King*, (New York, 1968), p. 225.
7. King, 'Behind the Selma March', *Saturday Review*, (3 April 1965), p. 16.
8. Gene Sharp, *The Politics of Nonviolent Action*, (Boston, 1973), pp. 109–13; 657–8.
9. M. K. Gandhi, *Non-Violent Resistance*, (New York, 1961), p. 134.
10. Farmer, *Freedom – When?*, p. 101.
11. Sharp, *Politics of Nonviolent Action*, p. 69.
12. King, *Why We Can't Wait*, p. 82.
13. James F. Childress, *Civil Disobedience and Political Obligation*, (New Haven, Conn., 1971), p. 213, n. 81.
14. King, *Where Do We Go From Here: Chaos or Community?* (New York, 1967), p. 37.
15. King, 'The Social Organization of Nonviolence', in Robert F. Williams, *Negroes With Guns*, (New York, 1962), pp. 14–15.
16. Farmer, *Freedom – When?*, chapter 3.
17. King, *Why We Can't Wait*, chapter 2.
18. Farmer, *Freedom – When?*, p. 55.
19. Richard Gregg, *The Power of Non-Violence*, new ed. (New York, 1944), chapter VII.
20. Ibid., p. 43.
21. William James, 'The Moral Equivalent of War', in *The Writings of William James: A Comprehensive Edition*, John J. McDermott, ed., (New York, 1967), pp. 660–71.
22. James Baldwin, *The Fire Next Time*, (New York, 1963), p. 21.
23. King, *Why We Can't Wait*, p. 27.
24. Fairclough, 'Southern Christian Leadership Conference', p. 185.
25. Henry David Thoreau, 'Civil Disobedience', in *Walden and Other Writings of Henry David Thoreau*, ed. Brooks Atkinson, (New York, 1965), p. 647.
26. Charles V. Hamilton, ed., *The Black Experience in American Politics*, (New York, 1973), pp. 155, 157.
27. Alan F. Westin, ed., *Freedom Now: The Civil-Rights Struggle in America*, (New York, 1964), p. 33.
28. Foreword to Burke Marshall, *Federalism and Civil Rights*, (New York, 1964), p. ix.
29. Joanne Grant, ed., *Black Protest: History, Documents and Analyses, 1619 to the Present*, (New York, 1970) p. 399.

30. Haywood Burns, 'The Federal Government and Civil Rights', in Leon Friedman, ed., *Southern Justice*, (New York, 1965), p. 235.
31. Schlesinger, *Robert Kennedy*, p. 318.
32. Ibid., p. 319.
33. Marshall, *Federalism and Civil Rights*, p. 50.
34. Pat Watters & Reese Cleghorn, *Climbing Jacob's Ladder: The Arrival of Negroes in Southern Politics*, (New York, 1967), p. 229.
35. Ibid., pp. 229–30.
36. Zinn, *Southern Mystique*, pp. 205–6.
37. Burns, 'The Federal Government and Civil Rights', p. 237. (Burns's italics).
38. Ibid., 231. (Italics in original).
39. Watters & Cleghorn, *Climbing Jacob's Ladder*, p. 230. (Italics in original).
40. Zinn, *Southern Mystique*, p. 207; Burns, 'The Federal Government and Civil Rights', p. 238.
41. Zinn, *Southern Mystique*, pp. 207–8.

9 A NEW DIRECTION: CHICAGO, 1966

1. Meier & Rudwick, *CORE*, p. 329.
2. *Revolution in Civil Rights* (Washington, D.C., 1968), p. 73.
3. King, *Where Do We Go From Here?*, p. 4.
4. Baldwin, *Fire Next Time*, p. 102.
5. 'From Protest to Politics', in Bayard Rustin, *Down the Line*, (Chicago, 1971), p. 115. (Rustin's italics).
6. Ibid., pp. 117–18.
7. Lee Rainwater & William L. Yancey, *The Moynihan Report and the Politics of Controversy*, (Cambridge, Mass., 1967), p. 75.
8. Ibid., p. 49.
9. Ibid. pp. 93–4.
10. Friedman, *Civil Rights Reader*, p. 267.
11. Albert Blaustein & Robert L. Zangrando, eds. *Civil Rights and the American Negro: A Documentary History*, (New York, 1968), pp. 560–1, 565.
12. Herbers, *Lost Priority*, p. 15.
13. King, *Why We Can't Wait*, p. 149.
14. Washington, *Testament*, p. 193.
15. Ibid.
16. Miller, *King*, p. 238.
17. Good, 'Bossism, Racism and Dr King', *The Nation*, (19 September 1966), p. 240.
18. Lewis, *King*, p. 314.
19. Westin & Mahoney, *King*, p. 192.
20. Manning Marable, *Black American Politics: From the Washington Marches to Jesse Jackson*, (London, 1985), p. 338, n. 48.
21. Kenneth B. Clark, *The Negro Protest: James Baldwin, Malcolm X, Martin Luther King talk with Kenneth B. Clark*, (Boston, 1963), p. 12.
22. Marable, *Black American Politics*, p. 209.

23. Oates, *Let the Trumpet Sound*, p. 379.
24. Lokos, *House Divided*, p. 229.
25. Garrow, *Bearing the Cross*, p. 448.
26. Sobel, *Civil Rights*, p. 397.
27. Garrow, *Bearing the Cross*, p. 457.
28. Miller, *King*, p. 235.
29. Bishop, *King*, p. 420.
30. Oates, *Let the Trumpet Sound*, p. 389.
31. Barbara A. Reynolds, *Jesse Jackson: The Man, The Movement, The Myth*, (Chicago, 1985), p. 46.
32. Ibid., pp. 46–7.
33. Lokos, *House Divided*, p. 234.
34. Bill Gleason, *Daley of Chicago: The Man, the Mayor, and the Limits of Conventional Politics*, (New York, 1970), pp. 42–3.
35. Garrow, *Bearing the Cross*, p. 465.
36. Oates, *Let the Trumpet Sound*, p. 393.
37. Lewis, *King*, p. 331.
38. Miller, *King*, p. 240.
39. Witherspoon, *King*, p. 194.
40. Bishop, *King*, p. 424.
41. Ibid., p. 428.
42. Miller, *King*, p. 241.
43. Coretta King, *My Life*, p. 277.
44. Sitkoff, *Struggle for Black Equality*, p. 213.
45. King, *Where Do We Go From Here?*, pp. 25–6.
46. Oates, *Let the Trumpet Sound*, p. 398.
47. King, *Where Do We Go From Here?*, p. 27.
48. Ibid., p. 28.
49. Sobel, *Civil Rights*, p. 392.
50. Allen J. Matusow, *The Unraveling of America: A History of Liberalism in the 1960s* (New York, 1984) p. 354.
51. Oates, *Let the Trumpet Sound*, p. 400.
52. King, *Where Do We Go From Here?*, p. 29.
53. Charles E. Silberman, *Crisis in Black and White*, (New York, 1964), p. 194.
54. Robert L. Allen, *Black Awakening in Capitalist America*, (Garden City, New York, 1970), p. 30.
55. *Malcolm X Speaks*, p. 9.
56. Ibid.
57. Ibid., p. 16.
58. Ibid., p. 26.
59. Ibid., p. 116.
60. King, *Where Do We Go From Here?*, p. 44.
61. Ibid., pp. 30–1.
62. Ibid., p. 31.
63. Ibid.
64. Garrow, *Bearing the Cross*, p. 489.
65. Paul Good, *The Trouble I've Seen*, (Washington, D.C., 1975), p. 261.
66. Lewis, *King*, p. 329.

67. Carson, *In Struggle*, pp. 210–11.
68. Meier & Rudwick, *CORE*, p. 412. (Italics in original).
69. Miller, *King* p. 249.
70. Oates, *Let the Trumpet Sound*, p. 405.
71. Meier, Rudwick, & Broderick, *Black Protest Thought*, pp. 596–8.
72. Robert L. Scott & Wayne Brockriede, *The Rhetoric of Black Power* (New York, 1969) p. 71.
73. Sobel, *Civil Rights*, pp. 382–3.
74. Bayard Rustin, *Down the Line* (Chicago, 1971), p. 154.
75. Sellers, *River of No Return*, pp. 171–2.
76. Bishop, *King*, p. 437.
77. Lokos, *House Divided*, p. 237.
78. Oates, *Let the Trumpet Sound*, p. 406.
79. Lewis, *King*, p. 334.
80. Sobel, *Civil Rights*, p. 398.
81. Lewis, *King*, p. 332.
82. Reynolds, *Jesse Jackson*, p. 58.
83. Lewis, *King*, p. 338.
84. Oates, *Let the Trumpet Sound*, p. 413.
85. Bayard Rustin, 'Convocation Address', 5 March 1968, at Clark College, Atlanta, Georgia, in *On Being Black: Writings by Afro-Americans from Frederick Douglass to the Present*, edited by Charles T. Davis & Daniel Walden (New York, 1970), p. 320.
86. King, 'The Last Steep Ascent', *The Nation*, (14 March 1966), p. 289.
87. Miller, *King*, p. 250.
88. Lewis, *King*, p. 342.
89. Ibid., p. 343.
90. Oates, *Let the Trumpet Sound*, p. 414.
91. Lewis, *King*, p. 346.
92. Ibid., p. 351.
93. Fairclough, 'Southern Christian Leadership Conference', p. 187.
94. Sobel, *Civil Rights*, p. 403.
95. Good, 'Bossism, Racism and Dr King', p. 238.
96. Lewis, *King*, p. 348.
97. Oates, *Let the Trumpet Sound*, p. 416.
98. Ibid., p. 418.
99. Louis Lomax, *To Kill A Black Man*, (Los Angeles, 1968), p. 167. (Lomax's italics).
100. Witherspoon, *King*, p. 203.
101. William Brink & Louis Harris, *Black and White: A Study of Racial Attitudes Today*, (New York, 1967), p. 41.
102. Lyndon Baines Johnson, *The Vantage Point*, (New York, 1971), p. 178.
103. Brink & Harris, *Black and White*, p. 41.
104. Garrow, *Bearing the Cross*, p. 524.
105. Lewis, *King*, p. 352.

10 KING TAKES A RADICAL STAND, 1967–8

1. David Halberstam, 'The Second Coming of Martin Luther King', *Harper's*, (August, 1967), in Lincoln, *King*, pp. 201–2.
2. King, *The Trumpet of Conscience*, (New York, 1968), p. 6.
3. Adam Fairclough, 'Martin Luther King and the War in Vietnam', *Phylon*, 45 (Spring 1984), p. 29.
4. John J. Ansbro, *Martin Luther King, Jr.: The Making of a Mind*, (New York, 1982), p. 253.
5. *New York Times*, (2 April 1967), p. 1.
6. King, 'A Time to Break Silence', in Washington, *Testament*, pp. 231–44.
7. Miller, *King*, p. 255.
8. Fairclough, 'King and the War in Vietnam', p. 34.
9. Ansbro, *King*, p. 254.
10. Washington, *Testament*, p. 408.
11. Ansbro, *King*, p. 254.
12. Ibid., p. 255.
13. Lincoln, *King*, pp. 217–18.
14. Ibid., p. 196.
15. Muse, *American Negro Revolution*, p. 299.
16. *Report of the National Advisory Commission on Civil Disorders*, (New York, 1968) p. 1.
17. Ibid., p. 203.
18. Ibid., p. 2.
19. Ibid., p. 23.
20. Ibid., p. 483.
21. Vincent Harding, *The Other American Revolution*, (Los Angeles, 1980), p. 191.
22. *Race Relations in the USA: 1954–1968*, Keesing's Research Report 4, (New York, 1970), p. 252.
23. King, *Where Do We Go From Here?*, pp. 174–5.
24. Ibid., pp. 36–7.
25. Ibid., p. 43.
26. Ibid., p. 44.
27. Frantz Fanon, *The Wretched of the Earth*, (New York, 1964), pp. 86, 94.
28. King, *Where Do We Go From Here?*, p. 54.
29. Ibid., p. 61.
30. Ibid., p. 58.
31. *New York Review of Books*, 9 (24 August 1967), pp. 3–6; *America*, 117 (22 July 1967), pp. 88–9; *Commonweal*, 87 (17 November 1967), pp. 215–16.
32. King, *Stride Toward Freedom*, p. 91.
33. Ibid., p. 94.
34. 'A Testament of Hope', in Washington, *Testament*, pp. 314–15.
35. 'The President's Address to the Tenth Anniversary Convention of the Southern Christian Leadership Conference, Atlanta, Georgia, 16 August 1967', in Scott & Brockriede, *The Rhetoric of Black Power*, pp. 161–3.

36. King, *Where Do We Go From Here?* p. 186; King, *Strength to Love*, (Philadelphia, 1963), p. 103.
37. 'The President's Address. . .', p. 162.
38. Adam Fairclough, 'Was Martin Luther King a Marxist?', in Lincoln, *Martin Luther King*, p. 236.
39. King, *Trumpet of Conscience*, p. 14.
40. Charles E. Fager, *Uncertain Resurrection: The Poor People's Washington Campaign*, (Grand Rapids, Michigan, 1969). p. 15.
41. Ibid., pp. 16–17.
42. King, 'Showdown for Nonviolence', in Washington, *Testament*, p. 65.
43. Ibid., p. 69.
44. Bishop, *King*, p. 469.
45. 'Martin Luther King, Jr. and the Promise of Nonviolent Populism', in John Hope Franklin & August Meier, eds. *Black Leaders of the Twentieth Century*, (Urbana, Illinois, 1982), p. 301.
46. José Yglesias, 'Dr King's March on Washington, Part II', *New York Times Magazine*, (31 March 1967), in *Black Protest in the Sixties*, edited by August Meier & Elliott Rudwick, (Chicago, 1970), p. 275.
47. King, 'Showdown for Nonviolence', p. 68.
48. Washington, *Testament*, p. 66.
49. Yglesias, 'Dr King's March on Washington', p. 270.
50. 'Memo on the Spring Protest in Washington, D.C.', in Bayard Rustin, *Down the Line*, p. 202.
51. Yglesias, 'Dr King's March on Washington', p. 272.
52. Rustin, 'Memo. . . .', *Down the Line*, p. 204.
53. Fairclough, 'Southern Christian Leadership Conference'. p. 190.
54. Garrow, *Bearing the Cross*, p. 583.
55. King, 'The Drum Major Instinct', in Washington, *A Testament of Hope*, p. 267.
56. Garrow, *Bearing the Cross*, p. 598.
57. 'Honoring Dr Dubois, in *W.E.B. Dubois Speaks*, vol. I *Speeches and Addresses, 1890–1919*, ed. Philip S. Foner, (New York, 1970) pp. 12, 18–20.
58. Coretta King, *My Life*, p. 313.
59. Gerold Frank, *An American Death*, (Garden City, New York, 1972), pp. 39–40.
60. Mark Lane & Dick Gregory, *Code Name 'Zorro': The Murder of Martin Luther King, Jr.* (Englewood Cliffs, New Jersey, 1977), pp. 99–102.
61. Bishop, *King*, p. 12.
62. Miller, *King*, pp. 270, 274; Kondrashov, *The Life and Death of Martin Luther King*, (Moscow, 1981), p. 226.
63. Garrow, *Bearing the Cross*, p. 615.
64. Oates, *Let the Trumpet Sound*, p. 480.
65. Bishop, *King*, p. 13.
66. Garrow, *Bearing the Cross*, p. 614.
67. Ibid., p. 613.
68. Matusow, *Unraveling of America*, p. 394.
69. Godfrey Hodgson, *America in Our Time*, (New York, 1978), p. 360.
70. Bishop, *King*, p. 33.
71. Washington, *Testament*, pp. 282, 286.

Select Bibliography

Abraham, Henry J., *Freedom and the Court: Civil Rights and Liberties in the United States*, 2nd ed. (New York: Oxford University Press, 1972).

Allen, Robert L., *Black Awakening in Capitalist America* (Garden City, New York: Doubleday, Anchor Books, 1970).

Alvarez, Joseph A., *From Reconstruction to Revolution: The Blacks' Struggle for Equality* (New York: Atheneum, 1971).

Ansbro, John J., *Martin Luther King, Jr.: The Making of a Mind* (New York: Orbis Books, 1982).

Ashmore, Harry S., *Hearts and Minds: The Anatomy of Racism from Roosevelt to Reagan* (New York: McGraw Hill, 1982).

Baldwin, James, 'The Dangerous Road Before Martin Luther King', *Harper's* 222 (February 1961), pp. 33–42.

——, *The Fire Next Time* (New York: Dial Press, 1963).

Barbour, Floyd B., ed., *The Black Power Revolt* (Boston: Porter Sargent, 1968).

Bardolph, Richard A., ed., *The Civil Rights Record: Black Americans and the Law, 1844–1970* (New York: Crowell, 1970).

Barnes, Catherine, *Journey From Jim Crow: The Desegregation of Southern Transit* (New York: Columbia University Press, 1983).

Bartley, Numan V., *The Rise of Massive Resistance: Race and Politics in the South During the 1950s* (Baton Rouge: Louisiana State University Press, 1969).

Bedau, Hugo A., ed., *Civil Disobedience: Theory and Practice* (New York: Pegasus, 1969).

Bell, Inge P., *CORE and the Strategy of Nonviolence* (New York: Random House, 1968).

Bennett, Lerone, Jr., *What Manner of Man: A Biography of Martin Luther King, Jr.*, 3rd ed. rev. (Chicago: Johnson Publishing Co., 1968).

Bishop, Jim, *The Days of Martin Luther King, Jr.* (New York: G. P. Putnam's Sons, 1971).

Blaustein, Albert P., & Robert L. Zangrando, eds, *Civil Rights and the American Negro: A Documentary History* (New York: Trident Press, 1968).

Blumberg, Rhoda L., *Civil Rights: The 1960s Freedom Struggle* (Boston: Twayne Publishers, 1984).

Bondurant, Joan V., *Conquest of Violence: The Gandhian Philosophy of Conflict* (Berkeley: University of California Press, 1965).

Bracey, John H., August Meier, & Elliott Rudwick, eds, *Conflict and Competition: Studies in the Recent Black Protest Movement* (Belmont, California: Wadsworth Publishing Co., 1971).

Brauer, Carl M., *John F. Kennedy and the Second Reconstruction* (New York: Columbia University Press, 1977).

219

Brink, William & Louis Harris, *The Negro Revolution in America* (New York: Simon & Schuster, 1964).

——, *Black and White: A Study of U.S. Racial Attitudes Today* (New York, Simon & Schuster, 1967).

Brockriede, Wayne L., & Robert L. Scott, eds, *The Rhetoric of Black Power* (New York: Harper & Row, 1969).

Brooks, Thomas R., *Walls Come Tumbling Down: A History of the Civil Rights Movement, 1940–1970* (Englewood Cliffs, New Jersey, Prentice-Hall, 1974).

Burns, Haywood, 'The Federal Government and Civil Rights', in Leon Friedman, ed., *Southern Justice* (New York: Pantheon, 1965).

Carmichael, Stokely, 'What We Want', *New York Review of Books'*, 7 (22 September 1966), pp. 5–8.

Carmichael, Stokely, & Charles V. Hamilton, *Black Power: The Politics of Liberation in America* (New York: Random House, Vintage Books, 1967).

Carson, Clayborne, *In Struggle: SNCC and the Black Awakening of the 1960s* (Cambridge, Mass.: Harvard University Press, 1981).

——, 'SNCC and the Albany Movement', *The Journal of Southwest Georgia History* II (Fall 1984), pp. 15–25.

Case, Clarence M., *Non-Violent Coercion* (New York: The Century Co., 1923).

Chafe, William H., *Civilities and Civil Rights: Greensboro, North Carolina, and the Black Struggle for Freedom* (New York, Oxford University Press, 1980).

Childress, James F., *Civil Disobedience and Political Obligation. A Study in Christian Social Ethics* (New Haven, Conn., Yale University Press, 1971).

Clark, Kenneth B., *Dark Ghetto* (New York: Harper & Row, 1965).

——, *The Negro Protest: James Baldwin, Malcolm X, Martin Luther King* (Boston: Beacon Press, 1963).

——, 'The Civil Rights Movement: Momentum and Organization', *Daedalus* 95 (Winter 1966), pp. 239–67.

Cleaver, Eldridge, *Soul on Ice* (New York: McGraw-Hill, 1968).

Cleghorn, Reese, 'Martin Luther King, Apostle of Crisis', *Saturday Evening Post* (15 June 1963), pp. 15–19.

——, 'Epilogue in Albany: Were the Marches Worthwhile?', *New Republic* (20 July 1963), pp. 15–18.

Cohen, Carl, *Civil Disobedience: Conscience, Tactics, and the Law* (New York: Columbia University Press, 1971).

Colaiaco, James A., 'The American Dream Unfulfilled: Martin Luther King, Jr. and the "Letter From Birmingham Jail" ', *Phylon* 45 (Spring 1984), pp. 1–18.

——, 'Martin Luther King, Jr. and the Paradox of Nonviolent Direct Action', *Phylon* 47 (Spring 1986), pp. 16–28.

Colburn, David R., *Racial Change and Community Crisis: St. Augustine, Florida, 1877–1980* (New York: Columbia University Press, 1985).

Cox, Archibald, Mark De Wolfe Howe, & J. R. Wiggins, *Civil Rights, the Constitution, and the Courts* (Cambridge, Mass.: Harvard University Press, 1967).

Davis, Charles T., & Daniel Walden, eds, *On Being Black: Writings by Afro-*

Americans from Frederick Douglass to the Present (Greenwich, Conn.: Fawcett, 1970).

Dorman, Michael, *We Shall Overcome* (New York: Delacorte Press, 1964).

Draper, Theodore, *The Rediscovery of Black Nationalism* (New York: Viking Press, 1970).

Eagles, Charles W., ed., *The Civil Rights Movement in America* (Jackson: University Press of Mississippi, 1986).

Fager, Charles E., *Selma 1965* (New York: Charles Scribner's Sons, 1974).

——, *Uncertain Resurrection: The Poor People's Washington Campaign* (Grand Rapids, Michigan: William B. Eerdmans Publishing Co., 1969).

Fairclough, Adam, 'The Southern Christian Leadership Conference and the Second Reconstruction', *South Atlantic Quarterly* 80 (Spring 1981), pp. 177–94.

——, 'Was Martin Luther King a Marxist?', *History Workshop* 15 (Spring 1983), pp. 117–25.

——, 'Martin Luther King and the War in Vietnam', *Phylon* 45 (Spring 1984), pp. 19–39.

——, 'Martin Luther King, Jr. and the Quest for Nonviolent Social Change', *Phylon* 47 (Spring 1986), pp. 1–15.

Fanon, Frantz, *The Wretched of the Earth* (New York: Grove Press, 1965).

Farmer, James, *Freedom – When?* (New York: Random House, 1965).

——, *Lay Bare the Heart* (New York: Arbor House, 1985).

Fleming, Harold, 'The Federal Executive and Civil Rights: 1961–1965', *Daedalus* 94 (Fall 1965), pp. 921–48.

Forman, James, *The Making of Black Revolutionaries*, 2nd ed. (Washington, D.C.: Open Hand Publishing Co., 1985).

Fortas, Abe, *Concerning Dissent and Civil Disobedience* (New York: New American Library, 1968).

Frank, Gerold, *An American Death* (Garden City, New York: Doubleday, 1972).

Franklin, John Hope, *From Slavery to Freedom*, rev. ed. (New York: Alfred A. Knopf, 1967).

Franklin, John Hope, & August Meier, eds, *Black Leaders of the Twentieth Century* (Urbana: University of Illinois Press, 1982).

Franklin, John Hope, & Isidore Starr, eds, *The Negro in the 20th Century* (New York: Random House, Vintage Books, 1967).

Friedman, Leon, ed., *Southern Justice* (New York: Pantheon, 1965).

——, ed., *The Civil Rights Reader: Basic Documents of the Civil Rights Movement*, rev. ed. (New York: Walker & Co., 1968).

Gandhi, M. K., *Non-Violent Resistance* (New York: Schocken, 1961).

Garrow, David J., *Protest at Selma: Martin Luther King, Jr., and the Voting Rights Act of 1965* (New Haven, Conn.: Yale University Press, 1978).

——, *The FBI and Martin Luther King, Jr.: From 'Solo' to Memphis* (New York: W. W. Norton, 1981).

——, *Bearing the Cross: Martin Luther King, Jr., and the Southern Christian Leadership Conference* (New York: William Morrow, 1986).

Gentile, Thomas, *March on Washington: August 28, 1963* (New Day Publications, 1983).

Gleason, Bill, *Daley of Chicago: The Man, the Mayor, and the Limits of*

Conventional Politics (New York: Simon & Schuster, 1970).

Goldman, Eric F., *The Tragedy of Lyndon Johnson* (New York: Alfred A. Knopf, 1969).

Goldman, Peter, *Report from Black America* (New York: Simon & Schuster, 1970).

——, *The Death and Life of Malcolm X* (New York: Harper & Row, 1973).

Good, Paul, 'Bossism, Racism and Dr. King', *The Nation* (19 September 1966), pp. 237–42.

——, *The Trouble I've Seen: White Journalist/Black Movement* (Washington, D.C.: Howard University Press, 1975).

Goodwyn, Larry, 'Anarchy in St Augustine', *Harper's* 230 (January 1965), pp. 74–81.

Grant, Joanne, ed., *Black Protest: History, Documents and Analyses, 1619 to the Present* (Greenwich, Conn.: Fawcett, 1968).

Gregg, Richard B., *The Power of Non-Violence*, 2nd ed. rev. (New York: Fellowship Publications, 1944).

Guthman, Edwin, *We Band of Brothers: A Memoir of Robert F. Kennedy* (New York: Harper & Row, 1971).

Halberstam, David, 'The Second Coming of Martin Luther King', *Harper's* 235 (August 1967), pp. 39–51.

Hamilton, Charles V., *The Black Preacher in America* (New York: William Morrow, 1972).

——, *The Black Experience in American Politics* (New York: G. P. Putnam's Sons, 1973).

Harding, Vincent, 'Black Radicalism: The Road from Montgomery', in Alfred F. Young, ed., *Dissent* (DeKalb: Northern Illinois University Press, 1968), pp. 319–54.

——, *The Other American Revolution* (Los Angeles: Center for Afro-American Studies, UCLA, 1980).

Harvey, James C., *Civil Rights During the Kennedy Administration* (Jackson: University & College Press of Mississippi, 1971).

——, *Black Civil Rights During the Johnson Administration* (Jackson: University & College Press of Mississippi, 1973).

Herbers, John, 'A Critical Test for the Nonviolent Way', *New York Times Magazine* (5 July 1964), pp. 5, 30–1.

——, *The Lost Priority: What Happened to the Civil Rights Movement in America?* (New York: Funk & Wagnalls, 1970).

——, *The Black Dilemma* (New York: John Day Co., 1973).

Hodgson, Godfrey, *America In Our Time* (New York: Random House, Vintage Books, 1978).

Howard, Jan, 'The Provocation of Violence: A Civil Rights Tactic?', *Dissent* 13 (Jan.–Feb. 1966), pp. 94–9.

Hubbard, Howard, 'Five Long Hot Summers and How They Grew', *Public Interest* 12 (Summer 1968), pp. 3–24.

Johnson, Frank M., 'Civil Disobedience and the Law', *Tulane Law Review*, Vol. XLIV, No. 1 (December 1969), p. 1–13.

Johnson, Lyndon B., *The Vantage Point: Perspectives on the Presidency, 1963–1969* (New York: Holt, Rinehart & Winston, 1971).

Kahn, Tom, 'Direct Action and Democratic Values', *Dissent* 13 (January–February 1966), pp. 22–30.

Kearns, Doris, *Lyndon Johnson and the American Dream* (New York: Harper & Row, 1976).

Keesing's Research Report No. 4, *Race Relations in the USA, 1954–1968* (New York: Charles Scribner's Sons, 1970).

Killian, Lewis M., *The Impossible Revolution?: Black Power and the American Dream* (New York: Random House, 1968).

King, Coretta Scott, *My Life with Martin Luther King, Jr.* (New York: Holt, Rinehart & Winston, 1969).

King, Martin Luther, Jr., *Stride Toward Freedom: The Montgomery Story* (New York: Harper & Brothers, 1958).

——, *The Measure of a Man* (Philadelphia: Christian Education Press, 1959).

——, *Strength to Love* (Philadelphia, Fortress Press, 1963).

——, *Why We Can't Wait* (New York: Harper & Row, 1964).

——, *Where Do We Go From Here: Chaos or Community?* (New York, Harper & Row, 1967).

——, *The Trumpet of Conscience* (New York: Harper & Row, 1968).

Kluger, Richard, *Simple Justice: The History of Brown v. Board of Education and Black America's Struggle for Equality*, 2 vols. (New York: Alfred A. Knopf, 1975).

Kondrashov, Stanislav, *The Life and Death of Martin Luther King*, rev. ed. (Moscow: Progress Publishers, 1981).

Kopkind, Andrew, 'Selma: Ain't Gonna Let Nobody Turn Me Round', *New Republic* 152 (20 March 1965), pp. 7–9.

Kunstler, William, *Deep in My Heart* (New York: William Morrow, 1966).

Lane, Mark and Dick Gregory, *Code Name 'Zorro': The Murder of Martin Luther King, Jr.* (Englewood Cliffs, New Jersey: Prentice-Hall, Inc., 1977).

Laue, James H., 'Power, Conflict and Social Change', in Louis H. Masotti & Don R. Bowen, eds, *Riots and Rebellion: Civil Violence in the Urban Community* (Beverly Hills, California: Sage, 1968).

Lawson, Steven F., *Black Ballots: Voting Rights in the South, 1944–1969* (New York: Columbia University Press, 1976).

Lester, Julius, *Look Out, Whitey! Black Power's Gon' Get Your Mama* (New York: Dial Press, 1968).

Levitan, Sar, William Johnston, & Robert Taggart, *Still A Dream: The Changing Status of Blacks Since 1960* (Cambridge, Mass., Harvard University Press, 1975).

Lewis, Anthony, *Portrait of a Decade: The Second American Revolution* (New York: Random House, 1964).

Lewis, David L., *King: A Biography*, 2nd ed. (Urbana: University of Illinois Press, 1978).

——, 'Martin Luther King, Jr., and the Promise of Nonviolent Populism', in John Hope Franklin & August Meier, eds, *Black Leaders of the Twentieth Century* (Urbana: University of Illinois Press, 1982), pp. 277–303.

Lincoln, C. Eric, *The Black Muslims in America*, rev. ed. (Boston: Beacon Press, 1973).

——, *Martin Luther King, Jr.: A Profile*, rev. ed. (New York: Hill & Wang, 1984).

Lokos, Lionel, *House Divided: The Life and Legacy of Martin Luther King* (New Rochelle, New York: Arlington House, 1968).

Lomax, Louis, *The Negro Revolt* (New York: New American Library, 1963).

——, *To Kill a Black Man* (Los Angeles: Holloway House, 1968).

Lynd, Staughton, *Nonviolence in America* (Indianapolis, Indiana: Bobbs-Merrill, 1966).

McAdam, Doug, *Political Process and the Development of Black Insurgency, 1930–1970* (Chicago: University of Chicago Press, 1982).

——, 'The Decline of the Civil Rights Movement', in Jo Freeman, ed., *Social Movements of the Sixties and Seventies* (New York: Longman, 1983), pp. 298–319.

——, 'Tactical Innovation and the Pace of Insurgency', *American Sociological Review* 48 (December 1983), pp. 735–54.

McMillen, Neil R., 'Black Enfranchisement in Mississippi: Federal Enforcement and Black Protest in the 1960s', *Journal of Southern History* 43 (August 1977), pp. 351–72.

Malcolm X, *The Autobiography of Malcolm X* (New York: Ballantine Books, 1973).

Malcolm X Speaks, ed. by George Breitman (New York: Grove Press, 1966).

'Man of the Year: Never Again Where He Was', *Time* (3 January 1964), pp. 13–16, 25–7.

Marable, Manning, *Black American Politics: From the Washington Marches to Jesse Jackson* (London: Verso, 1985).

Marshall, Burke, *Federalism and Civil Rights* (New York: Columbia University Press, 1964).

——, 'The Protest Movement and the Law', *Virginia Law Review* 51 (June 1965), pp. 785–803.

Matthews, Donald R., and James W. Prothro, *Negroes and the New Southern Politics* (New York: Harcourt, Brace & World, 1966).

Matusow, Allen J., 'From Civil Rights to Black Power: The Case of SNCC, 1960–1966', in Barton J. Bernstein & Matusow, eds, *Twentieth Century America*, 2nd ed. (New York: Harcourt, Brace, Jovanovich, 1972), pp. 494–520.

——, *The Unraveling of America: A History of Liberalism in the 1960s* (New York: Harper & Row, 1984).

Mehta, Ved., 'Gandhism Is Not Easily Copied', *New York Times Magazine* (9 July 1961), pp. 8ff.

Meier, August, 'On the Role of Martin Luther King', *New Politics* 4 (Winter 1965), pp. 52–9.

Meier, August, & Elliott M. Rudwick, *From Plantation to Ghetto* (New York: Hill & Wang, 1966).

——, *Black Protest in the Sixties* (Chicago: Quadrangle Books, 1970).

Meier, August, Elliott Rudwick, & Francis L. Broderick, eds, *Black Protest Thought in the Twentieth Century*, 2nd ed. (Indianapolis, Indiana: Bobbs-Merrill, 1971).

Meier, August, & Elliott Rudwick, *CORE: A Study in the Civil Rights Movement, 1942–1968* (Urbana: University of Illinois Press, 1975).

Messner, Gerald, ed., *Another View: To Be Black in America* (New York: Harcourt, Brace, & World, 1970).

Miller, William R., *Nonviolence: A Christian Interpretation* (New York: Association Press, 1964).

——, *Martin Luther King, Jr.: His Life, Martyrdom, and Meaning for the World* (New York: Weybright & Talley, 1968).

Monroe, William B., 'Television: The Chosen Instrument of the Revolution', in Paul L. Fisher & Ralph L. Lowenstein, eds, *Race and News Media* (New York: Praeger, 1967).

Morris, Aldon D., *The Origins of the Civil Rights Movement: Black Communities Organizing for Change* (New York: Free Press, 1984).

Murray, Pauli, 'Protest Against the Legal Status of the Negro', *Annals of the American Academy of Political and Social Science*, No. 357 (January 1965), pp. 55–64.

Muse, Benjamin, *The American Negro Revolution: From Nonviolence to Black Power, 1963–1967* (Bloomington: Indiana University Press, 1968).

Myrdal, Gunnar, *An American Dilemma*, rev. ed. (New York: Harper & Row, 1962).

Navasky, Victor, *Kennedy Justice* (New York: Atheneum, 1971).

Niebuhr, Reinhold, *Moral Man and Immoral Society* (New York: Charles Scribner's Sons, 1932).

Oates, Stephen B., *Let the Trumpet Sound: The Life of Martin Luther King, Jr.* (New York: Harper & Row, 1982).

O'Neill, William L., *Coming Apart: An Informal History of America in the 1960s* (Chicago: Quadrangle Books, 1971).

Oppenheimer, Martin, and George Lakey, *A Manual for Direct Action* (Chicago: Quadrangle Books, 1964).

Parmet, Herbert S., *JFK: The Presidency of John F. Kennedy* (New York: Penguin Books, 1984).

Parsons, Talcott, & Kenneth B. Clark, eds, *The Negro American* (Boston: Beacon Press, 1967).

Peeks, Edward, *The Long Struggle for Black Power* (New York, Charles Scribner's Sons, 1971).

Piven, Frances F., & Richard A. Cloward, *Poor People's Movements: Why They Succeed, How They Fail* (New York: Pantheon, 1977).

Polenberg, Richard, *One Nation Divisible: Class, Race and Ethnicity in the United States Since 1938* (New York: Penguin Books, 1980).

Powledge, Fred, *Black Power – White Resistance: Notes on the New Civil War* (Cleveland, Ohio: World Publishing Co., 1967).

Raines, Howell, *My Soul Is Rested: Movement Days in the Deep South Remembered* (New York: G. Putnam's Sons, 1977).

Rainwater, Lee & William L. Yancey, *The Moynihan Report and the Politics of Controversy* (Cambridge, Mass.: M.I.T. Press, 1967).

Rakove, Milton L., *Don't Make No Waves, Don't Back No Losers: An Insider's Analysis of the Daley Machine* (Bloomington: Indiana University Press, 1975).

Report of the National Advisory Commission on Civil Disorders (New York: Bantam Books Edition, 1968).

Revolution in Civil Rights (Washington, D.C.: Congressional Quarterly Inc., 1968).

Reynolds, Barbara A., *Jesse Jackson: The Man, The Movement, The Myth* (Chicago: Nelson-Hall, 1975).

Ricks, John A., ' "De Lawd" Descends and Is Crucified: Martin Luther King, Jr., in Albany, Georgia', in *The Journal of Southwest Georgia History* II (Fall 1984), pp. 3–14.

Roberts, Adam, 'Martin Luther King and Nonviolent Resistance', *World Today* 24 (June 1968), pp. 226–36.

Rose, Arnold M., 'The American Negro Problem in the Context of Social Change', *Annals of the American Academy of Political and Social Science*, No. 357 (January 1965), pp. 1–17.

Rowan, Carl T., 'Martin Luther King's Tragic Decision', *Reader's Digest* 91 (September 1967), pp. 37–42.

Royko, Mike, *Boss: Richard J. Daley of Chicago* (New York: E. P. Dutton, 1971).

Rustin, Bayard, 'The Meaning of Birmingham', *Liberation* 8 (June 1963), pp. 7–9, 31.

——, 'The Meaning of the March on Washington', *Liberation* 8 (October 1963), pp. 11–13.

——, 'From Protest to Politics: The Future of the Civil Rights Movement', *Commentary* 39 (February 1965), pp. 25–31.

——, ' "Black Power" and Coalition Politics', *Commentary* 42 (September 1966), pp. 35–40.

——, *Down the Line* (Chicago: Quadrangle Books, 1971).

Schlesinger, Arthur M., Jr., *A Thousand Days: John F. Kennedy in the White House* (Boston: Houghton Mifflin, 1965).

——, *Robert Kennedy and His Times* (Boston: Houghton Mifflin, 1978).

Schulke, Flip, ed., *Martin Luther King, Jr.: A Documentary – Montgomery to Memphis* (New York: W. W. Norton, 1976).

Schulke, Flip, & Penelope McPhee, *King Remembered* (New York: W. W. Norton, 1986).

Selby, Earl & Miriam, *Odyssey: Journey Through Black America* (New York: G. P. Putnam's Sons, 1971).

Sellers, Cleveland, with Robert Terrell, *The River of No Return* (New York: William Morrow, 1973).

Sharp, Gene, *The Politics of Nonviolent Action* (Boston: Porter Sargent 1973).

——, *Gandhi As A Political Strategist* (Boston: Porter Sargent, 1979).

Shridharani, Krishnalal, *War Without Violence* (Bombay: Bharatiya Vidya Bhavan, 1962).

Silberman, Charles E., *Crisis in Black and White* (New York: Random House, 1964).

Silver, James W., *Mississippi: The Closed Society*, new ed. enl. (New York: Harcourt, Brace & World, 1966).

Sitkoff, Harvard, *The Struggle for Black Equality, 1954–1980* (New York: Hill & Wang, 1981).

Skolnick, Jerome H., *The Politics of Protest: Violent Aspects of Protest and Confrontation* (New York: Simon & Schuster, 1969).

Sobel, Lester A., ed., *Civil Rights, 1960–66* (New York: Facts on File, Inc., 1966).

Sorenson, Theodore C., *Kennedy* (New York: Harper & Row, 1965).

Spitz, David, 'Democracy and the Problem of Civil Disobedience', *American Political Science Review* 48 (June 1954), pp. 386–403.

Stiehm, Judith, *Nonviolent Power: Active and Passive Resistance in America* (Lexington, Mass.: D. C. Heath, 1972).

Stoper, Emily, 'The Student Nonviolent Coordinating Committee: Rise and Fall of a Redemptive Organization', *Journal of Black Studies* 8 (September 1977), pp. 13–34.

Thoreau, Henry David, 'Civil Disobedience', in *Walden & Other Writings of Henry David Thoreau*, ed. Brooks Atkinson (New York: Random House Modern Library Edition, 1965).

Thornton, J. Mills, 'Challenge and Response in the Montgomery Bus Boycott of 1955–1956', *Alabama Review* 33 (July 1980), pp. 163–235.

Vander Zanden, James W., 'The Non-Violent Movement Against Segregation', *American Journal of Sociology* 68 (March 1963), pp. 544–50.

Von Eschen, Donald, Jerome Kirk, & Maurice Pinard, 'The Disintegration of the Negro Non-Violent Movement', *Journal of Peace Research* (1969) no. 3, pp. 215–34.

——, 'The Conditions of Direct Action in a Democratic Society', *Western Political Quarterly* 22 (June 1969), pp. 309–25.

Waldron, Martin, 'After Dark in St. Augustine', *The Nation* 198 (29 June 1964), pp. 648–51.

Walker, Wyatt T., 'Albany, Failure or First Step?', *New South* 18 (June 1963), pp. 3–8.

Walton, Hanes, Jr., *The Political Philosophy of Martin Luther King, Jr.* (Westport, Conn.: Greenwood Publishing Co., 1971).

Walton, Norman W., 'The Walking City: A History of the Montgomery Boycott', *Negro History Bulletin* 20 (October 1956), pp. 17–21, (November 1956), pp. 27–33, (February 1957), pp. 102–4, (April 1957), pp. 147–52, 166; 21 (January 1958), pp. 75–6, 81.

Warren, Robert Penn, *Who Speaks for the Negro?* (New York: Random House, 1965).

Washington, James M., ed., *A Testament of Hope: The Essential Writings of Martin Luther King, Jr.* (San Francisco: Harper & Row, 1986).

Waskow, Arthur, *From Race-Riot to Sit-In* (Garden City, New York: Doubleday, Anchor Books, 1967).

Watters, Pat, 'St. Augustine', *New South* (September 1964), pp. 3–20.

Watters, Pat & Reese Cleghorn, *Climbing Jacob's Ladder: The Arrival of Negroes in Southern Politics* (New York: Harcourt, Brace & World, 1967).

Watters, Pat, *Down to Now: Reflections on the Southern Civil Rights Movement* (New York: Pantheon, 1971).

Weinberg, Arthur, & Lila Weinberg, eds, *Instead of Violence* (Boston: Beacon Press, 1963).

Westin, Alan F., ed., *Freedom Now! The Civil Rights Struggle in America* (New York: Basic Books, 1964).

Westin, Alan F., & Barry Mahoney, *The Trial of Martin Luther King* (New York: Thomas Y. Crowell, 1974).

White, Theodore H., *The Making of the President – 1964* (New York: Atheneum, 1965).

Wilhoit, Francis M., *The Politics of Massive Resistance* (New York: George Braziller, 1973).

Wilkins, Roy, *Standing Fast: The Autobiography of Roy Wilkins* (New York: Viking Press, 1982).

Williams, John A., *The King God Didn't Save* (New York: Coward-McCann, 1970).

Williams, Juan, *Eyes On The Prize: America's Civil Rights Years, 1954–1965* (New York: Viking Penguin, 1987).

Williams, Robert F., *Negroes With Guns* (New York: Marzani & Munsell, 1962).

Wilson, James Q., 'The Strategy of Protest: Problems of Negro Civic Action', *Journal of Conflict Resolution* 5 (September 1961), pp. 291–303.

Wirmark, Bo, 'Nonviolent Methods and the American Civil Rights Movement, 1955–1965', *Journal of Peace Research* 11 (1974), pp. 115–32.

Witherspoon, Wm R., *Martin Luther King, Jr. – To The Mountaintop* (Garden City, New York: Doubleday, 1985).

Wofford, Harris, *Of Kennedys and Kings: Making Sense of The Sixties* (New York: Farrar, Straus, & Giroux, 1980).

Wolk, Allan, *The Presidency and Black Civil Rights: Eisenhower to Nixon* (Rutherford, New Jersey: Fairleigh Dickinson University Press, 1971).

Woodward, C. Vann, 'What Happened to the Civil Rights Movement?', *Harper's* 224 (January 1967), pp. 29–37.

——, *The Strange Career of Jim Crow*, 3rd ed. rev. (New York: Oxford University Press, 1974).

Wright, Nathan Jr., *Black Power and Urban Unrest* (New York: Hawthorn Books, 1967).

Yglesias, José, 'Dr. King's March on Washington, Part II', *New York Times Magazine*, (31 March 1968), pp. 30ff.

Zashin, Elliot M., *Civil Disobedience and Democracy* (New York: Free Press, 1972).

——, 'The Progress of Black Americans in Civil Rights: The Past Two Decades Assessed', *Daedalus* 107 (Winter 1978), pp. 239–62.

Zinn, Howard, *SNCC: The New Abolitionists* (Boston: Beacon Press, 1964).

——, *The Southern Mystique* (New York: Alfred A. Knopf, 1964).

——, *Disobedience and Democracy: Nine Fallacies on Law and Order* (New York: Random House, 1968).

——, *The Twentieth Century: A People's History* (New York: Harper & Row, 1984).

TELEVISION TRANSCRIPTS/FILMS

The six part public television series, *Eyes on the Prize: America's Civil Rights Years*, A Production of Blackside, Inc. (Boston: Massachusetts, 1986).

Transcript of television show, 'Recollections of Dr. King: *A Like It Is* Special' WABC-TV, New York, 4 Parts (5, 12, 19 January, and 2 February 1986). A discussion among six of King's closest associates (Ralph Abernathy, Dorothy Cotton, Fred Shuttlesworth, C. T. Vivian, Wyatt Walker and Andrew Young), hosted by Gil Noble.

King: A Filmed Record: From Montgomery to Memphis, produced by Ely Landau (1970).

Index